BEING A ROCKEFELLER

EILEEN ROCKEFELLER is the youngest daughter of David and Peggy Rockefeller, and a great-granddaughter of John D. Rockefeller. A pioneer in catalyzing the fields of mind/body health and social and emotional learning, she is also a founding chair of the Rockefeller Philanthropy Advisors and the Growald Family Fund. She is the mother of two grown sons and lives on a small organic farm in Vermont with her husband.

Praise for *Being a Rockefeller, Becoming Myself*

"[A] surprisingly candid and insightful account of an emotionally wounded girl ... Throughout the story [Eileen Rockefeller] deals with her deep sense of isolation and her search for recognition and self-worth beyond her wealth and iconic name. As the daughter of David and Peggy Rockefeller, and the great-granddaughter of John D. Rockefeller, founder of Standard Oil, she struggled to establish her own identity and confidence. But she succeeded through mind/body therapy, social and emotional learning, and a love of nature and the outdoors."　　　　　　　　—Sandra McElwaine, *The Daily Beast*

"Eileen Rockefeller has always sought the true, the real, the authentic. To read her beautiful book is to join her in a journey toward your own truth, your own real self, your own authenticity. What could be more important?"
　　　—Timothy Shriver, chairman and CEO of Special Olympics, and chair of
　　　　　　　　　Collaborative for Academic, Social, and Emotional Learning

"Weaving together a lifetime of navigating her own family bonds and traveling among diverse people throughout the world, Eileen Rockefeller explores the common threads of human pain and joy in this lyrical memoir, proving that no one is immune from suffering and doubt, and that no one finds happiness without ingenuity and effort. An inspiring, fascinating, heartening read."
　　　　　　　—Martha Beck, author of *Finding Your Own North Star*
　　　　　　　　　　　　　　　　and *Expecting Adam*

"A fascinating and frank look at the world of privilege and power by one to the manner born, who nevertheless strikes out to discover the power and privilege of being her own person. Engagingly written, honest, intimate, we follow a journey, not only of self discovery, but a journey of the heart from a woman committed to use her power and privilege to serve and help others. And this Rockefeller has her own additional legacy to gift us, her readers, this inviting memoir."

—Julia Alvarez, author of *A Wedding in Haiti* and *In the Time of the Butterflies*

"A beautifully written book that will touch many people in a very personal way. In Eileen Rockefeller's stories we learn not only that love heals but that *only* love heals, and that being fortunate in life has nothing to do with material goods but lies in being truly loved for yourself, exactly as you are."

—Rachel Naomi Remen, author of *Kitchen Table Wisdom* and *My Grandfather's Blessings*

"Eileen Rockefeller shares a fascinating, moving, and revealing tale of growing up in the midst of power and wealth, and moving on to find a True North star in life. Any one of us, no matter our roots, will learn much about living with authenticity and compassion, and becoming the person we want to be."

—Daniel Goleman, author *Emotional Intelligence*

"Eileen Rockefeller shows us that life's many projections—internal and external—ultimately do not show us who we truly are. Regardless of what comes with a name, the soul still has to find its unique expression in the world. This engaging book is an extremely detailed and honest look at one woman's search for safety of place and nuance of meaning in a world that often prefers boxes and labels."

—Peter Buffett, musician, philanthropist, and author of *Life Is What You Make It*

"This beautifully written memoir is deeply moving. It inspires self-reflection and a passion for human connection. *Being a Rockefeller, Becoming Myself* models honest communication and the benefits of sharing feelings in constructive and loving ways. Readers will enjoy learning about the Rockefeller family, and more importantly learn valuable ways to relate compassionately to family members, friends, and themselves."

—Roger P. Weissberg, PhD, president and CEO, Collaborative for Academic, Social, and Emotional Learning

"Eileen Rockefeller has written a thoroughly engaging, perceptive, and warm-hearted memoir, deftly weaving together the threads of family history and personal journey in the story of her own coming of age. There is beautiful writing here, along with a fresh and energetic voice and a narrative that goes far beyond the inevitable resonances of fame and fortune and into a complex family landscape where, luckily, our guide not only is familiar with the territory, but is also compassionate, loving, and very wise."

—Reeve Lindbergh, author of *No More Words* and *Under a Wing*

"While few of us grew up in a famous family, most of us have experienced a struggle to find our own way, one that could include mutual acceptance and loving understanding. In this wise, sometimes humorous, and remarkably candid memoir Eileen manages to share fascinating stories that make her personal journey reflect lessons in our universal longing for meaning, giving to the greater good, and belonging."

—Kare Anderson, author of *Moving From Me to We*

"In this poetic memoir, *Being a Rockefeller, Becoming Myself*, Eileen Rockefeller courageously shares what it was like to grow up the youngest child of six in one of America's most storied families. 'Do I have value beyond my last name?' she asks. As Rockefeller leads us on her life journey—from early academic challenges, to finding her voice inside her family, to youthful environmental advocacy, to pioneering work in the field of emotional intelligence, to finding her husband and soul mate—she finds her lights, and resolutely puts her singular gifts to work in making the world a better place. Her challenges are very specific; her quest for selfhood universal."

—Wanda Urbanska, author of *The Heart of Simple Living*

"*Being a Rockefeller, Becoming Myself* is everything a memoir should be: endowed with engaging characters, rich in detail, enlivened with episodes and stories, and above all, intensely personal. And add one other thing: courageous. Eileen Rockefeller has not held back in describing her family dynamics or her own feelings, thus has shared with us fascinating and utterly honest insights into her sometimes perilous journey toward unconditional love and acceptance."

—James A. Autry, author of *Love and Profit* and *The Servant Leader*

"Eileen Rockefeller's exquisitely written, compelling memoir takes the reader on a deeply moving, inspiring journey of self-discovery. Beyond the details of her fascinating life as a member of a world-renowned family, she courageously reveals her inner self, her struggles, and her triumphs. In so doing, she beckons us all to understand ourselves and our lives more fully and to remember, once again, the power of love."

—Julie Kidd, president, Christian A. Johnson Endeavor Foundation

"Eileen Rockefeller played a seminal, creative, and catalytic role in two as yet little known but revolutionary emergences in our culture: 1) the rise and mainstreaming of mind/body medicine, and 2) the development and dissemination of Social Emotional Learning (SEL) in schools. Both are based on robust scientific evidence that her efforts contributed to significantly. Both deserve major kudos. In this memoir, Eileen now reveals the human being behind these accomplishments. Her story is unusual, since she was born into a family dynasty that brought with it a karmic load that encompassed nothing short of the good, the bad, and the ugly, all of which she experienced from a very early age. The result: a compelling 'inside story' of the developmental trajectory of a young girl born into an extraordinary and complex family, compelled to find a way to ultimately become herself and contribute in her own unique and meaningful ways to the larger world."

—Jon Kabat-Zinn, author of *Full Catastrophe Living*
and *Wherever You Go, There You Are*

"*Being a Rockefeller, Becoming Myself* is an extraordinary book about a most remarkable woman who transformed her life and the lives of those around her. Insightful and inspiring!" —Dean Ornish, MD

BEING A ROCKEFELLER, BECOMING MYSELF

A Memoir

EILEEN ROCKEFELLER

P

A PLUME BOOK

PLUME
Published by the Penguin Group
Penguin Group (USA) LLC
375 Hudson Street
New York, New York 10014

USA | Canada | UK | Ireland | Australia | New Zealand | India | South Africa | China
penguin.com
A Penguin Random House Company

First published in the United States of America by Blue Rider Press,
a member of Penguin Group (USA) Inc., 2013
First Plume Printing 2014

P REGISTERED TRADEMARK—MARCA REGISTRADA

THE LIBRARY OF CONGRESS HAS CATALOGED THE BLUE RIDER PRESS EDITION
AS FOLLOWS:
Rockefeller, Eileen.
Being a Rockefeller, becoming myself: a memoir / Eileen Rockefeller.
p.   cm.
ISBN 978-0-399-16408-8 (hc.)
ISBN 978-0-14-218137-9 (pbk.)
1. Rockefeller, Eileen.   2. Women philanthropists—United States—Biography.
3. Philanthropists—United States—Biography.   4. Rich people—United States—
Biography.   5. David Rockefeller, 1915-.—Family.   6. Rockefeller, John D.
(John Davidson), 1839–1937—Family.   7. Rockefeller family.   I. Title.
HV28.R546A3   2013   2013015407
361.7′4092—dc23

Printed in the United States of America
10   9   8   7   6   5   4   3   2   1

Original hardcover design by Meighan Cavanaugh

*Penguin is committed to publishing works of quality and integrity. In that spirit, we are proud
to offer this book to our readers; however, the story, the experiences, and the words are the
author's alone.*

To my grandmother Abby Aldrich Rockefeller,

who gave me the dream of becoming myself,

and to Paul, my beloved husband,

for standing by my side every inch of the way

Contents

❧

Author's Note: The Presence of Peonies   *xiii*

1. THE STORY I DIDN'T WANT TO TELL   1

2. WELCOME HOME   9

3. SETTING THE STAGE   14

4. FIRST LOSS   22

5. FEELING DIFFERENT AS A FAMILY   28

6. THE SMALLEST COUNT   34

7. "YOU SHOT THE RABBITS?"   39

8. MAID TO ORDER   50

9. A SAFE HARBOR   58

10. STAYING AFLOAT   71

11. A PLACE TO RELAX   77

12. JAGGED EDGES   86

13. THROUGH A DOOR IN THE WOODS   91

14. IT DOESN'T MATTER WHERE YOU START   100

15. PULLING TOGETHER   104

16. MUSIC LESSONS   112

17. CULTIVATING LOVE   117

18. YOU CAN LEAD THEM TO THE WATER . . .   127

19. ROADBLOCKS   133

20. GRADUATING   140

21. GIFTS GIVEN   143

22. LEARNING RESILIENCE   149

23. GEORGIA O'KEEFFE SPEAKS   156

24. MALE MENTORS   161

25. DREAMING MY HUSBAND   170

26. THE FIRST YEARS   177

27. GORILLA ON MY SHOULDER   181

28. TIME FOR BEING   186

29. LAUNCHING THE MIND/BODY FIELD   197

30. AT THE FOOT OF THE LADDER   204

31. IN THE FIRE   209

32. DANCING AMONG THE STARS   219

33. PRIMAL PARENTING   223

34. A Good Christmas   231

35. Working with Emotional Intelligence   238

36. I Wouldn't Admit It If I Were You   243

37. In the Nest of My Heart   247

38. Putting the Heart into Practice   251

39. Tearing Down the Fence   258

40. Cleaning House   266

41. Passing the Torch   270

42. Planting Seeds   281

43. Out of the Canyon   288

44. Courage   300

45. One Last Look   307

   Acknowledgments   317

Author's Note:
The Presence of Peonies

❧

Each fall my peonies collapse, flattening to the ground like tired balle-rinas. Without a sound they surrender their youthful beauty to the cold. By the time snow covers them they have disintegrated and started turning back into soil. It is hard to remember them as blowsy hedges around our circle drive.

Six months later, when spring arrives, the plants send up new shoots as fast as the birds return. Their leafy abundance, flouncing pink and white flower heads in the breeze, catches my breath mid-step.

For me, awareness is like this. It awakens naturally from its dor-mant state. I still remind myself to let it grow in its own time.

When I was a child I thought the duration of a meaningful experi-ence or the length of time I knew someone was in direct proportion to its impact. I have been surprised by this misconception, having often experienced the opposite. The school I spent the least time attending shaped my life the most. A woman I once spent only one week with as a teenager still influences the way I listen to others.

Sometimes I find awareness in a single flower petal. If I stop to savor the spoon of its creamy flesh, the whole day blossoms, just like a peony.

1.

THE STORY I DIDN'T
WANT TO TELL

❦

John D. Rockefeller was my great-grandfather. For years, my siblings and I tried to keep this a secret because his name created such a buzz. Adulation, judgment, envy, and endless curiosity flew around us like a swarm of bees. I was afraid of the sting. People saw us as different, and that set us apart. Their preconception of my family as akin to royalty contributed to my sense of isolation and loneliness.

I live with anxiety and gratitude, just like the generations of Rockefellers before me. Without anxiety and the desire to heal it, I would not be writing this story.

The physical comforts and circumstances of my life were undeniably different from most people's. I grew up in big houses with lots of servants. I was given an allowance that could probably be considered large, and I went to school in a chauffeur-driven limousine. We called it the "hearse" or "curse" because, before the oldest ones left for boarding school, we needed a car large enough to carry all six of us. It had two jump seats in back. My siblings and I (and, it turns out, my cousins, too) jumped out a block or two before we arrived at school so we could walk up to the door just like everyone else. We tried to hide who we were because we wanted to fit in, and also because my mother trained us not to stand out.

As an heir to the Rockefeller legacy I have found that real richness and power comes not from the amount of money but from our connection to ourselves and one another. I am just as much "Eileen" as I am "Rockefeller." I struggle with my weight. I am getting more lines in my face every year. I have fights with my husband, I get really impatient when I have to wait for a long time in the grocery or gas line, and I hate going through airport security. Sound familiar? And just like you, I am also unique.

I am part of a long line of venture capitalists and philanthropists. It's hard to talk about my grandfathers without them taking over. Their accomplishments overwhelm me. I feel small and insignificant in comparison.

I come from a family of ledger keepers. We have been practicing for over 150 years. It started in 1855, during the Great Awakening of our nation, a strong religious revival movement among Protestant denominations. A fifteen-year-old boy felt compelled to drop out of Cleveland Central High School. He would have had to have studied Greek and Latin to qualify for college. That wasn't his plan. He needed a steady income to support his mother and siblings. His father, William, was a charismatic land speculator, referred to as "Big Bill." He occasionally sold stolen horses and left home for extended periods of time, selling snake oil remedies, which he promoted as medicinal cures. William was rumored to appear in marketplaces acting as a mute. He held a sign that read: "Dr. William A. Rockefeller, the celebrated cancer specialist, here for one day only. All cases of cancer cured, unless too far gone, and then can be greatly benefitted." He also cultivated a second, simultaneous family. His philandering lifestyle, compounded by absence and scant amounts of money, left John D. Rockefeller, the boy, extremely anxious. He kept track of every penny, but it often wasn't enough to pay the bills; he vowed to be more reliable than his father. The family's well-being depended on it. He wrote down his minister's advice in his little book: "Get money, get it honestly, and then give it wisely."

Just weeks prior to graduation he left high school, bypassed college, and enrolled in a nearby business school, pushing himself to finish the six-month program in half the time. Careful bookkeeping was key. His first job at the age of sixteen was as an assistant bookkeeper for Hewlett and Turtle, a firm selling products on commission, in Cleveland. They paid him nothing for the first three months, waiting to see how he would do. He was so relieved at the opportunity to support his family that he celebrated his first day of salaried work, September 26, 1855, for the rest of his ninety-seven years.

The daily practice of noting the inflow and outflow of money had begun. He applied the discipline to himself as well, creating a set of books in which he tracked his personal finances. They have been carefully preserved in the family archive. In reading them, I imagine him walking to his desk in a sparsely furnished room. Each night he strikes a match to the whale-oil lamp and turns up the wick. The shadow cast by its light elongates his tall, slender frame and straight-angled nose across the wooden floor. He lifts his tailcoat neatly over the back of the chair and, with his head bent, he dips his quill into the inkwell and notes the day's expenditures:

January 2	1 week's Board	3.00
January 2	2½ yards cloth for pants	3.13
January 5	Making of same	2.25
January 5	1 Pare [sic] of rubbers	1.25
January 6	Donation to Missionary Cause	.06
January 6	Donation to the poor in the church	.10

The pants were well earned, he reassures himself, even if they did cost more than a week's salary. He can afford them now. Just before Christmas, the firm paid him fifty dollars for his first three months of work and set his salary at twenty-five dollars a month. He is on his way. His mother's fears will be eased, but he needs to remain diligent and to present himself well as the honest and hardworking man he has become.

His thoughts drift to Laura. He heard that she had been the valedictorian of their class. What had she thought about his dropping out? Or had she even noticed? "I Can Paddle My Own Canoe" was the title of her address to the class. What did a woman like her value in a man? A respectable pair of pants wouldn't hurt, but she would be looking for something more. She was a churchgoer, a Congregationalist, and had progressive principles; that was clear. Hopefully, she had come to appreciate that he did, too, and did not mind his Baptist roots. Maybe he would speak with her after church sometime soon. But no more daydreaming; there was work to be done.

❧

Great-Grandfather not only spoke with Laura. He also began courting her, sometimes with his ledger books in hand. I envision them sitting together on a bench in the garden of her parents' home on a Sunday after church, turning the pages and talking quietly. It's not my idea of a romantic courtship, but it had to start somewhere.

I wonder what the ledgers revealed to her? What evidence of character, worthiness, or desirability did he hope they would convey? Of which entries was he most proud? Was it his first paycheck? Was it giving money to a black man in Cincinnati so he could buy his wife out of slavery? I wonder what he read to Laura that pulled her heartstrings? I never knew him, but my father did. He keeps a picture by his bedside that he took in Ormond Beach, Florida. John D. Rockefeller's slender frame is seated in a wooden wheelchair with a plaid blanket on his lap and boney fingers clasped on top. His eyes look lovingly, though somewhat vacantly, toward my father. He died just weeks after the picture was taken. I can see his whole life scanning before him, from his courtship to his favorite grandson.

In 1864, my great-grandparents, John Davison Rockefeller Sr. and Laura Celestia Spelman, married. America was at war with itself over issues of division, enslavement, and morality. John D. would deal with some of these same issues internally. The laws of family and tithing, learned at the knee of his Northern Baptist mother, Eliza, called for daily Bible readings and persistent self-examination. He believed his work was a calling from God. His wife is best known for her and John's major contribution in 1881, to Spelman College, in Atlanta, Georgia, to educate black women.

Young men, like his brother, Frank, were walking down country roads with heavy guns slung across their shoulders when Great-Grandfather's Cleveland company started extracting oil for kerosene that would light the soldiers' encampments at night. It was the start of a new era. John D. borrowed from his father's entrepreneurial spirit and predilection for cure-alls in developing the greatest snake oil of the modern world. He consolidated oil production and distribution on a scale that would spawn both cures and cancers, lighting the way to modern transportation, road networks, and industry. He could not have known then that one hundred and some years later, burning oil would contribute to the warming of Earth's atmosphere.

Senior apparently wanted his children to learn temperance from ledger keeping. They earned allowances and noted inflow and outflow line by line in their own ledgers. Luxuries were not in evidence. John D. Jr., the youngest of five and the only son, wore his sisters' remade hand-me-downs until he was eight. When he became a father, he taught the third generation to be ledger keepers as well. My own father's ledger shows him earning two cents apiece for swatting flies, being docked five cents for lying, and spending his first dollars at age eleven on a little pot made by a Pueblo Indian woman.

My great-grandfather's success in the oil business made him the world's first billionaire. The abundance of money more than compensated for his early fears of scarcity. Yet, throughout his life he kept scrupulous ledgers, balancing everything he earned, spent, or gave away to the point of obsession. As a devout Baptist, he practiced tithing—giving away 10 percent of his income. He passed this tradition down to his son, and together they taught the next generation a philosophy of philanthropy that continues to this day: save one third, spend one third, and give away one third.

My great-grandfather called upon the assistance of his son and advisers in giving away the equivalent of tens of billions in today's dollars. Grandfather, John D. Jr., graduated Phi Beta Kappa from Brown University in 1897, and after working for thirteen years at the Standard Oil Company, spent every day of the rest of his life helping to give away his father's money. His fervent sense of loyalty and duty would help shape his father's and his image while doing good throughout America and the world. He lived in a time of expansionism, when the very word *America* represented a land of opportunity and hope. His work was not without its consequences, however. Despite father and son's unprecedented success, they were periodically subject to public excoriation over the practices of some of their businesses. They contracted what might have been stress-induced illnesses.

In his early fifties, Senior suffered permanent hair loss from a viral disease called alopecia, sometimes associated with stress. Junior had his first nervous collapse at the age of thirteen. I suspect it stemmed from the expectations and implications of being his father's only son. He was given a year of hard physical labor to regain his emotional strength. This would be the first of periodic collapses throughout his life, along with crippling headaches. Nature became his therapy and he passed along its value to subsequent generations.

I like to think he found some relief in the time he spent with his grandchildren. My only memory is of visiting him at his house in Maine when I was six or seven years old. He came to the door to greet me. I remember his wire-rimmed glasses, and he smelled faintly of cedar. He sat down on a chair next to me and taught me how to play Chinese checkers. I was allowed to choose the yellow marbles, yellow being my favorite color.

The list of his accomplishments for the benefit of the common good is a book in itself, and many have been written. Though most of us in my extended family no longer keep ledgers, we still practice philanthropy and service, balancing questions of worth and relationship with opportunities and responsibilities. We are free to spend our money as we wish, but we have inherited the values passed down from my great-grandfather, to give no less than a third of our income away annually, and to give our time to causes such as social justice, the arts, and land conservation. We have promoted innovations in medicine, education, and science. Philanthropy is the glue that has bound us through seven generations.

My great-grandfather and the two generations that followed him set the bar high for my cousins and our offspring. "It is easy to give money away," my grandfather and father used to say, "but it is not easy to give it well." The truth of this statement follows my family around like a bee that won't quit buzzing. We have been given enormous opportunities, but they come with an equal measure of expectation. It takes a family as large as mine to balance the ledger of my grandfathers' legacy. Personal stories help me to see us not as icons but as ordinary human beings.

My great grandfather, John D. Rockefeller's childhood home in Moravia, NY

2.

WELCOME HOME

❧

My paternal grandmother, Abby Aldrich Rockefeller, enjoyed people of every age and background. She loved just as much the beauty of art, from ancient to modern expressionism to simple folk art, seeing value in communication, regardless of recognition or fame.

I have been exposed to many kinds of beauty since I was old enough to say Cézanne. Monets and mountains, Buddhas and butterflies are as familiar as mother's milk, yet my relationship with art, until recently, has been like an unresolved sibling relationship. I need it; it feeds my soul; but at home growing up I competed with it for attention. My four middle siblings showed artistic talent for drawing, inherited from my mother's side, but the pictures we gave to my parents ended up in the closet. I later found my own talent as a weaver of yarns and a connector of people and ideas. Grandmother's story has helped give me peace with art and its place in my home and heart.

Abby Aldrich Rockefeller passed on four years before I was born.

She earned respect during her lifetime as a collector of art, particularly modern and folk art, and was a driving force in establishing the Museum of Modern Art in New York City. Her interest in preserving cultural traditions led to the founding of the Folk Art Museum in Colonial Williamsburg, Virginia.

People who knew her often say I remind them of my grandmother. I had my first-ever dream about her the night my oldest uncle, John D. Rockefeller III, died. He was killed in a car crash in 1978 while I was hiking with a friend in the Selway Bitterroot Wilderness in Idaho. I was twenty-six at the time and cell phones did not exist, so I had no way of knowing my uncle's fate. The next day I heard a helicopter overhead and wondered if something had happened in my family, thinking the helicopter might be trying to find me.

In my dream, Grandmother came to visit me at the house I had recently inherited in Maine, known as the Guest Cottage. My grandparents had originally built it as the superintendent's cottage for their estate, below the vast winged summerhouse up the hill, known as the Eyrie, or eagle's nest.

I dreamed Grandmother arrived in a lacy mid-calf dress and pearls and elbow-length kid gloves. She wore a small veiled hat over her curly, alabaster hair. Her presence was comforting as she walked with me around the interior of my house looking with interest at everything. In the house were several Arthur Davies watercolors, inherited from her. She told me that they, and the Japanese prints, which in real life she had personally collected and placed there, were now mine. She told me I should feel free to change them about or remove them as I wished. I woke up feeling she had given me permission to become my own person. This dream marked the beginning of a long road in healing my relationship with family and art.

Two days later, when I hiked out of the wilderness, I called home. My mother told me that Uncle John had died in a car crash on July 10, the date of my dream. She said she had considered trying to find me but felt it would be too much trouble to bring me so far when I had not known him well. My grandmother found me anyway. She has been with me in spirit ever since.

I remembered this experience when I was asked to give a talk to the Cosmopolitan Club in New York City about my mother's and grand-mother's roles in the Club. My grandmother had been a charter founder of the Club and had given a speech there, in 1927, entitled "The Perpetuation of the Home as One of the Main Hopes of Civilization." Her words were like a continuation of my dream. She spoke of "the power and value of beauty in our home life." She believed "a home has no nationality; it is simply the place in which the people you love *most* happen to be living."

Despite the disruption of the average home from how she knew it almost a century ago, she said, "I am undismayed because I believe in human nature—both masculine and feminine; I trust the power of love and the hope that lies hidden in every heart that some day peace and justice shall reign."

Grandmother lived her values. She saw it as her duty not only to welcome our country's newcomers but to honor the family artifacts and keepsakes from their country, which often lay hidden away.

The story I love best takes place in the 1920s or '30s. Immigrants at that time were expected to assimilate if they wanted to be accepted as Americans. Grandmother thought otherwise. She honored cultural diversity and took it upon herself to personally welcome newly arrived families to the United States who were working for the Standard Oil Company in New Jersey.

Her chauffeur drove her to their homes around teatime. I imagine her stepping out of the car in her flowing dress, flowered hat, ivory gloves, and long string of pearls and ringing the bell. A frightened woman would open the door. "Good afternoon," my grandmother would say. "I am Mrs. John D. Rockefeller Jr. I have come to welcome you to the United States of America."

My grandmother's name was familiar. The woman would invite her in, no doubt with some apology about her meager furnishings. Several children might appear shyly from behind a bedroom door. My grandmother loved children, especially babies, and would ask to hold one on her lap. Something pretty usually caught her eye. "What a lovely tablecloth," she'd comment. "Is this a picture of your family? How many of you are here in the United States?"

The woman of the house would put the kettle on for tea. A sense of ease would fall about the house and the children would busy themselves with homemade toys like cardboard boxes and wooden spoons. Tea would be poured. My grandmother would thank her and continue, "What country have you come from? Tell me, how have your first days and weeks been?" She was interested in people regardless of rank, race, or religion. Her curiosity and warmth opened their hearts.

At some point in the conversation she would ask her favorite question: "Did you bring an object of art from your country? I would be so pleased to see whatever you brought." The mother of the family would hurry to the back of the apartment and return with a pot, weaving, carving, or a cherished vase inherited from her mother or father. Grandmother held whatever was presented with great respect. She wanted to know its history and importance to the family.

She would close by saying, "I hope you will find this lovely piece a place of honor in your home. Don't ever lose sight of your roots. They are the foundation for your future as an American."

She would return her teacup to its saucer and thank the woman of the house for her time. She believed that beauty was central to the sanctity of the home. In her speech to the ladies at the Cosmopolitan Club she said, "A theory about the brotherhood of man, about social hygiene, or child welfare, is not enough. There must be a place, a home, which will safeguard the children and provide comfort for the old . . . a good home is created by love and sacrifice, by good taste, and self-control, and devotion to high ideals."

I am inspired by her attitude; home is the first mirror through which we form our identity. Beauty, art, and nature help us to find our place of belonging. When I feel I belong, I dare to expand my horizons. I didn't feel I belonged for much of my early life, but Grandmother's spirit gave me the first ray of hope.

3.

SETTING THE STAGE

❧

I am the youngest child of six. For many years there was not enough love to go around, and I competed for attention. No matter how many ways I tried, I didn't feel accepted by my siblings. Belonging meant subjugating myself to their whims or will. I alternately relented and refused before siding with my parents. They were bigger and more powerful, but not much more welcoming. Life in my family was lonely.

By the time I arrived, my father was busy climbing the ranks of the Chase Manhattan Bank, where he would eventually become chairman and chief executive officer. My mother was still learning how to be the wife of a Rockefeller. She and my father met when they were both twenty, at a party in New York. After a five-year courtship, they were married in St. Matthew's Episcopal Church, in Bedford, New York. My mother liked to tell how she pestered my father to pose the question. When he finally did, she told him she would have to take twenty-four hours to think about it. She knew how to hold the reins. Perhaps this was her compensation for not having gone to college or kept a check-book until they were married. She had no experience in managing a staff, and no one to teach her except for gentle hints from her mother-in-law. Mum spoke of Grandmother with great affection and gratitude, but it was a steep learning curve, one that cost her some friends. She told me about one time, when several women she had grown up with arrived un-announced at the gates of the family estate in Tarrytown, New York, and were turned away. Her casual country living had changed overnight into a more formal lifestyle. The friends never returned.

My maternal grandmother, Neva van Smith McGrath, took advantage of her daughter's new status and money. She demanded a key to the Upper East Side town house and would arrive unannounced to make her long-distance calls from my mother's desk. In those days phone calls were expensive. My grandmother ruled not only my mother, but also the help, giving orders to the cook, the kitchen maid, the laundress, the butler, the nannies, and two maids, as if they all worked for her. She played out a fantasy at the expense of her daughter. My mother finally changed the locks. Wealth sometimes requires that one keep others out.

My mother's identity as a country woman from an aspiring upper-middle-class background was more aligned with her passion for garden-ing, animals, and the solitude of nature than it was with the growing responsibilities of raising six children; running three houses (and later more); scribbling dozens of handwritten letters of invitation, thanks, or comfort before breakfast; and dressing up at the end of the day for the incoming tide of people who would advance my father's career. Her twinkling eyes, huge talent for storytelling, and a wealth of fierce resil-ience masked the feeling of insecurity and defeat that would periodi-cally plunge her into deep depression. From the outside, no one knew, but her unpredictable rages toward those of us living and working under the same roof were all too familiar. The apple didn't fall far from the tree.

My grandmother frightened me. I didn't know her very well, but my mother told me that she wanted to be seen as an aristocratic lady who did not work, played bridge . . . and shot wild dogs. Danda, as we called her, was known for shooting dogs. Even her neighbors knew. I went to high school with one of them, and when she learned that Neva Mc-Grath was my grandmother, she asked, "Did you know she used to hunt stray dogs in the neighborhood?" I admitted I did, and in that moment I realized I had mixed feelings about Danda. I was proud of her bravery and skill, but the story reminded me of the one time I can remember her babysitting me, when she furrowed her brow as she told me about people who let their dogs chase innocent deer. I was confused because she referred to her mother as "Dear," and I was too young to know this had a different meaning.

Danda loved animals more than people. The people she respected most mirrored her own ferocity, courage, and daring, but in the animal world she defended the weak and wounded. She took revenge against dogs that chased herds of terrified deer through her backyard. I suspect she would have preferred to kill their owners, as she considered it a crime that they had not cared properly for their dogs in the first place. For this reason she kept a .22 rifle in the front hall closet of her white colonial home in Bedford, New York.

My friend Peggy Read, who lived next door to Danda, remembered going over to my grandmother's house on Halloween. She said Danda always seemed to have forgotten the date. When Peggy knocked, the door opened to Danda's puzzled scowl and haphazard arrangement of white hair, a few strands dangling over her face like a spiderweb. Peggy bravely held out her bag and said, "Trick or Treat." Danda was the neighborhood Halloween Scrooge. She would mutter as she turned to her kitchen for a sprinkling of raisins or a homegrown, wrinkled apple.

I never went trick-or-treating to my grandmother's, and I'm just as glad. Danda's face was etched with anger. Perhaps she still carried resentment over her father having died in 1903 without leaving his family any money. Danda was eighteen years old when she was left to fend for herself, with her mother and younger sister. Her father had led his family to believe that, as a vice president of the B&O Railroad, he had lots of money. They were shocked and ashamed to discover he had left them nothing.

As my mother told the story, Danda became the primary breadwinner. She was a fine artist and painted portraits of anyone who could pay her. Danda's discerning eye often pointed out flaws in the design of her subject's dress and she would offer to make a few alterations to improve it. The response was so positive, she recognized the greater potential for profit in dress designing. She enlisted her mother and sister in creating a business in New York called Chez Ninon. It was so successful that ten years later, at the start of the First World War, she sold it to a Paris firm for a million dollars. That would be close to twenty-five million in today's dollars. There is a difference of opinion in the family lore about whether it was Danda or her mother, Dear, who actually founded the business, but Danda maintained it was she, and referred to her mother as "a helpless, weepy female."

When Danda married Sims McGrath, an up-and-coming New York lawyer, she handed him her money to manage, hoping he would do better than her father. He was a short man, barely clearing five feet, and my mother was the apple of his eye. She shared his quick wit and intelligence, but by the time my mother was fourteen, he lost most of the family money in the stock market crash of 1929. Danda never forgave him. He was the second important man in her life to betray her.

Danda was too proud a woman to let people know that much of her wealth was lost. She sold furniture she thought wouldn't be noticed by their friends. She even sold my mother's beloved horse, Soldier: anything to keep up appearances.

Sadly, Danda never felt pride in her accomplishments. She was more impressed by the memory of her brief fling as a wealthy aristocrat than what her work represented. No achievement on the part of her lawyer husband could make up for the loss. I suspect that what she most wanted was the protection and security that was twice lost at the hands of men. Perhaps that's why she shot wild dogs.

This was the backdrop of the stage on which I grew up. My parents bought their Manhattan town house in 1948 to accommodate their growing family. My father still lives there today. Despite its four floors and double-size lot, it was not an easy house to play ball in. Our home accommodated all six children, but it was also bought for displaying art and for entertaining. The rooms were tidy at all times. Ball playing was restricted to the narrow hallway of the fourth floor.

I can still see the six of us, as if in a play. We descend a spiral staircase and enter the long, chestnut-paneled living room on the second floor; dutiful, rebellious, reserved, obliging, distracted, subservient. Each of us takes a bow or curtsies before running off to change costumes. Add to stage right a staff of hundreds. Fifty people, each requiring face and name recognition, might bustle in and out of our house every day carrying papers to sign, messages to deliver, and dinner plates to clear. Stage left is crowded with throngs of friends and extended family.

Backstage one can hear the murmurs and skirmishes of children.

They enter the room, dressed for a party. The littlest girl, age four, wears a white smocked dress with leggings. Her three older sisters have on matching velvet frocks with lace collars. Her two brothers are dressed in pants and starched white shirts. The ten years between the oldest and youngest becomes evident as the six children skip around a dining-room table set for eight. They pinch and push one another as they play musical chairs. They laugh as they circle the table, but their faces are drawn tight. No hitting or crying is allowed in public. It is considered vulgar to ask for attention.

Our parents call us by name to come say hello. We children are for the moment well behaved. Not conforming would later provoke the consequences of our mother's shaming lectures.

I curtsy and shake hands around the room. I've been taught to look in everyone's eyes, but I feel too shy to gaze above their mouths. The press of people is like a vise, and I try not to breathe too deeply, for the expensive perfume is too strong for my sensitive nose, and I don't like the smell of cigarettes and martinis. The burble of conversation floods the room in an artificial tide of names and titles. Some guests are sitting primly on couches and chairs, talking intently or laughing nervously. Even at my young age, I am aware of their discomfort, their desire for approval, and their worry of not measuring up to a preconceived image of the Rockefellers.

My mother puts them at ease, regaling them with funny stories, mostly told as jokes about herself. People gather around her in obvious enjoyment. She knows how to make them laugh and my father looks over at her adoringly. He is grateful for their partnership.

Curtains rise and fall over changing scenes and years. At ten, I am asked to pass the hors d'oeuvres. People thank me and think I'm cute. I'm glad for the attention. I also know that I won't be allowed to have an appetizer until I have passed them first to everyone else. The littlest one goes last. There is a constant din in this Brueghel-like scene, and night after night there is barely room to breathe. This is how my father built his business.

Most often the guests stay for dinner, and only those of us old enough to carry a conversation are invited to join them. This leaves out the youngest three: we eat at six thirty with the nannies. I will not be invited until I am ten, but on this night the guests have left, and we will eat with our parents.

I worry I will not find a seat at the table. My next-in-age brother, Richard, sees the anxious look on my face and taunts me. "There aren't enough places and you will be in starvation corner anyway." This means I will be served last by the maids and butler who will pass platters of food with delicately balanced silver utensils. I cry and am told to hush. My oldest brother, David, takes my hand, knowing all too well the shared rejection from the middle four who have formed a pact that excludes David and me. We are the bookends. The scramble to be included is abruptly truncated by the tone of my mother's voice as she commands, "Your father will seat us." Whenever she uses the term *your father*, we know she means business. The skirmish is quieted but not without feeling the hands of my three sisters pushing me away.

❧

In my forties, I asked a healer to do soul retrieval with me. She was small and strong. She laid me down on the floor on an alpaca blanket and told me to breathe into the percussive sounds of drums, rattles, and feathers from Native Americans. I closed my eyes. Inside, I felt like a great spirit was hovering above me.

I'm not sure how long I lay there, but when it was over, she told me she saw my soul as a three-year-old girl, standing outside a large country house on an expansive lawn. She did not know we had a house in Tarrytown with a back lawn large enough for a soccer field. When she described the scene, I knew right away that I was peering through the bay window of its living room. She recounted her conversation with the lost soul of my little girl.

"What are you doing?"

"I'm looking for someone."

"But there are many people inside."

"Yes, but there's no one home."

When I heard her words I cried so hard I thought I would throw up. I had not wanted to see my childhood this way. I wanted to hold on to the fantasy that it was just a bad dream. Her words confirmed the dreaded truth. I was an outsider looking in, craving to belong.

My family did not show emotion openly. They took their feelings underground and expressed their anger through sullen silence or debate. I was not constructed to be reserved or rational. I was alternately loud and sulky, clownish and stormy. I was not part of the pack but my feelings were proof that I was alive.

I felt like Cinderella, running errands, being helpful, and caring for my mother. There was no other choice. When she was stressed, which was much of the time, she was scary, just like her mother. If any of us dared cross her, she shamed us with guilt about the privilege of being a Rockefeller and lectured us, sometimes for an hour. If we protested, she turned on us, saying, "You stop that right now. You must always remember that as a member of this family you will get double praise or double blame." We learned to step cautiously into the world.

4.

FIRST LOSS

❧

In the late 1950s, Ringling Bros. and Barnum & Bailey Circus sold turtles by the tray. Vendors marched up and down the darkened aisles waving their tiny white flashlights while shouting, "Turtles! Live turtles for sale! Twenty-five cents a turtle." My five-year-old hand shot up in the dark. A hard shell with no head or legs was extended to me in exchange for my mother's quarter. It fit perfectly in the palm of my hand. Herman was my first animal friend.

Turtles were so cheap, they sold hundreds in a night. I was too little to wonder how or where they found them, or whether turtles were en-dangered. I did not even know it was a red-eared slider turtle. No one told me about those things back then. I was fascinated by its emerging head with red spots on either side of its pointed beak face.

Intermission was over. Live brass music played from the bandstand to our right and my attention was momentarily drawn from my turtle to six white horses with no bridles trotting to the middle ring, straight below us. I was entranced by a lady wearing a tutu who jumped on and off their backs with the ease of a bird. The horses cantered in a slow, rhythmic cadence, seemingly oblivious to their intermittent passenger.

I watched with great interest until I felt something scratching the palm of my hand. I looked down to see, through the dim light, four tiny legs emerging from the dark green shell. The circus was forgotten as the turtle explored my hand. He seemed to like the warm sweat on my palm that my mother had told me was a sign of emotion and something to hide. Normally, I would have pulled back. But I knew from our pond that turtles live in water part of the time, so this one must be happy on my wet palm. His head pushed out from the fold around his neck. He reminded me of the clams I had held in Maine. They, too, had a hard back and long neck. But turtles were different. I could see his little black eyes.

Herman lived in a glass tank in my room in New York City. The first weekend after he came home, I collected gravel from the driveway of our country house to put on the bottom of his tank. My nurse, Gibby, told me that turtles like to hide. (In those days we called nannies nurses.) I found a turtle-size log he could climb partway out of the water on or dive under for cover. Gibby helped me pull some water plants from our pond and we put them in there, too, so he could feel extra safe.

Herman's shell had a hopscotch pattern of lines and squares in different shades of green and yellow. His belly was mostly yellow with black dots, just like the freckles on my face. I wished I could crawl in his shell right next to him. It looked so safe. I backed myself into a pillowcase instead and pretended I was Herman's sister.

Every day, when I came home from kindergarten, I went straight to Herman's tank. I could tell he knew I was coming because he would paddle up to the surface of his tank and pop his head out of the water to say hello with his beady black eyes. His face dripped water from the green and yellow stripes leading from his mouth and eyes toward the hidden part of his body. I took a pinch of turtle food from the can and flicked it onto the water's surface. Herman snapped it up and looked for more. He really liked me. He didn't mind when I lifted him out of the water and stroked his back. He just pushed his little claws out and tickled my hand.

Sometimes I would put him on the rug to see how fast he could move. If the cat was there he refused to go anywhere and tucked his head, feet, and tail right back in his shell. But the moment I picked him up to take him back to his tank, he would pop his head out again and look at me as if to say, *Thank you.*

I could really communicate with my turtle. I was the only one he poked his head out of the water for when I came into the room. My brothers or sisters would try to tell me he did that for them, too, but that was only because I was coming in the room with them. I know he didn't do this for anyone else. They were just jealous.

Apparently, my mother did not know how well Herman and I communicated. One day, before I left for school, I noticed he was looking sad. He did not pop his head up quite as usual when I came to give him food. I decided he was still sleepy. After all, I was, too. I trudged off to kindergarten and didn't think of him again until I came home.

The moment I walked into my bedroom I knew something was wrong. No matter how tired Herman was, he always looked up out of the water at me. But this time he just swam down under the log and started digging for something among the pebbles. This was not like Herman. In fact, this wasn't Herman. A sudden chill went through my body and my hands broke into a sweat.

I called for my mother. "Where's Herman?" Her steps seemed all too slow as she approached the room. Her brow was furrowed above her thick glasses, and her mouth looked scrunched up, like she was trying to hide something.

"What happened?" I pressed. Tears were already forming in my eyes in anticipation of the news I did not want to hear.

"Well, darling," she started, looking down at me like a cat that has just swallowed the family fish. "Gibby saw he wasn't feeling well this morning so we went to the pet store to get you another."

"But where's Herman?" I demanded, hating the unspoken truth.

"Now don't be upset, darling. I'm sure you will like this turtle, too," she soothed.

Yeah, right, I thought to myself. *Just like I'll like the hairballs that come off the cat after he dies.*

Mum tried to comfort me. She understood how it felt to lose an animal you love.

"After Gibby walked you to school this morning, she returned to find Herman belly up, floating on his back in the tank. We know how much you loved your turtle. We decided we must find a replacement before you came home, so we hurried down the street to the Lexington Avenue Pet Shop. We spent a lot of time huddled over the turtle tank, trying to choose a twin to Herman."

Even at my age I knew that twins have their differences. Children sense the truth.

I wanted to toss this turtle out the window. But eventually I learned that the pain of loss is not something you can toss. Loss has to heal in its own time, just like the slow plodding of a turtle.

I was seven when Miss Margaret Turk arrived from Scotland to be my nurse. Gibby was too tired from helping the older children to be my full-time nanny, so she recruited a friend of hers for her days off. Miss

Turk was a pleasantly round woman, and I liked cuddling on her lap while she read me poems and stories. She had quiet energy. While my siblings played cards or dress-up with "the other mother," as Gibby was called, Miss Turk took me by the hand to Central Park. I loved going to the park. Sometimes I roller-skated along the paved paths, feeling momentary strength in the push and glide. Other times, as I watched people sail their miniature boats in the pond, I imagined myself the captain of a tiny ship on a big sea. *Let her out*, I could hear myself commanding, and my crew would fly to the lines to slack the sails, like in *The Borrowers Afloat*. In this fantasy of freedom and control I sniffed the scent of my own power. It mingled with the smell of apple blossoms and newly mown grass.

I remember one occasion when Miss Turk and I walked among the trees together and a few white blossoms floated into my hair. I picked one out and was looking at the delicate petals when I heard a terrible cry. It was not the sound of a human being but of an animal struggling for its life. Brutal laughter and savage grunts followed the sound as four boys came running over the hill. They had long sticks in their hands and were chasing a badly beaten and much frightened squirrel.

My fingers dug into Miss Turk's arm and I screamed to her at the top of my lungs, "PLEASE, MISS TURK. STOP THEM!" My words pelted like hailstones. In that moment, I was the squirrel. I felt its pain, its fear, and the precariousness of its life. I couldn't bear to look yet I watched through webbed fingers as she gathered herself and stomped over to the boys on her stumpy legs, waving her pudgy arms at them.

"You go away now. Be off with you! Stop your cruel ways." Her voice found power in the depth of her lungs and she rolled her *r* with conviction. The boys dropped their sticks and ran off. I have loved the Scottish accent ever since.

Miss Turk was breathing heavily. I sobbed. She put her soft arms around me, holding me tight to her breast. I could feel the adrenaline still pumping through her veins.

"It's time we go home now, dear Eileen."

How could that voice, which had wielded such power just minutes before, become so soft and comforting? No one had ever called me "dear Eileen" before. I vowed to myself that when I grew up I would be as brave and strong and kind as Miss Turk.

5.

FEELING DIFFERENT
AS A FAMILY

⟿

In the sixties it was embarrassing to be rich. It was even more embarrassing to be "Rockefeller rich." I never saw a Toulouse-Lautrec in anyone else's bathroom or a Cézanne portrait hanging over their living-room couch. We were different.

My father did not play ball and he never took out the garbage. I first saw a black-and-white television in our house when I was five, and we only watched it as a family on the first night. I learned early on that we were among the last families to own a TV, and to still have maids *and* finger bowls.

When friends our age came over for dinner and the main course was replaced with purple-glass finger bowls served on top of doilies on early nineteenth-century Spode plates, my siblings and I watched our wide-eyed friends shifting in their chairs. Sometimes we told them, with forced straight faces, that we were supposed to drink out of the bowls. Our mother had taught us that practical jokes and humor were levelers. They also relieved stress. Occasionally, we lifted the round bowls to our mouths, as if to drink from them, just to see if our guests would follow suit. It was very satisfying when they did. We laughed until our sides hurt, before explaining that the large velvety leaf of mint geranium floating on top was not for eating but to scent our hands should they need washing after picking up lamb chops with our fingers. We showed them how to place the finger bowls on their doilies to the upper left side of the plate. The real dessert was then served and our differences no longer felt so uncomfortable.

There were six of us siblings within a ten-and-a-half-year age span. David was given my father's name and became David Rockefeller Jr. Three sisters followed him: Abby Aldrich, named after my paternal grandmother; Neva Goodwin, named after my mother's mother; and Peggy (Margaret) Dulany, named after my mother. My brother Richard Gilder Rockefeller was named after my father's best friend from college, who died in World War II, and I was named after my mother's sister, Eileen McGrath. We each struggled to find our uniqueness. We wanted to be different from one another as a way of being seen, but being too different could be lonely.

My mother felt like an outsider amid her husband's family. She taught us, through her discomfort, to fit in wherever we went by wearing understated clothing, carrying our own bags, not driving fancy cars, and making friends regardless of others' wealth or status. We enjoyed going barefoot, hunting for mussels and mushrooms, getting our hands dirty, and wearing one another's hand-me-downs. She encouraged these behaviors as a means of normalizing us and liberating herself from the constraints of aristocracy.

My father was less complicated. He didn't seem to question whether or not he fit in. When asked how he felt about the name, he said, "I like being a Rockefeller," and expected us to feel the same. Somehow he also recognized that people of every background, race, and religion belonged equally. When I was a child, he quoted my grandfather, saying, "If there were five men in a boat which turned over in a storm, and each of them was of a different religion, would God have saved only the Christian? Of course not." Dad treated the chauffeur or taxi driver the same as a king or secretary of state. We learned these values from him daily, observing how he smiled and held out his hand to greet the butler when he arrived home as genuinely as he shook the hand of King Faisal of Saudi Arabia.

Friends of my parents, Linda and Bob Douglass, told me recently of a time when they went sailing with my parents in the Gulf of Maine. The weather turned bad and they had to find a safe harbor for the night. They were near the Bay of Fundy, where the tides can rise up to fifty-two feet. It was near low tide as they pulled up to the pilings of a dock. My father climbed some forty feet up a ladder. He was welcomed at the top by a toothless lobsterman wearing dirty, fish-scented foul-weather gear. My father reached out his hand as usual. "Hello. I'm David Rockefeller." The man looked him up and down and replied, in a thick Maine accent, "Well, I'll be damned."

My mother and their friends followed up the ladder and were soon in conversation with the lobsterman. After exchanging stories about the weather and how they came to be there, the man invited them up to his house to meet his wife of forty years. My parents and friends returned an hour later with a blueberry pie in hand for their supper and exclaimed that nothing had ever tasted so good. The next day they delivered a bottle of wine and a jar of homemade jam in exchange for their generosity.

These were the kinds of visits that my parents told us about at the dinner table. The message was always the same: treat everyone with humility and respect. There was another, unspoken message underlying it: *We are the American royalty. We have an extraordinary inheritance of both money and service. Do not disappoint.*

We children were not so comfortable inside the size of our name. *Rockefeller* has four syllables. At school during roll call, my name seemed to go on forever: "Eileen Rock-ef-ell-er?" I see the heads turning in fourth grade at the Brearley School in New York City. The memory still makes my hands sweat. I would slouch in my chair, hoping I could disappear as I answered in a soft voice, "Here." I often wished my family name could just be changed to "Rock."

Two of my three sisters and I did change our names after we reached our twenties. We used our given middle names. Neva took Goodwin. Peggy took Dulany, and I tried out McGrath. Abby stuck to Rockefeller, ready to challenge anyone who asked her an impertinent question. Children who aren't rich often feel entitled to ask the rich and famous questions as invasive as "How much money do you have?" This is kind of like going up to an obese person and asking, "How much do you weigh?" It's hard to imagine what might hurt when you're on the other side of the fence.

My father felt our voluntary name changes were disloyal, as if we had disaffected from the clan. In part he was right, but it was a necessary step in finding our own identity.

McGrath became my legal name for six years while I went to group therapy, studied transactional analysis and gestalt therapy, and tried to figure out who "Eileen" was apart from any other name. I became a professional weaver in my twenties, and sewed cloth labels onto all my pieces that read "Handmade by Eileen McGrath." I lived in Cambridge, Massachusetts, and felt very proud of myself for earning most of my income from weaving and teaching. I supplemented it with my trust fund when necessary but kept my self-earned income in a separate account.

I received my master's degree in early childhood development from Lesley College at age twenty-four and split my time between a paid teaching position at Milton Academy Lower School and selling my weavings in shows and commissions, both locally and in the Midwest.

No one to whom I sold knew my real last name, but living as a McGrath showed me how dependent I had become upon my Rockefeller name for instant identification. I felt uncomfortable meeting new people. *Rockefeller* had given me a starting place, an uncomfortable but familiar root in the ground from which to grow a conversation, and sometimes a relationship. Yet I could not always tell the difference between those who liked me for who I was and those who were simply curious to know me for what I symbolized.

"What's in a name? That which we call a rose by any other name would smell as sweet." Thank you, Shakespeare! I have carried this quote with me like a well-worn flannel shirt. It is good comfort on a gray day of inner turmoil.

The infatuation with my incognito name changed one night when I was at a party in Cambridge. I was doing the usual rounds of "Hi. I'm Eileen McGrath," expecting the usual "Nice to meet you" before they moved on. One person stopped me in my tracks when he asked, "Wait a minute. Are you related to the governor?" There was no governor by the name of McGrath at that time, but I felt like a deer in the headlights. Was he misinformed, or did he know I was related to the governor of New York State? Sigh . . . Whatever the reason, I took it as a sign that I had better go back to my given name. It was less confusing to have it right out there, with no ambiguity, than to play the guessing game of Do They Know Already? and wonder what they were really thinking.

Different or not, I reclaimed the Rockefeller name.

6.

THE SMALLEST COUNT

∽

We went to our country home every weekend. My mother wanted us to become familiar with animals and nature, and as my father had grown up across the road on the larger family estate, he was happy when his only sister sold him her house and five hundred acres. We had enough horses for all of us to ride, a donkey, named Cleopatra, that my mother brought home in the back of her station wagon, one goat, named Cricket—a herd of black angus cows, sheep, chickens, and a few pigs. Abby and Neva got in trouble for riding the sheep when the animals were pregnant, so my sisters turned their attention to one of the black angus cows they named Antonia. They improvised a harness for her and tried to teach her to pull a little red wagon. The cow ran away with Abby and Neva inside it, but my sisters got right back in every time. Peggy's goat regularly escaped its pasture and ran up to the house to find us. We often saw Cricket with her front feet resting on the windowsill outside our dining room when we were having lunch. Animals and nature were part of every weekend; this included beetles.

When I was small my father's attention was usually on his work, but on weekends at our farmhouse in Tarrytown, I remember looking for beetles with him. He had a huge collection of them in the basement. The beetles had been killed in alcohol, pinned and labeled, and lined up neatly in his beetle boxes. He took my hand as we walked out the front door of the Georgian-style brick house and, with his head already bent, his eyes scanned the ground like searchlights for little things that crawled and flew. Sometimes, one of our four Norwich terriers tagged along as we walked past our round swimming pool and out along the back lawn overlooking the Hudson River in the distance.

I was no older than six when my dad taught me to say *coleoptera*, the name of the order of the class Insecta. Beetles are hard-cased, with six legs. They are the most numerous species on earth, totaling 350,000, and representing 40 percent of all known insects. Dad was as proud of his growing collection of beetles as he was of his six children. He kept a glass "beetle bottle" in hand, just in case we found a good specimen.

Dad first became interested in beetles through a woman who tutored him in Maine the summer he was nine. Beetles were even smaller than he felt as the lonely youngest child in a family of six. The beetles in his collection down in the basement were lined up like schoolchildren or friends. For him I think it was the numbers that counted. To me it meant being together. My dad's passion for beetles became our first bridge of connection. As he's grown older, he's made it clear that nothing pleases him more than to be with family.

During his thirty-five years traveling around the world to help open branches for the Chase Manhattan Bank, he became famous for carrying his bottle on every trip, showing off his beetles with as much enthusiasm as I felt for a doll he brought me from South Africa or a tortoiseshell comb from Spain. In Africa, he collected three-inch-long rhinoceros or dung beetles, from the family Scarabaeidae. To my awe-struck six-year-old eyes they resembled the prehistoric *Tyrannosaurus rex*, on six legs. In South America, he collected five-inch-long longhorn beetles, from the family Cerambycidae. My seven-year-old eyes widened at their resemblance to a hard-shelled cockroach. He might just as easily return home with a rove beetle (family Staphylinidae), no bigger than a scrap of thread on the end of a pin. By then, my eight-year-old eyes were well trained to see even the smallest specimens. I took them down to the "beetle room" to look at them under the microscope with our beetle man, Freddie.

Freddie Solana became a close friend of my father's during his fresh-man year at Harvard University. Dad met him while doing social work in a poor section of Boston. He took a group of disadvantaged high school students on a field trip and showed them beetles. Freddie be-came deeply interested. Dad asked whether he could pay him to help organize his collection. Freddie readily accepted the invitation and soon came to share my father's fascination. Dad later helped him go to college. Freddie studied business, and after graduating he worked week-days at the Chase Manhattan Bank and spent weekends working on my dad's beetle collection, identifying them, pinning and labeling them, and lining them up in wooden boxes.

All six of us children could be heard yelling to my father on a Satur-day afternoon, "Look, Daddy! I found a Curculionid!" No sooner had we found one and popped it in alcohol for a quick death than we ran to show him. I was disappointed that his enthusiasm for my discoveries was never as strong as for his own. Luckily, Freddie was always de-lighted with everything we found. My brothers and sisters and I spent many hours with him, learning their Latin names, their body parts, and how their hard exoskeletons provided a kind of armor for protection. I marveled at their clearly perceptible mandibles, head, thorax, and abdomen and was fascinated by how big their eyes were in proportion to their bodies.

My father was not interested in these things. I competed with my siblings for his attention over who had the most, whose were the best-labeled, or who had the biggest or prettiest. Freddie helped us see that each of our specimens was beautiful, and I loved him for it.

Sometimes I envied beetles' hard shells, and wished I could crawl under a leaf with them. I wondered how it would feel to be part of a family that belonged everywhere on earth. Some of them were jewel-like iridescent greens, pinks, or purples, from the jungles of South America or the bark of a tree outside my window. In examining beetles I grew curious about the world. As we were taught their many family names, I learned there was an order of things, much smaller than us but far more powerful in proportion to their size. They work in harmony to recycle life by tearing down the flesh of dead animals and plants. I envied their clear purpose and rightful place in the larger web of life.

Many years later, when I was at my dad's house recovering from surgery, I asked him why he had been attracted to collecting over 150,000 specimens. His answer is a lesson:

"Beetles teach one about the extraordinary variety and organization of nature. You can go anywhere in the world and find beetles that you can identify. As I travel I find friends. How is it that nature has provided this extraordinary variety of animals that can be found anywhere you go? The world isn't just a conglomerate. It has order and structure. I find that rewarding, refreshing, and significant. If you know a little about nature, you can know a little about things around the world. We live in a world where man is the predominant force, but the fact is there are vastly more species of beetles than humans."

Through beetles my father has found his own sense of humility. He has had many successes in the business world and long associations with conglomerates of capitalism, but he has kept his eye to the ground, to the little things in life that really run the world. His interest and perspective have taught me to keep my eyes open, to look with wonder at the natural world, and to treasure beauty and relationships wherever I find them.

7.

"You Shot the Rabbits?"

∿

The third week of July my family's bags filled the spacious front hall of the house in Tarrytown, waiting to be transported to Maine. A din of excitement filled the air for days as we each pulled clothes out of drawers and stuffed them in our suitcases. Packing was something my parents taught us to do ourselves, just like they did. Maine was the place we felt most free. We spent six weeks there each summer, until the end of August. I was three the last summer we traveled by overnight train. Thereafter, we drove and later flew on the family plane.

Our dinner table in Maine was noisy. The blue-and-white wallpaper of the dining room did little to dampen the sound of excited voices above the clatter of china plates and glasses. Until I was five, when my siblings started heading off to boarding school, there were often no fewer than ten people for meals. This included my parents, the six of us children, and two nurses. Summertime was more casual and I was included at the adult table even at dinner. Given the age span in our conversations, tones of voice varied and the rhythm of emotions undulated like a pennywhistle. Perhaps it was for this reason that my mother developed her talent for storytelling. She was one of a family of four children with bright and articulate parents, all of whom were good storytellers. Whether she consciously developed her talent or stumbled upon its effect, the response from us was the same. My mother's stories brought our storms of competition, isolation, hurt, and anger to a lull. The waves of sibling rivalry would quiet as we watched her face soften in preparation for a story. Her eyes would lift up and to the right as she recalled the images she was about to paint in words.

On one such occasion during the summer, when we were having Sunday lunch in Maine, she told us a story that had all of us on the edge of our seats. She and my father had just returned from a cruise on their sailboat and their skins were salty as they kissed us hello in the gravel driveway. We gathered around them like puppies, as my mother told us with emphasis, "We shot the rapids." My siblings and I had never seen rapids so this statement did not win them the sympathy they were looking for, especially since we misunderstood a crucial word. Loud wails of accusative questioning were heard from the older ones. "What? You shot the *rabbits*? That's so mean." It took some time before my mother could calm us down enough, between her laughter and tears of relief to be home alive, to tell us the whole story. But finally, we were seated for lunch, and after the meat and vegetables had been passed, she explained.

In those days their version of cruising was more like today's backpacking. Their thirty-six-foot boat, called the *Jack Tar*, was sleek in the water, slender at her girth, and had no motor or electricity. Built in 1915, the same year they were born, the R class boat was primarily built for racing, but it could accommodate two people sleeping on narrow bunks below. My parents attached a charcoal grill off the stern for cooking. They used a washbasin for the dishes and a bucket for their toilet. They did not mind the simplicity for it was a welcome contrast to the complexity of their normal lives. They loved being out on the ocean together in the wilderness of weather and water. With the hoisting of their sails by hand winches and the drop of their mooring, they were off. Their boat was so sensitive to wind that it could drift on a breath of air as easily as it could churn waves behind it in a sudden gust.

A wonderful Mainer, named Donald Bryant, drove their forty-foot motorboat at some distance behind them just to make sure they did not get stranded on a rock in the thick of fog. They would set off before him to enjoy their privacy and freedom, so coveted by my mother. Donald would wait for several hours or more before turning on the engine and cruising at twelve knots in the *Tartan* to catch up with them by late afternoon or evening. When my parents found a harbor and dropped anchor, they would wave Donald over to raft the boats together for the night and make dinner. They grilled off the stern of the *Jack Tar* and cooked everything else on board the motorboat, for it had a gas stove, running water, and a head. While my mother prepared dinner, my father made martinis, and they sat on deck, recounting the adventures of the day. These moments, a long way from their usual responsibilities, brought deep inhalations and easy conversation, as soft as the night. I know, because in later years I often went with them.

The weather and tides were not always so conducive to relaxation. This time they had sailed into the Bay of Fundy, between New Brunswick and Nova Scotia, where the reversing tides push as much water through a narrow entry passage in one cycle as all the freshwater rivers of the world combined. This equals about one billion tons of seawater, squeezed through a narrow passage with such force that it forms whirlpools and waterfalls on the ingress or egress. My parents had heard about these tides and decided to sail up the coast. Donald motored behind them at a respectful distance. The adventure was more than they bargained for and they were still looking a bit ashen when they returned to tell the tale.

"Well," she began. "Your father and I have had the worst experience of our lives."

The room fell silent, all eyes and ears turned in her direction.

"First of all," she said, swallowing her *r* as usual to make it sound more like *fwyst*, "the Bay of Fundy has the highest tides in the world. They rise and fall fifty-two feet every six hours. So you can imagine how much water has to run through the narrow passage up to the head of the bay before it turns around. We had been warned that the only way to get through alive in a boat such as ours was to pass through the narrows at slack tide. But somehow we miscalculated the time. The water moves so fast that it literally makes whirlpools and falls through the narrows."

Our eyes widened as we tried to imagine this place of imminent danger. She looked around the table to punctuate the gravity of the situation before continuing.

"We discussed our plans with Donald and he suggested tying a line between his stern and our bow, so as to pull us through if we got stuck. I felt strongly that this was not a good idea. Your father and Donald argued with me for some time, but I held my ground on instinct."

My mother did not believe in God, but she did believe in her instinct and intuition.

"As it turned out, had we been tied to the *Tartan* we would not be here to tell this story."

My mother had a knack for drama and her stories were made larger by exaggeration, but in this case she was probably telling the truth.

"After some discussion, they finally consented, as we knew that the longer we talked, the faster the tide would be running. At least it was going out and we would be able to ride the waves in the right direction. We hoisted our sails and, with the wind against us, tacked our way toward the rippling water. Donald had motored ahead of us as planned, and we heard him gun the engine while we watched in horror as the boat turned in circles with the force of the whirling water. He had just enough power to push his way through the tide rip, and he shot through the rapids.

"Now, children, I don't mean we shot the *rabbits*," she emphasized, as a smile returned briefly to her face. I could not be sure, but it seemed that her curly brown Afro-like hair was standing on end even farther from her head. The mounting tension created electricity in the room that mixed with the salt air outside and seemed to crackle in the space around my ears. I could not imagine how their sailboat would make it through after her description of the *Tartan*. I looked around the table and noticed we were all leaning in closer over our plates. You could hear a fork drop.

"As soon as Donald was through the rapids, he turned the *Tartan* around to see what we would do. From where I sat, holding the jib, I could tell he was pretty shaken. The wind was picking up and we had to tack our way to the rapids to keep some control of our direction, even though the tide was by now sweeping us on at an alarming rate. Your father was at the tiller, his face tense as we started to enter the first whirlpool. It turned our boat counterclockwise and our bow started heading for a rock on one side of the narrows. By now the jib and main were luffing as our boat bobbed helplessly, caught in the wind and waves, which were now crashing at our sides and lurching us into the next whirlpool. It was clear we were going to be propelled into the rocks at the right side of the narrows. Then, just as we were within an inch of our lives, I yelled to your father, 'PUSH THE TILLER AWAY!' At that very moment he had the same instinct and pushed with all his might."

In recalling this moment, my mother's eyes glistened with tears. I could see the looming rock, the crashing of waves, and the relentless pull and twirl of water. The fear on my tongue tasted like metal. I could hardly wait for her to continue.

"With the sudden, violent push of the tiller our boat whipped to the left and in a blink of an eye we shot the rapids. I must admit that your father and I were shaking all over. When we looked up to see Donald in the *Tartan*, he was white as a ghost. But we made it. And we're glad to be home."

I left my chair and went to sit on my mother's lap. I tried to think of something I could give her so that she would never leave home again, but nothing worked. She went on many trips as I was growing up, and I never stopped missing her.

ভ

Sailing together is a crash course in familiarity. The Baltic cruise my parents took my pal Margie Erhart and me on in 1967 turned out to have the emphasis on *crash*. They invited their friends Dick and Bunny Dilworth and chartered a boat with a captain, Torstein Lord, to help navigate the rocky waters.

Dick Dilworth was head of our family office. He and Bunny were nervous by nature and Dick often worked himself to exhaustion. My parents thought this week would be a relaxing vacation for the four of them. Margie and I were along for the adventure.

Our boat was sixty feet long and drew a good seven feet from her keel. She belonged to a Swedish friend of my parents, Marcus Wallenberg, a banker and industrialist. We spent the first night at his house in Stockholm. I had never before seen the midnight sun and I remember him coming into Margie's and my room to show us how to turn the wooden shutters so we could sleep. But it was not the light that kept us awake so much as the excitement.

I met Margie in fourth grade at the Brearley School in New York. She was blond as the Swedes and marched to her own drummer. She did one hundred push-ups daily. Physical activity kept her wiry, and she was up for anything.

The next day Mr. Wallenberg took us down to his boat. It had fine teak decks and a large cockpit. There was ample space between the cockpit and the hatchway for the living quarters. Margie and I were given twin bunks just aft of the stairway. We stowed our clothes and came up above to look at a chart that Torstein was showing my parents of the many islands through which we were going to be sailing.

North of Stockholm, Sweden has a prolific archipelago, dotted with evergreen islands. The shores of the islands are so steep, you can tie your boat to a tree on land and anchor from the stern. This was a first for us, as Maine islands have more gradual shores and anchoring is usually farther out.

We explored new islands each day to stretch our legs, and we pored over charts to see where we would go next. In contrast to my parents' and the Dilworths' usual chock-a-block lives, there was no definite plan. The only destination was our final one, the port of Mariehamn, the capital of Åland. Mariehamn is an important port for both Sweden and Finland and, as an autonomous territory under Finnish sovereignty, a popular destination for sailors. Margie and I helped trim the mainsail and my parents took turns on the jib. The Dilworths huddled together like two cats curled up in the sun. Their faces already looked less harried.

My mother was full of laughter, as always on a boat. Her joy was infectious. She was a superb cook and had an iron stomach well suited to sailing. I was her sous-chef and learned most of my skill from her while cruising. She taught me how to make soups from scratch as well as vegetables, meats, and dessert crepes. We were both most comfortable improvising. Her mother left behind recipes on scraps of paper that gave bare essentials. One recipe for stewed apricots and prunes listed the basic ingredients of apricots, prunes, sugar, grated orange peel, a dash of Kirsch, and no quantities. She cooked everything by taste and intuition, just the way she led her life.

Cooking was a liberating experience for me, in sharp contrast to the exactness with which I had been taught manners or the expectations for correctness in conversational knowledge. I am an intuitive and feeling person, so this kind of cooking was right up my alley.

The afternoon we were headed to Mariehamn we saw a sailboat race appearing and disappearing around islands. There was a brisk breeze and we heeled over, going a steady clip of ten knots. The boat weighed fifty tons and left quite a wake behind her.

My father was at the wheel, as usual, with Torstein at his side. Dick Dilworth was standing to windward on the port side of the deck near the closely trimmed mainsail, his hand resting on the boom. Bunny was sitting behind him above the cabin. Margie was crouched on the stern and my mother was kneeling just in front of the hatchway with me behind her. We were looking for sailboats.

All of a sudden, there was a loud bang. The boat came to a jolting stop, listing on her side. I was thrown forward against something blunt and felt my cheek swelling, but I was more concerned about my mother. She was curled over, holding her head. The left lens of her glasses was shattered beside her and her eye was bleeding. She was very quiet, as she became when something was serious.

I handed her Kleenex from my pocket, and as I looked up before hurrying down below to get more, I noticed both Dick and Bunny standing together, dripping blood from their foreheads. I turned around on the stairs to see Torstein at the wheel and my father holding his head. There was no blood, thankfully, and Margie came to his side. She and Torstein did not seem to have been injured.

The next few minutes passed like a slow-motion film. I came up from the cabin with paper toweling and ice. At fifteen, I had learned enough about first aid from seeing my older brothers and sisters get hurt, and observing my mother's quick response, to know that ice and clean paper or cloth was a good first step. My mother was afraid to touch her eye because she thought there was a piece of glass in it. I picked up her glasses from a growing pool of blood and handed toweling and ice to her and the Dilworths. My father came to my mother's side and shouted to Torstein, "Where is the nearest hospital?" Torstein assured him we were already headed for it.

Margie and I were now the only functioning crew. Torstein turned on the engine and managed to get the boat off the rock. We later learned it was not on the charts. No leaks so far, so he came up into the wind and asked Margie and me to take the sails down. I was glad Margie had done all those push-ups. Adrenaline pumped more strength into both of us and before long we had the jib and main down. We were furling the main as the little sailboats came around the point of an island. The people looked at our large boat and waved. I remember feeling angry.

I wished they knew we were in the middle of an emergency, but there was too much to do and I could only wave quickly before tying the ties around the main as fast as I could.

The rest of the trip into the port is a blur. Margie and I were darting back and forth to get the bumpers set out on the rail lines in case there was room at a dock. My dad asked me for more ice for my mother and more towels, too. The only thing she said was, "I hope it didn't cut my eye." My mother's vision was so poor, she was almost legally blind. She could not afford to lose an eye. I was moving too fast to cry or to feel much of anything.

In those days there were no cell phones and Torstein couldn't call on the ship-to-shore radio because he was busy navigating a safe passage into port. It turned out there was no space available at a dock so we had to pick up a mooring. Margie got out the boat hook and together we managed to pull the heavy line onto the foredeck and secure it around the large cleat. This seemed to take forever. Torstein asked Margie and me to stay on board while he took them to the hospital by taxi.

After they left, we sat down for the first time and my legs began to tremble. We looked around. Blood was everywhere, staining the beautiful teak decks. We looked at each other and our glances exchanged something like a prayer.

To keep our fear at bay, we found two scrub brushes and hauled up buckets of seawater to swab the decks while talking all the while about the boats out there beyond the harbor, the shock of hitting the rock, and how amazing it was that our boat slid off without springing a leak. All the while I was wondering how badly hurt my mother was and whether she had lost her eye. I scrubbed hard to keep from panicking.

When we had the boat looking pretty good, we sat down to ponder what to do next. Margie was great in a crisis. She kept her cool, and even her sense of humor. She said, "I know. Let's make them some drinks for when they return."

"That's a great idea," I responded. "How about some Bloody Marys?" Neither of us had ever made a drink before, but I had spied some Bloody Mary mix in the bar and knew from watching that they used vodka. We put an ample splash in each glass, piled in ice, and poured Bloody Mary mix over the top. The irony of this drink after swabbing the decks had not yet sunk in, but when the adults returned soon thereafter, the sight of red drinks provided comic relief.

My mother told me that the glass sliver had cut within a hairbreadth of her eyeball, but there was no damage to her eye. I looked at the tiny stitches and breathed a sigh of relief. The Dilworths both had a railroad track of stitches across their foreheads. Bunny's was a lateral wound and Dick's was vertical. We joked at how together they made a plus sign. My dad had a very swollen cheek and was starting to get two black eyes. We contemplated various scenarios to tell the folks back home and soon our nerves were eased as we giggled over fighting off pirates at sea. I looked at my mother and realized that had she not been in front of me, I would have been the one with stitches. I did not know until that day that I was good in an emergency. I had crossed an important threshold toward adulthood.

8

MAID TO ORDER

❧

My mother was famous for her pranks. A favorite story of mine is the time she and her childhood friend Lila Nields dressed up as maids and served dinner to my grandfather Rockefeller. He and my grandmother had invited ten prominent people to dinner at their house at 10 West Fifty-Fourth Street in New York City.

Grandfather was strictly punctual and he was clearly irritated when my mother and her friend did not show up on time. At two minutes past the hour, he insisted the group sit down without them.

The table was set with some of Grandfather's best blue-and-white Crown Derby china. No sooner were napkins drawn to laps than two gray-haired maids with black uniforms and white aprons appeared with bowls of soup. True to protocol, my grandfather was last to be served. The maid holding his bowl of soup was wearing pince-nez glasses. Her hands and head had such a vigorous tremor that the old-fashioned glasses fell into the soup before him. She shrieked a little too loudly and plucked them out of the soup before my grandfather's widening eyes. The maid was my mother.

Her friend Lila was waiting behind the screen at the entrance to the pantry. As my mother disappeared, there was a loud *crash!* of dishes falling to the floor. Grandfather winced as he heard his fine china shattering. My mother decided it was the time to reveal Lila's and her identities. They came out from behind the screen and collapsed in laughter as they held their gray wigs in one hand and their pince-nez in the other. The dinner party erupted with glee and my mother explained that the broken china was just cheap plates they had bought for the occasion. My grandfather's relief was palpable. After seeing he was the brunt of the joke and that no harm had been done, he joined in with good humor. The normally formal atmosphere had loosened like a tie.

My mother's predilection for practical jokes had a long history. She boasted to us how one winter, as a rebellious adolescent at the Rippowam School in Bedford, New York, she slipped a wedge of Limburger cheese behind the radiator of her classroom. The stench grew so strong that they had to close the entire school for two days before discovering the cause. No one ever found out who did it.

Sometimes Mum encouraged us to conspire with her. I still remember the horrified look on my father's face one night at our house in New York City. My mother enlisted Peggy, Richard, and me to help in turning each painting upside down in the morning room. It took two nights, and my mother's prompt after dinner, "Why don't we have our coffee in the morning room?" before Dad noticed. "We haven't sat there in awhile," she coaxed cunningly, her tone as smooth as honey. We children could hardly contain ourselves as we giggled behind our hands.

Dad sat down and looked around. His eyes blinked twice, as if he was having a dizzy spell. He turned to Mum and said in a mildly reproachful tone, "Why, darling, what have you done? This is shocking beyond belief." I believe he coined the phrase then and there, but what amazed us most was it had taken him a day to notice. In retrospect, he probably had a lot on his mind at the office, and the Matisse looked pretty good either way.

The next summer my mother thought up another prank. She asked Donald, who was a born mechanic, to help her find some pieces of metal in a nearby junkyard and weld them together into a modern sculpture. They came home with an old tailpipe and several other pieces, looking like two schoolchildren who had just put Limburger cheese behind the radiator. Her plan was to see if she could fool my father into buying her "sculpture" from our art dealer friend, Mr. David Thompson, who summered in Seal Harbor. He had helped Dad discover several new artists and Mum asked him to be in on the joke. He agreed.

They set up shop in the garage and I helped hand rusty metal shapes to Donald as he welded the pieces together at Mum's direction. By the time the piece was finished, we thought we had one up on Brancusi's *Bird in Space*. The rather clumsy rendition of an abstract person with a very long esophagus and a bow tie at the top was wrapped up and brought over to Mr. Thompson's house. He placed it on a stand in front of the sliding door, with a towel over it, so the light from behind would shine on the steel when it was unveiled.

At Mum's request, Mr. Thompson invited my parents to lunch along with the three younger children for a viewing of "a very interesting piece by an up-and-coming young artist." Mr. Thompson served martinis to the grown-ups. Small talk ensued. He waited until Dad was partway through his martini before disrobing the piece. "What do you think, David? Only five thousand."

Dad looked at it with mild interest at first, but as he took another sip, and looked at my mother's approving eye, he cocked his head and spoke with typically measured tone. "Well, I think five thousand is not an unreasonable price." This was a most satisfactory answer to all of us scamps, most of all my mother, who could no longer contain her laughter. Tears poured down her cheeks under her glasses and we all joined in the merriment, to the detriment of my gullible and very forgiving father.

In my dad's defense, most of the time he had clear and well-studied views on art, but he thought very highly of Mr. Thompson's opinion and even more of my mother's. He and Mum always bought art together. When all was said and done, he still contended, perhaps for his pride as much as the truth, "But I still think it's quite a wonderful piece." We kept it in the garage for years afterward.

My favorite story of all was when Mum convinced Peggy, Richard, and me to steal a ram from an island in Maine. We were sailing overnight on my parent's forty-foot Hinckley yawl and had just put down anchor in between Merchant and Harbor Islands. Dad stayed on the boat while Peggy, Richard, Mum, Donald, and I rowed ashore to Harbor Island. We had seen sheep grazing and wanted to try to pet one.

It was the late sixties, and everyone seemed to be blasting through the edge of conformity. Streakers ran through executive boardrooms, women burned their bras in public, and men dodged the draft. So what was the harm in stealing a ram for a little boat ride?

I was twelve at the time and Peggy and Richard were in their midteens. We pulled the dinghy up on the beach and headed toward the grazing sheep. They turned out to be quite tame, and as the ram came forward to protect his flock, Mum had a sudden inspiration. "Let's take him up to the boat to see if your father will believe us that we want to have lamb chops for dinner." She might as well have said, "Let's eat the whole tub of ice cream." We were in. Donald shook his head with amused resignation and grabbed the ram's horns while Mum straddled it. Richard, Peggy, and I flanked the poor beast, helping to push and pull our captive down to the water's edge.

I steadied the rowboat while the others lifted the astonished animal into the bow. Mum quickly removed her blue jean jacket and held it over the ram's head before he could think about where he was or whether he wanted to jump out. She sat in front of him on the bow. Peggy and I sat to either side at midships and dug our fingers into the ram's thick fleece on either side of his back to help steady him. His wool smelled sweetly of lanolin and sea lavender. Richard took the oars from the stern as Donald pushed us off with a twinkle in his eye. The four of us and the blindfolded ram put the water up to the gunnels. We hoped our stowaway would not protest as we headed for my father and his sailboat.

Dad had somehow missed all the commotion. When we came alongside the *Jack Tar II*, my mother yelled for him in her most endearing tone, "David? We have something for you for dinner." He came quickly then, and when he saw what we had in the boat his eyes widened large as crabs. "Why, darling, what have you done?" The ram was beginning to squirm, but she was undaunted. "We just thought you might like some lamb for dinner." Her smile belied her impishness, and we all waited for his refrain. "But this is shocking beyond belief! You can't steal a sheep from someone else's island!"

Even as he said this, he knew she would relent. The ram was already increasingly agitated, swaying from one side of the dinghy to the other. He would soon have us in the water if we didn't row him back quickly. We returned to the island and the ram jumped right out, shaking his coat with indignation. We traded him for Donald. Laughter trailed over the water in the quiet of dusk as we grilled lamb chops off the stern and hoisted a small pirate's flag up the mast, just in case anyone was looking.

Mum's stories gave me early permission to try my own practical joke. An idea came to me one Saturday when I was eight, while visiting with my father's beetle man, Freddie Solana.

Freddie was my pal. He had a soft spot for children, and my friend Lisa Diethelm and I liked being around him. We tromped down the stairs to the basement and found him amid the smell of camphor and cedar wood organizing my father's collection of coleoptera. In between the lineups of carefully pinned and labeled beetles he gave bucking bronco rides on hands and knees to my siblings, friends, and me. He was our playmate and teacher. When we visited him, he often had some especially interesting specimen pinned under the microscope for us to see close up. We learned that beauty is not always apparent at first glance.

One of the most familiar beetle families is the ladybug (family Coccinellidae), which nests in windowsills. In the beetle room on one particular Saturday morning my friend Lisa and I chanted, "Ladybug, ladybug, fly away home. Your house is on fire. Your children are alone." Freddie listened while hunched over the label he was painstakingly penning with permanent ink in tiny but neat handwriting.

I loved to lie on my stomach at the edge of our pond and watch the whirligig water beetles (family Gyrinidae) twirling like tops on the surface. As a girl in the basement with Freddie I practiced being a whirligig on the rug behind his chair. At other times I imitated the dung-rolling scarabs (family Scarabaeidae), pretending I was in the African savannah walking behind an elephant. Freddie was the elephant. My favorite was the blue metallic jewel beetle (family Buprestidae). This wood borer comes in many different colors, from green with purple heads, to stripes of yellow, blue, green, and red, to glossy metallic blue. It is also a large beetle. Lisa and I dressed up as Buprestids, donning extra swaths of shimmering material from the dress-up drawer to dance around the beetle room. Freddie admired us and we felt like jewels.

One day, Lisa and I decided to surprise Freddie with a different kind of costume. It was February and for my eighth birthday I had been given a cowboy outfit, complete with leather chaps, fringed vest, gloves, and cowboy boots. I put them on and buckled up my holster and toy metal gun over the chaps. I felt just like Red, the cowboy who managed my uncle Laurance's ranch in Wyoming. Lisa found a cowboy hat in the dress-up drawer and I coiled up a rope to give to her for a lasso. We stomped down the linoleum-covered stairs to the beetle room, feeling very tall and tough. Freddie heard us and turned his bald head toward us, laughing. His voice sounded like velvet.

Lisa's father was a doctor. He was gone from home almost as much as my father. She and I did not understand the connection between our yearning for our fathers' company and Freddie, but he was a good stand-in and he was not going anywhere. We would make sure of it. We asked if he would let us tie him up, just for a little while. His work must have reached a slow point, for he agreed.

First, we tied his ankles to the legs of his chair. Lisa took one side and I took the other. I used my best wrangler knots. Red would have been proud of me. When we finished, the knots looked like snakes wound around his ankles.

Next, we took his arms and put them behind the chair, crossing one wrist over the other, like we had seen in cowboy movies. He struggled a little bit and we assured him we would untie him very soon. I loved Freddie for his patience. He let us put slipknots around his wrists, tying them together. We took the remainder of the rope and made more square knots.

There was only one more thing to do. We tied a red bandana around Freddie's mouth, just to make sure he did not kiss us.

Just then my mother called downstairs to tell us lunch was ready. We had to come right away. We were hungry and, not daring to delay, we hurried upstairs, promising Freddie we would be right back.

Lisa and I kept our conquest a secret. We looked at each other across the dining-room table during lunch and smothered giggles amid the din of conversation between my mother, several brothers and sisters, and our nanny. When Mum asked who wanted to go riding after lunch, Lisa and I forgot everything and eagerly raised our hands. We were cowboys, after all. We had forgotten that Freddie was still downstairs, trying fervently to untie himself while calling for help. His voice was muffled under the bandana and no one heard him.

It took Freddie two hours to untie himself before going home. He probably wasn't too pleased at the time. Perhaps he blamed himself for being so gullible. How could two eight-year-olds have tied him up so well? He clearly underestimated our skill in knot tying. Lisa and I had underestimated the strength of our desire for a father at home.

My biggest fear was that Freddie would stop coming on Saturdays. The next week, when he appeared as usual, I quickly offered to give *him* a bronco ride. He politely declined, putting extra camphor in the corners of the cedar boxes as an added protection against invasive pests and little girls. He lined up the specimens on pins in neat rows, like schoolchildren, on the white cork surface. I was glad I was not a beetle. When he offered me another bucking bronco ride, I knew he had forgiven me and I quickly promised never to tie him up again.

9.

A SAFE HARBOR

~

Every family is an island, but not every family gets to own one. Buckle Island was the backyard of my summer childhood fun. Located about fifteen miles by sea from our home on Mount Desert Island, in Maine, my parents discovered it one day in 1961 while sailing through Jericho Bay. A storm was brewing from the east and they had no motor on their slender R boat. Their chart showed a safe harbor just ahead by Buckle Island. They sailed in and dropped anchor. One of the happiest phases of my childhood was about to begin. My family and the many friends who joined us on the twenty-acre island over the next ten years spent time there without pressure or responsibility. Buckle Island became a safe harbor for us all.

On that first stormy day when my parents rowed ashore, my mother told me she felt a déjà vu. Something about the island caught her fancy, or perhaps she recognized a longing in herself, like Mole in *The Wind in the Willows*, who smells his home after returning from adventures with his friend the river rat. She sniffed drifts of balsam wafting from the dark woods and pungent seaweed covering mud-soaked clams at half tide. She heard the warning screams of gulls overhead as the sky darkened. The impending storm did not scare her, for she felt safe on the island, as if encountering an old friend.

I like to imagine my parents dragging the rowboat up above the tide line and tying the painter line around a pink granite rock. Farther up onshore they sight the white-flecked remains of Indian clamshell middens partially covered in grass and earth. They explore the dense wilderness of balsam and spruce, mossy outcroppings, and tracks of deer and raccoons. Above the high tide beach they discover a fisherman's shack and peer through its windows at rusted cans and broken glass on the floor. My mother dreams aloud to my father. "David, wouldn't it be fun to buy this island and build our own cabin on it?" They stand together dreaming, shoulder to shoulder.

Later that year, my mother bought Buckle Island from a lobsterman for three hundred dollars. Carl Lawson lived on neighboring Swan's Island, along with several hundred other people, year-round. The ferry between Swan's Island and Mount Desert Island had been built just the year before, opening up the island to summer people. Each year more sailboats dotted the ocean as cruising became a refined form of wilderness camping.

It was a sunny, blue-sky day when my parents, and Richard and Peggy and I, sailed in my parents' new Bermuda 40 from Seal Harbor to Buckle Harbor. No sooner had we dropped anchor than Mr. Lawson's lobster boat came sputtering around the end of the island. We were downwind of it, and the smell of dead fish rushed up my nostrils as he slowed to a drift alongside our sailboat. My parents waved and shouted hellos. Mr. Lawson extended one hand with three missing fingers while his good hand held the wheel. He pulled his boat up alongside ours, and I could see that his well-worn overalls were speckled with fish and salt.

"Glad to see you, Carl," my mother shouted, ignoring the smell. "How are you?"

"Oh, not too bad, considering all the fog we've been havin'." A toothless smile cracked his stubbled face. "Did you hear about the boat that dragged anchor last night out of Seal Cove and went on the rocks? It took three fishin' boats to pull her off. You must have brought the sun today." He spoke with an accent thick as fog, words rolling over his toothless gums, unself-consciously, as he and my parents talked on like old friends. Sometimes he was hard to understand. But one thing was clear as the sky above. Mr. Lawson loved my parents, and his life.

He did not have much in the way of material goods and we knew he must earn the equivalent of minimum wage, but he insisted on giving us lobsters anyway.

"Really, Carl. You mustn't," insisted my father.

"Nope. I was hopin' you'd come by as I had some extra. Glad you're here." Mr. Lawson seemed to profit more from our company and the stories. The exchange became a ritual each time we visited.

My mother reached for a box. "We brought you some fresh vegetables from our garden and we need to get rid of this extra beer, for the ice in our ice box is melting." She knew just how to thank and repay him simultaneously. Mr. Lawson might be poor in pocket, but he was rich at heart and my parents valued his friendship as much as any leader from around the world.

We visited often after that because my mother had bought a prefabricated cabin and planned to erect it on the site of the old fisherman's shack. This was the beginning of our family project.

We came in the forty-foot motorboat, bringing boatloads of wood, nails, bags of cement for footings, tar paper, saws, hammers, and other equipment. None of us except Donald, who drove the motorboat, had built anything like this before. Donald knew engines and carpentry like Mr. Lawson knew lobstering. His modest nature and hands-on experience made him a natural teacher and guide. He knew how to stay one step behind us, allowing us the pleasure of discovery. Yet he was there with a measuring tape when plans went askew.

The summer we began, I was twelve, Richard was fifteen, and Peggy was sixteen. It was 1964. My parents were in their forties and my older siblings had all left home. There was something for each of us to do and we had enough combined energy to work for hours at a time. Once the shack was removed, my mother held up a window frame to determine which view she wanted to build the house around. Then we laid the foundation.

The project spanned several summers. In addition to the cabin, we constructed a rock wall around a small vegetable garden and built an outhouse about one hundred feet away. The cabin was furnished with a table, benches, chairs, and bunk beds, all made by my mother and Donald. We put a woodstove in one corner and set a wooden barrel outside to collect rainwater for washing dishes. Kerosene lanterns hung from the walls and my mother chose sturdy colored tin cups and plates along with iron frying pans and pots. Eventually, we attached an additional room with a double bed. After the final touch—a pump organ for music—we named our cabin "Buckle Botel" as a pun on *hotel*. We could not house many people at a time, but it was a home of our own making, and, having been one of the builders, I edged my toe through the door with fresh confidence.

Once the cabin was built and furnished, we cleared trails around the island. When we got too hot we separated boys from girls, found our respective beaches, and jumped in without clothes. Maine water wakes you up in a hurry. After a skinny-dip we took time to let our tingling skin dry in the sun.

My mother was more at home in this landscape than any other. Buckle Island became the realization of her dream of independence and freedom. She absorbed herself in projects of her own choosing, and whenever she talked about them, rapture spread like dawn upon her face.

Our adventures stretched into days and weeks and dreams. Buckle Island occupied my thoughts as I worked on math problems over the winter. It brought me to the page of my poetry long before I knew I could write. It was a place where fantasies blazed trails through the darkest part of the island of self. Buckle Island was a safe harbor for all kinds of exploration. Friends who had never spent time in the countryside or wilderness learned how to get their hands dirty, digging clams with their fingers or making rafts out of driftwood and recycled nails. It was an island without plumbing, electricity, or stores. But it had all the ingredients for a good life.

Over time, we got to know Buckle Island in every season. One February my mother took my brother Richard, my friend Holly Duane, and me to Maine for our school vacation. The temperature had been well below freezing for several weeks and my mother was looking for ways to occupy us. She decided it would be fun to spend a night in Buckle Botel. Visions of ice-encrusted windows, cold feet, and the stir of adventure ran a shiver down my spine. I loved camping and backpacking but being on an island in winter was going to be a first for all of us. "This will be an adventure," said Mum. Nothing pleased her more than to brave the elements in hopes that normal schedules would be disrupted. Excitement was in the air as she put together the food. We each packed an extra set of clothes and bundled up in long underwear, blue jeans, flannel shirts, mittens, hats, and parkas. Richard and I wore the red Scandinavian sweaters Mum had knit for us. She drove us to the dock and we trundled down the ramp like overstuffed penguins on a migration march. The cold air bit my nose.

The only boat able to take us through the freezing and partially frozen water was a scallop dragger. It was ten o'clock in the morning when it drew alongside the family dock. We hoisted our few duffel bags and baskets of food into the boat and headed out to sea. Holly and I soon joined the others inside the cabin of the dragger. We gazed in silence at ice floes skimming the water and waves. They formed ice chips and flew off either side of the bow.

Beneath the cold we could smell the stench of aging scallop juice. Holly and I wrinkled our noses at each other and giggled, as thirteen-year-olds do when tasting the unfamiliar. Richard, who was three years older, was intent on the scallop man, watching him deftly navigate the ice and swells. My mother cleaned her fogged-up glasses and kept a conversation going with our captain. "It must be awfully cold to work at times like this, Marvin," she said, one eyebrow arched.

"It's not too bad most of the time, but today's some cold."

The conversation chopped from one subject to the next. My mind drifted to visions of wood in the stove and hot cocoa.

Two hours and many ice floes later, we slowed down in Buckle Harbor. How different it looked from summer. The water's edge that I knew so well, and had last seen flowing with seaweed like my own long hair, was now caked with salty blocks of ice and snow. Soft waves that had lapped at the shore in the ebbing tide were now tinkling and clashing with ice meeting ice.

Marvin tossed the anchor and backed his boat to catch the bottom.

Once it held he turned off the engine. His eyes met my mother's, as if to say, *Are you sure you want to do this?* But she was already gathering up a basket of food and her duffel. "Come on, children, pick up a bag and let's get in the dinghy." Nothing was going to stop her now.

Richard took the oars and rowed us to the high tide beach, closer to the cabin. Holly and I sat in the stern and I held the line to an extra dinghy tied behind us to have in case of an emergency. I tried to imagine what that would look like. We were just staying overnight so what could go wrong? The cold air quickly froze my hands and I envied my brother's active tug at the oars, keeping his hands warm. I looked forward to getting the fire going in the woodstove.

It took two trips to get us and all our bags unloaded on the beach. Richard and I pulled up the extra dinghy and tied it to a tree. The scallop man said, in his thick Maine accent, "You take cayah now. I'll be back tomorrah if the weathah holds."

This last sentence was not very encouraging. I looked at Holly with a half smile and shrugged. Her eyes had grown wide. I was glad to have her company. Richard was already walking up the beach when my mother replied, "Thanks very much, Marvin. We'll be fine." She was all smiles as she turned with us to trudge through the snow. I looked back to see our scallop man give one final wave before hopping back in his dinghy.

Buckle Botel was no more than ninety feet from shore, but drifts of snow across our path made it seem twice as far. Cold air followed us indoors. I slid the glass door shut behind us, clinging to the illusion that indoors would be warmer.

When we had finished the cabin the previous summer, the air was warm and the grass was green. Now it was white and cold and unfamiliar. I put the small cooler I had been carrying down on the kitchen table and flung my duffel onto the bunk bed in the corner that would be for Holly and me. My mother had asked Richard to sleep on the floor on a mattress. She would be in the extra room with the double bed on the other side of the wall from the woodstove.

Mum and I rolled up last summer's newspaper to stuff in the stove. We stacked kindling on top and Richard lit a match. Holly and I unpacked our food. The smell of salami and gingerbread made me hungry. We decided to have lunch right away. Richard sliced the salami as I cut into the block of Cheddar cheese. Holly placed bread on a plate and my mother poured water from a gallon jug she had brought with us. We were far away from potable running water, indoor plumbing, or other comforts of home, but we were feeling very self-reliant, warming ourselves by the fire and sharing in the work of food preparation.

The wind was picking up. It rapped at the windows and blew through the cracks around the trim. Had we listened to the weather forecast before coming, we might have thought twice. But that was not my mother's way.

When lunch was over we decided to shovel a path to the outhouse, a distance of a hundred feet. We realized it would seem a lot farther if the snow was deep. I felt the first flakes melt on my nose and looked up to see gray clouds. No sooner had we started to shovel than we were engulfed in a blizzard. There was nothing to do but go back in and wait.

Richard got out his guitar and played some Peter, Paul and Mary tunes while Holly and I played cards. Mum found the storm relaxing and took a nap.

Wind screamed through the sliding door each time one of us needed to use the outhouse. This was going to be a long, cold night. Luckily, we had plenty of firewood stacked inside. I was glad we had cut so much last summer. Even with the cold nosing through the cracks, we were warm indoors.

My mother was in an unusually good mood when she awoke. She was happiest when on Buckle Island, and the storm put her over the top. Her mood cast a spell on us. We eased into our chairs, stared out the windows, and felt secure in the envelopment of snow outside and peace within. Conversation centered on whether the boat was going to get here tomorrow. I knew my mother was hoping it would not and I was beginning to feel the same way. It was fun surviving together. I felt needed and I liked that we had to work together to survive. My mother's values went deeper than possessions and stuff. She wanted to give us experience in testing our mettle.

Mum put another log in the stove and took an iron frying pan out of the cupboard to sauté some onions for the steak. She removed another pot and filled it with water to boil the string beans, and said with just a hint of excitement in her voice, "I think we will probably have to cross over to Swan's Island tomorrow to get some extra supplies. We will not have enough food if we get stranded." Tomorrow was Sunday and stores would not be open. I wondered how we were going to buy our food.

Snow continued to pile up around our cabin until after dinner. Then in a breath it stopped, and the temperature plummeted to far below freezing. We did not have a thermometer, but it was cold enough to burn your throat when you inhaled outside. I discovered this when I went to the outhouse before bed. The half-moon was up, spreading its reflection across the still water. Waves were not moving the way they usually did. Could the harbor be freezing over?

I told everyone and we went down to the high tide beach to have a look. Sure enough, the surface spreading from shore was solid. Where blocks of ice had floated in the harbor the day before, they now joined together, forming heaves and ridges. Our breath was steamy as we listened to the uncommon silence. Time stopped. We felt the great body of ocean groaning under the weight of ice, forcing upward fingers of frozen water, as if trying to push back a much too heavy blanket.

The next morning the entire harbor was frozen solid. My mother was uncommonly cheerful. She asked Holly and me to go with her to Swan's Island while Richard stayed at the cabin "to keep the home fires burning." I understood the full meaning of the expression. Without him it would be cold by the time we returned. We ate our share of bacon, eggs, and toast, put on our warmest clothes, and lumbered down to the beach.

The extra rowboat was now stranded above the tide. We undid the stiffened painter from around the tree and slid the boat down to the edge of the frozen water, making a trail in icy sand and seaweed. Everything was slippery with ice. Between Swan's Island and us was a cluster of pink boulders with a tiny copse of trees on top. The tide was so far out that the mussel flats were a field of ice. Holly and I took one side of the boat, my mother the other, and we very carefully slid our way over the flats and onto the ice.

Years later, Holly and I compared memories of how we crossed Buckle Harbor. She swears we rowed in open water. I swear we pushed the boat all the way across the harbor on top of the frozen waves.

One thing we do agree on was that the walk into town was very, very long. We took turns with my mother, breaking trail through the knee-deep snow. Our conversation was muffled by the dense white of winter hanging on every branch. Rambling reminiscences, random observations about birdsongs, and the exertion of walking through deep snow helped keep our morale high. We giggled at the sight of us, marching single file through woods in search of civilization.

By the time we arrived at the town, the streets were plowed but the sidewalks were empty. Our weary legs welcomed the easy walking. Mum knew only one person on Swan's Island. Carl Lawson lived on the other side of town. She was banking on their friendship as collateral for convincing someone to open the general store on a Sunday. We were by this time very hungry, and returning to the island empty-handed was not an option.

The street was lined with houses and trees, all spaced well apart around the harbor of the little fishing village. We walked past several doors, hoping to find someone looking out a window, but not a soul was in sight. Halfway down the street was a faded yellow house with white trim, similar to others on either side, but with a glass front. We peered through the darkened window and spied shelves of canned food.

"Now, if only we can find someone to open it up," my mother said. She sounded as if she had just found the first clue on a treasure hunt. We looked up and down the street wondering whose door to knock on. A light was glowing three houses away and my mother decided to take the chance. We followed behind her as she knocked on the door. A man opened it, and when he saw us fringed with snow, his mouth dropped open, revealing several missing teeth. "You lost?" he asked.

"Not exactly," Mum answered, smiling, and reached out her hand. "I'm Peggy Rockefeller. We are staying on Buckle Island and have run out of food." She made it sound like that would answer everything. His quizzical expression was grounds for embellishment.

"I wonder if you know the person who owns the store. My friend,

Mr. Carl Lawson, told me there was a grocery here, and while we realize it is Sunday, we'd be awfully grateful if we could buy some food."

The man looked from my mother to Holly and me, as if a strange new species had just shown up in town. I couldn't tell if he recognized our last name or whether it made any difference, for his mouth fell slack for what seemed like an eternity.

Perhaps he took pity on us. Or maybe the feeling of being needed had just spread beyond Buckle Botel.

"You come right with me, Mrs. Rockefeller," he said, pulling on a jacket from a hook just inside the door. "We'll go ask Carl's brother and I bet he'll open her up. Where did you say you came from?"

If we weren't a new species we were aliens, but any kind of stranger is welcome news on a cold winter day on an island in Maine.

"From Buckle Island," my mother repeated, her voice slightly higher, as if it would shrink the distance we had walked. "We came out to spend the night and were supposed to return today, but the man whose boat we were going on never arrived. I guess there was too much ice."

"Ayup. It is some cold. But you walked a long ways. And you're fixing to walk all the way back, too?"

"Yes, indeed," my mother answered. "I've got two strong helpers here." Holly and I looked at each other and grinned.

We had arrived at a house five down from his. He knocked on the front door. It opened to a larger man dressed in overalls. Before we could say hello, our knight in shining armor launched into a story.

"Harry, this is Mrs. Rockefeller, a friend of Carl's. She and her girls have just walked from the Buckle and they need some food. Can you open up your stowa? They've run clear outta food." His last sentence explained how stories on Maine islands get bigger over time.

Harry looked from us to his neighbor, gently shaking his head as if to say, *"Don't know what they was doin' in the first place,"* but he took us on as a welcome project in his otherwise quiet day.

"Well, I think I can arrange that. Just let me get my key and I'll open her right up."

I looked at my mother as if she had just found the combination for the treasure chest. The first turn of the dial had brought us to Buckle Island. The second had produced the storm. The third got us safely into town. We opened the door to food and survival. The three of us smiled like Cheshire cats.

10.

STAYING AFLOAT

⚬

R afts are good metaphors for life. The more buoyant the material, the easier it is to stay afloat. When a girl from Harlem spent a week with my family on Buckle Island, I learned that buoyancy has as much to do with attitude as equipment.

I have built at least five rafts in my life. Two of them were for river races when I was at Middlebury College. The first, made out of beer kegs, held four of us successfully until the corks came out ten minutes after the gun went off. The next year we used tractor tires covered by plywood. This worked well until the makeshift rudder hit a rock and came flying up over the floorboards, causing us to lose our steerage. Four of us paddled madly with our hands to avoid a trestle. People stopped their cars on the bridge above to watch as we bumped into the cement pillars and moved on downstream like a whirligig. We lost other essential parts in the rapids long before the finish line, but we still had our sense of humor as we towed our bedraggled vessel ashore.

The most successful raft I ever built was in 1963, when I was eleven. It was a team effort with Richard and Peggy, and her friend Gloria from Harlem. My sister Peggy had demonstrated an early interest in people from other cultures, economic levels, and racial backgrounds. She had spent two summers living with a family in the slums in Brazil before working in Harlem during the spring semester of her junior year at Milton Academy. I admired her desire to see people from the inside out, close-up.

While tutoring in Harlem, she befriended sixteen-year-old Gloria and asked my parents if she could invite her to Maine. They agreed and took all of us on the motorboat to Buckle Island.

This was Gloria's first trip outside New York City. The prospect of sharing our island with a city girl from a culture different than mine filled me with excitement and anticipation.

Low tide found us knee-deep in mudflats, teaching her how to pull clams with our hands from six inches beneath their air holes. First we poked a finger down the hole until we felt the clamshell's razor edge. Then we plunged our hand beneath the clam. The trick was in going fast enough to grab but not so fast we'd get sliced. With our fingers clamped around the shell, we pulled against the suction. This was the clam's only defense except an occasional squirt in our eyes. When it surrendered, it came out of the hole with a sucking sound. Each clam was a victory. We washed them and examined their size, showing Gloria how each ring in the shell represents a year of growth. I noticed that the rinsed clams had contrasting stripes of black and white on their shells, similar to Gloria's white teeth against her black skin. The mud was less evident on her forearms than on mine. We laughed at how our physical differences were no more than one clam to another, and I wondered how Gloria felt about being different from people around her. I was too shy to ask if she ever experienced racism or exclusion. I didn't know what it was like to feel racial discrimination, but in my own way I knew what it was like to feel falsely singled out by strangers or excluded by my siblings. People's assumptions often have nothing to do with the person inside. I felt a kinship with Gloria and I admired her willingness to jump into the unfamiliar.

The next day Richard suggested we all build a raft. He showed us sketches he had drawn of a sail with skull and crossbones. It was going to be a pirate's raft, the natural sequel to treasure hunting for clams the day before. Richard found a hammer and nails while Peggy and Gloria rowed out to our boat to bring back some rope. We needed to find enough logs that, when tied together, they would keep all of us afloat. It was important that each log float on its own or it would diminish the overall buoyancy. Like connections between people, every log made a difference to the whole. We assembled a large pile and tested each one before lining it up against the others.

When we had enough to keep us all afloat, the raft was about eight feet square. This would surely hold us. Richard took the rope and wove it over and under the logs while the rest of us held them in place. Our effort was so engrossing, we were surprised when my mother called us for lunch. She and my father had been having their own adventure, building a low stone wall for a garden just outside the cabin.

We helped cut cheese, red onion, salami, and tomatoes to put on bread. It was our favorite picnic lunch. Gloria told us she had never had a homegrown tomato before. I wondered what new experiences I would have if I visited her.

The afternoon was spent securing errant logs that popped out of the harness when we pushed the raft into the water. We had to build close to the water to slide it in. Fourteen or fifteen trees together, even when dead and dry, make too heavy a load for four teenagers to budge without the help of water. It took many tries, but with the tide on our side, water crept up our ankles just as we were ready to float the raft. We jumped aboard. Richard first, Peggy second, then Gloria. As I was last, I swam out a little way to join them. The raft was barely visible on top of the water but did not sink. My parents heard our loud shrieks of glee and came to the water's edge to share in our moment of triumph. We still had the sail, rudder, and tiller to make, but the foundation was built. We were more or less afloat.

The following day we stripped one of the beds of its white sheet. My mother conspired with us, donating it to the cause of piracy for a sail. We stretched it over the table in the cabin and Gloria and I held it taut while Richard and Peggy drew skull and crossbones in black ink. My mother had a good supply of felt-tip pens and we used up most of them coloring our pirates' emblem.

That afternoon we erected a mast for the sail. It was not so easy securing it between two logs forward of the raft's center, but with much effort and lots of opinions we finally pushed and wiggled it into place. Richard pounded some long nails at an angle around the mast to secure it at right angles into the horizontal logs.

The next morning we fashioned a rudder and tiller to the stern. I had found a wide board in my original search for logs that turned out to be just the right size for a rudder. Richard carved a hole near its top for a small tree pole, two inches in diameter, to fit through. This became our tiller.

We were ready to set sail and head out to sea in search of more treasure. There was only one small problem. In the two days since we had built the raft, several of the logs had soaked up water. The raft still held two of us, but any more than that and it submerged a good two feet.

Maine water is too cold to stand in for more than a few minutes. We decided to take turns in pairs while the others posed as conspirators rowing at a distance behind.

My mother took a photograph of Peggy and Gloria on the raft. She kept it on her desk in New York City until her death in 1996. Its colors faded over the years, blurring the differences between the two girls as seen from the back on a slightly submerged platform. Above them a white sail with black skull and crossbones bellies in the wind.

Two years after Gloria spent the week with us, my father gave her a full scholarship to college. My mother often spoke to me with eyes brimming over about how she admired my father's ease with people from all backgrounds and his generosity in helping them to stay afloat.

The year we built the raft my parents planted daffodils. The flowers have returned each spring, even though my mother has long since gone. Their flouncy yellow heads bob in the wind like little sails, each one bearing witness to the memory of adventure. My father has sailed to Buckle Island every year since my mother died. Sometimes I join him. We come to see the daffodils and to remember my mother's green thumb. When my dad and I look at the flowers she planted, I can see her light brown eyes dancing with satisfaction. I think back to that summer. Gloria's and Mum's joy were as bright as the daffodils. I don't know what happened to Gloria, but I suspect that she and my mother are still laughing somewhere. Like a raft, chuckling is a good way to stay afloat.

The Gift of Daffodils

A thousand eyes from heaven
peer out across the sea-blown field,

like mute trumpets heralding spring
on her beloved Buckle Island.

My dad and I pick bouquets;
white petticoats, orange kisses,
lemon-chiffon skirts and yellow trumpets
are my names for them.

They are my mother's gifts
from thirty years ago.
Once a dozen bulbs or so
deftly planted by her hands

have multiplied each year
giving her permanent residence here.
Generations of her artistry
stand tall as my knee.

Such young faces recall her
concentrated frown and quick hands
loving the earth she kneeled upon
above the tidal rocks and sand.

And she is here again
winking her yellow eyes
abundantly
as we pluck her to our hearts.

11

A Place to Relax

〜

The other island we befriended as children was Saint Barthélemy, in the French West Indies. My family first started going there in the late 1950s. My father was the first American to buy land on St. Barts, long before it became known to vacationers from the northern hemisphere. We owned the peninsula at the far end of the island, named Colombier. It was to be our winter getaway, a place for family and friends to relax among the tropical breezes and turquoise water, with no phones or television, and only accessible by boat.

My first memories of St. Barts are of women sitting in brightly painted doorways weaving straw birds, barefooted men riding donkeys, and the only vehicle on the island, a Jeep, driving up to the chartered plane to greet us. There were no cars when my family first arrived on this French-speaking island in 1957. The only way to fly in was over a very steep volcanic mountain. The pilot circled the airstrip once to scare off a herd of goats before swooping down over the precipice to land on the grass runway. He cut the engine as our wheels touched ground, braking hard so we didn't dive into the water at the end of the pasture.

We initially stayed at the Eden Rock Inn, owned by an alleged former smuggler. From the main town of Gustavia, we took a twenty-minute boat ride to Colombier, to see the site of the new house my parents planned to build. It would be their only modern home.

Colombier is a wide, arching peninsula, with a soft, sandy beach rimming the shoreline. The hill on the near side of the beach had long been windswept and clear of trees, a perfect place to build a house. My parents enlisted Nelson Aldrich, an esteemed New England architect and one of my father's cousins. They decided to hire local people to build their house, though they had to import several stonemasons from Italy to train them, as stone had not been used to build houses on the island before. My parents' house became the incubator for masonry, a growing source of income on the island since then.

The house at Colombier was deemed Nelson Aldrich's most imaginative design. Its parabolic arches were built to withstand hurricanes, salt, heat, and wood-boring insects. Its undulating, nearly flat roofs blended with the landscape, resembling a curving wave or the wing of a very large bird. The bedrooms were separated from the living and dining rooms by serpentine stone pathways, punctuated by flowing water pools and banana trees. Red and green hummingbirds zipped back and forth among orchids, bromeliads, and hibiscus along the paths. My parents placed several pieces of art in the garden, including a black Calder sculpture, resembling a bird coming to roost, and an iron stork made in Bali, with one leg holding a miniature of itself in the form of a bell. A bronze Tibetan gong hung outside the dining room and we children competed to strike it before meals.

My mother did not use a decorator. She enjoyed her eclectic taste and loved applying her artistic talent to interiors. She chose modern Scandinavian furniture for the five bedrooms lining one side of the interior garden and the spacious living room, whose thirty-foot floor-to-ceiling windows looked out over the bay. She and my father bought several modern paintings, including a large Kenzo Okada that resembled a beached plane on an ice floe in the Arctic for the dining room. The ceiling between the dining and living rooms undulated and joined into serpentine stone walls, which formed several nooks for sitting. Outside on the patio hung three egg-shaped basket chairs from mahogany timbers. They were my favorite reading chairs. I liked to pretend I was still inside my mother's womb.

In 1961, when the house was mostly finished, my family hosted a housewarming party for all the local builders and their families. I remember a swarthy crowd of people arriving in bare feet, wearing simple dresses and well-worn khaki pants. Many were missing some teeth, but they were full of smiles as my parents and we six children held out our hands in a line to greet them. Ours was the first party of this magnitude given on the island, and since everyone was related to at least one member of each builder's family, it appeared that the entire island population came to celebrate. Several women gave handmade palm frond cranes to Peggy, Richard, and me, a treasure we later learned to copy. We served lemonade and passed hors d'oeuvres. It was a joyous occasion.

The next year, my friend Holly Duane joined me on our first official vacation with my parents and my five siblings. We sailed from the nearby island of Saint Martin on my uncle Laurance's ninety-four-foot ketch, the *Wayfarer*. Laurance was busy building Caneel Bay in the US Virgin Islands and had loaned us his new boat for the trip.

Warm waves splashed over the bow as Holly and I stood on deck and looked over the azure water toward the approaching Colombier peninsula. A volcanic mountain rose behind our new house, like a gigantic poodle's head. Palm trees swayed at the edge of the land, waving their welcome in the tropical wind.

One hundred feet from shore the *Wayfarer*'s gigantic anchor plunged into the sea and a smaller boat motored out from our newly built stone dock. The waves were rough and water splashed between the two boats as we loaded the many bags. I inhaled the warm, sticky air. My long blond hair was already tightening into curls. I licked my lips and loved their salty flavor.

Holly and I put our bags in our room and ran to the living room. We curled up in the high-backed swivel chairs, tucking our feet under us as we spun around and around. Each chair was a different color: bright red, yellow, or orange. I can still smell the woolen upholstery and rugs, dampened by the salt air. The modern furniture blended well with a Chinese lacquer chest that held our board games and two Japanese screens depicting red, white, and blue waves, which brought the ocean to the room on opposite walls. An oversize yellow daybed lined with colorful silk pillows was fitted to a curving interior rock wall that defined the two-tier boundary between the living room and dining room. It was a perfect place for Holly and me to sit while we put suntan lotion on each other's backs.

Each morning after breakfast, Holly and I put on our bathing suits and took our towels, snorkels, and masks down to the beach. At ten years old we were allowed to snorkel alone as long as we stayed close to the shore. I loved floating with the drift of water, watching schools of angelfish dart in and out of crevices in the volcanic rock just three feet below me. I felt soothed by my sibilant breath underwater, exchanging air through my snorkel. Whole families of fish moved together. I marveled at how they knew just when the others were turning, as if they were all one.

Our fingers eventually crinkled with saturation and we surfaced to dry out on the beach. Hermit crabs scuttled between our toes as we looked for shells. We filled our hands and towels with cowries and butterfly wings, as we called the light pink ones that clung to their twin by a single hinge.

At St. Barts my siblings and I developed our own forms of entertainment. Richard learned to scuba dive and spearfish. Peggy and Abby enjoyed the empty beach for nude sunbathing and spent time looking over the hillside for boys. Neva took a special interest in underwater photography, and David spent hours sailing our twenty-five-foot trimaran. I continued to snorkel.

One afternoon, David took Holly and me out on the trimaran. We went so fast, it took my breath away. I loved it when David didn't have a girlfriend. Not only did I get to sail with him, but he was also a great partner in playing games at night. Parcheesi was the first game I ever won against my siblings. I spoke to the dice as I shook them in the can and it seemed to work, for I frequently got the right number on each throw.

St. Barts was the only place I was included in the games we played together. Other families might have spent their holidays at resorts, going to discos, watching TV or movies, but we played games, put on records, and danced in our living room.

My family's favorite game was charades because we played in teams. The total points accrued for either team was less important than the collaborative spirit and hilarity of acting "Gone with the Wind" or "She's got ants in her pants." I loved having David on my team. His puns and dry wit were even funnier when acting out a book or movie title or famous quote. We all laughed until our bellies ached. I felt like one of those fish swimming in drifts along the reefs.

For the next twenty-five years, our expanding family arrived the day after Christmas for ten days' vacation. My mother was invariably exhausted after her annual task of spending weeks shopping for and wrapping over two hundred presents for family and friends. Christmas in our house was a chore performed with a stiff upper lip.

By the time we arrived at Colombier, her face was pale and taut, with lines around her mouth pulled into a grimace. It took her at least five days to recover. During that time she spent her mornings writing thank-you letters at the living-room desk for all of the Christmas presents they had received. We wrote our thank-you letters, too, but I never had more than five to write.

My mother did not write cards. She wrote four-page letters extolling the virtues of a new set of napkins and place mats they didn't need, or a pair of gloves resembling her favorite well-worn ones, which she would describe as "just perfect for the winter." She had a way of making others feel they had chosen the very gift she'd been waiting for, while all she wanted was to curl up in bed and sleep. She gave to others what she needed for herself, heaps and heaps of carefully thought out, personalized appreciation and attention.

We children bore the brunt of her exhaustion and stayed clear until the finished letters on her desk in the living room had reached a foot high. When she pushed back her chair and went to put on her bathing suit, the real vacation began. Our French cook, Mme. Genet, would pack a picnic of pâté and cheese, fresh tomatoes, salad, and French bread, and we went by boat to the main town of Gustavia. We were met by several cars that transported us to another remote parcel of land my father bought on the opposite end of the island.

Gouverneur Beach was reached by a little footpath, stretching down over sand dunes to the water. The waves at Gouverneur were much stronger than at Colombier. They rolled and heaved in from the ocean, perfect for body surfing.

My parents had hired caretakers for the additional property who were brother and sister. They lived together in a little shack on the side of the hill. Monsieur and Mademoiselle Brin were missing some teeth but they did not lack for words. Whenever we arrived they ran to greet us, talking excitedly over each other. They had no children, which might have accounted for their joy in seeing us. I can still hear Mademoiselle's deep guttural laughter as she ran barefoot before her brother down the hillside, her breasts bobbing loosely as she leapt into the water with her dress still on. Her brother climbed a coconut tree in bare feet, bearing a machete, and dropped several coconuts on the sand where we were standing, all eyes looking upward in a circle. He shinnied down, hacked them open, and passed them around for us to drink. We each took a sip of this tropical nectar as if taking Communion. It became the family initiation to unbridled freedom.

Afternoons, back at the house, were often spent resting or reading to help digest the meal before another round of activities. St. Barts was the one place I felt I had permission to read during the daytime. No one bothered me if I wanted to read on the couch all afternoon. I never felt that luxury in our other homes for there were always people coming and going and I was on call to help my mother throughout the day.

Mum did not have the luxury of relaxation in St. Barts for, in addition to her letter writing, she had to manage the staff and keep track of six children gone wild. Had she been able to delegate the responsibilities to a chief of staff and join us on our adventures and lazy afternoons, she might have felt differently. But it was not her way. She couldn't let go of the responsibility she married into. I believe she felt it was payback for being given such good fortune in my father's love and all that came with it.

She resented the French for introducing us to bikinis and sexual pleasures during our teenage and young adult years. It did not help that she suspected M. Genet, the caretaker of the house, of surreptitiously looting wine from our cellar to sell in town. She confronted him and he protested too much for her comfort. Mum had very good intuition, and her suspicions were soon confirmed. That night, when she got up to go to the bathroom, she opened the door and felt something metal fall against her leg. Turning on the light, she found a large hunting knife, which she recognized as belonging to M. Genet. It had been placed menacingly on top of the door.

Mum arrived at breakfast the next morning, looking white as coconut meat. She could no longer trust M. Genet, and he and his wife were summarily dismissed and replaced the following year by a highly recommended couple named Salazar. They came from Algiers, where he had retired as a Foreign Legion officer and she had run a four-star restaurant. M. Salazar brought with him his German shepherd police dog, which he used to patrol the beach and deter the increasing numbers of trespassers.

Mme. Salazar was the best cook we ever had. She was famous for her potages, the thick vegetable soups she served at lunch and dinner, but my favorite was her cold langouste, the spiny lobster caught by a fisherman that morning, which she served rimmed by quail eggs in aspic. The main course at both lunch and dinner was succeeded by cheese and crackers before the final climax of soufflé or some sort of cake for which we could no longer find room.

My mother appreciated the meals, but she felt guilty for eating too much and struggled with self-image. She had the additional burden of sun-sensitive skin from years of youthful suntanning, so she had to wear long sleeves outdoors. St. Barts was not for her.

My father's dream home for family winter vacations, and an oasis from travel, work, and business entertaining, came to an end in 1985. He sold the place because, although he loved the island and the French, and gathering his family and friends there to enjoy good food, wine, and relaxation, he recognized that it was a burden to his beloved wife. My siblings and I were sad to say good-bye, but I appreciate Dad's love of our mother, and the irreplaceable memories of family, natural beauty, and relaxation.

12.

JAGGED EDGES

ᖇ

My room in our summer home in Seal Harbor, Maine, was named the shoe-box room. I liked everything about it except that it was next to the playroom, where my siblings gathered each night.

Our three-story house was built for a large family, including servants. Like all summer houses on Mount Desert Island, it had a name. Westward Cottage had white clapboard siding and light blue trim. It sat across the road from the ocean with a circle drive in front. My family had summered here for two generations. Grandfather Rockefeller found restoration and relaxation in the granite peaks and balsam forests of Seal Harbor.

Grandfather understood landscape. The trip he and Grandmother took to the Far East in 1921 awakened their deep passion and appreciation for Asian philosophy and art in the natural landscape. They learned that the interactions of humans and land can be viewed as a series of concentric circles. Grandfather saw their house, a sixty-five-room

Tudor "cottage," as the center. The next circle was the pink-walled East Asian, English garden that he and Grandmother built in consultation with the famous landscape architect Beatrix Farrand. They purchased bronze Buddhas and stone lanterns and statuary to place in and around the garden, and rescued fluted orange tiles from a rubble pile outside the Forbidden City, in Peking, to place on top of the perimeter wall. The interior was planted as an English cutting garden with cool colors on one side and hot on the other. The effect was a secret garden blending Eastern and Western traditions.

Grandfather personally laid out fifty-seven miles of carriage roads connected by stone bridges, and from 1913 to 1940 he hired nearly one hundred men to build them. He saw the carriage roads as the next concentric circle and purchased eleven thousand acres of land for the final circle, which he gave to the government. Acadia, on Mount Desert Island, became the first national park on the Eastern Seaboard.

My father and his four older brothers and sister spent every summer of their childhood in the Eyrie. It was perched like an eagle's nest on a granite ledge overlooking the approach to Seal Harbor. When my parents began their own family they were given Westward Cottage, and my uncle Nelson was given a private dock and land on the promontory at the mouth of the harbor. He built his house just down the road from the Edsel Fords. Abby, John 3rd, Laurance, and Winthrop chose other places to spend their summers.

Over the years my parents gave or sold family land to their friends as a way of creating their own community. They joined their friends at the saltwater pool and tennis courts of the Seal Harbor Club, which was built by my grandfather for the summer people on the condition that the Club would remain alcohol-free. In those days summer residents kept separate from year-around Mainers. My mother sought to close that gap by inviting the children of local employees to meals at our house. Our dining-room table was constantly expanding. The succession of guests resulted in our needing a larger family room.

The second floor of Westward Cottage had a large playroom and five bedrooms, including a bedroom for the nurse. The shoe-box room, named for its size, was where I slept during my preteen years. It lay at the end of the hall from my parents' bedroom, and the head of my bed was on the other side of the wall from the playroom and opposite an ocean-facing window. I listened each night to the sounds of waves on the rocky beach across the street and could tell when it was low tide from the smell of salt and kelp.

A small closet across from the side of my bed made me uncomfortable. I remembered my sisters' stories about owls. One of them started a rumor that owls were dangerous, and if we asked our mother about them as she was putting us to bed, we could have just a few more seconds of her attention. I decided one might be living in my closet. Every night I asked my mother, "Mummy, what do owls do to you?" Her answer was always the same. "Nothing, darling. Sleep tight."

"But I'm sure there's one in my closet."

"No darling. Who ever heard of such a thing? Now go to sleep."

Sigh. At least I had her for a moment longer. I picked at the wallpaper until it hung in shreds by my pillow.

I could hear my siblings talking and giggling through the wall of the playroom next door. One night I poked my head in and asked them to please be quiet so I could go to sleep. "Okay. All right," Abby said impatiently. She and Peggy were huddled together chuckling at something Abby had been reading aloud. I went back to my room.

A few minutes later the noise began again. I lay on my back, waiting for them to stop. Even the hoot of owls would be better than their laughter. It was too dark to pick the wallpaper. I tried listening to the clock ticking on my bedside table, hoping its steady rhythm would soothe me to sleep. No luck. I trudged down the hall and opened the door again.

Peggy looked up and said, "We're not making any noise."

"Stop bugging us," Richard added. Neva was giving him a back rub. This was their exclusive club and I wasn't part of it.

I settled grudgingly into bed and listened to the lapping of waves onshore. Nature was my comfort. A friend was coming over tomorrow. I would take her to my own secret room on top of the cliffs behind our house. There were shards of blue-and-white China dishes buried there. We would dig for treasure and I wouldn't let my brothers and sisters even see it. If it was a rainy day, we would do jigsaw puzzles inside, all by ourselves.

My family collected Pastime Puzzles by Parker Brothers, vintage 1908–1958. Each one was hand-cut from wood. Jigsaw puzzles were the video games of today. They captivated my imagination and drew me into their story. Unlike videos, there was no music accompanying them other than the scratch of an occasional record in the background or introspective mumblings around the table, such as "Well..." or "Now I have it...."

When doing a jigsaw puzzle, I like to make a plan and then break the rules. I find freedom within the structure of piecing something together, like pieces of my life. Whether I choose to fit the edge pieces first, or sort by color or picture, whatever plan I make usually changes depending on the way in which the puzzle grows. Jigsaw puzzles are a lot like life. Finding the right place for each shape is like finding where I fit. Each piece I look for becomes a part of me. Sometimes I find jagged edges, other times smooth and round. I love the rounded loops and curves and occasional figure pieces of real-life shapes like stars, a don-key's head, or a bugle. I can see myself in these shapes as a twinkling light in the dark, a silly ass that loves to giggle, or a master of the hounds, calling all riders to start.

By the time I was old enough to put puzzles together, pieces were often missing, just like parts of me. I concentrated hard, able to carry a shape or color in my mind until I found the right fit. I enjoyed the sub-tleties of shapes and colors and could spend hours alone without feeling lonely.

I made order of the pieces by sorting out the edges and fitting them together first. They were a good place to begin because Pastime Puzzles always had straight edge pieces. When the outline was complete I got a sense of the whole, a lesson that would serve me well in many other as-pects of life.

As I grew older, I found that if I also sorted pieces by color it would save me time later on. Colors and shapes hold my attention. I'm now drawn to connecting clusters of colors and jagged pieces from anywhere in the puzzle. Confidence expands my options. I no longer depend so heavily on my usual sense of order, finding it more interesting to work from the inside out. Puzzles have taught me to flow with whatever fits in the moment.

13.

THROUGH A DOOR
IN THE WOODS

～

Fog curled over the trees as we started up a trail in Acadia National Park at the end of an August afternoon. My sister Abby was in the lead, barefoot as always. Before she left the driver's seat of the car, I had noticed her stuffing two ripe bananas into the army surplus backpack she wore under her long mane of brown hair. No one else was carrying any food.

I was ten at the time of this foray into the wild with my four older siblings. Abby, Neva, Peggy, and Richard were nineteen, eighteen, fourteen, and thirteen. David probably felt too old to be interested in such an adventure. I idolized him and felt safe in his presence, but on this night he was probably out with friends after racing his sailboat. I wished that he were with us.

I had never before been invited on an expedition with my siblings, and I went with mixed emotions. I was glad to be included but frightened by their style of adventure. I liked to know the plan. They were happiest when there wasn't one.

Abby was a student at the New England Conservatory of Music. By 1962, she had already crafted her identity as antiestablishment. She disagreed with most of what our father and his friends stood for and spent hours arguing heatedly with him about the flaws of capitalism. She had a significant influence on her three next youngest siblings, and I learned years later that she was hurt I would not fall sway as well. I often heard her lecture to Neva, Peggy, and Richard in the playroom as I was trying to sleep, denouncing the Vietnam War, lambasting the establishment, and blaming our parents. I was not part of those conversations, but they splintered my family and frightened me. I was not old enough to be an equal player so I sided with my parents as the best chance of feeling safe and defended them against my siblings. This did not endear me to them.

In retrospect, I think Abby brought a healthy challenge to our family's image in the world. She kept us questioning. None of us wanted to be seen as part of the establishment from which we came.

My siblings took awhile to get organized and the sun was setting. We planned to sleep out, but the incoming fog was chilly and none of us had brought more than a sweater for warmth. We had no sleeping bags, only three water bottles, and, so far as I could see, only two bananas for the four of us. Abby believed in roughing it, and she wanted the rest of us to fall into line like the comrades of the Communist Party she had been studying. Going barefoot symbolized freedom to Abby. I wondered if it was her gesture of empathy for common laborers of the world who had no shoes.

Abby's toughened feet felt their way without hesitation. Peggy was next, then Richard and me, with Neva taking up the rear. I was the only one still wearing shoes and I was glad for my sneakers as others blurted *ouch* when they stubbed their toes on a root or rock. I liked being barefoot, but I felt too vulnerable to take mine off, afraid we would lose our way and be hungry and cold. Neva made up stories to keep me going. Peggy followed at Abby's heels with Richard in tow.

Rock cairns near the top of the mountain marking the path to Sargent Pond loomed out of the fog. We came to a signpost and Abby rummaged around in her pack to find a flashlight. It didn't provide much comfort. I was sure we were lost. I felt lost in so many ways in my life already. Night hiking with my daredevil sisters and brother was a nightmare. I started to sob. "Stop being such a crybaby!" Abby snapped. Her words stung. I had no choice but to put my head down and keep going.

It felt like an hour before we reached the pond. No one else was there, and it was way past my bedtime. The other four ripped off their clothes and jumped into the cold water. Yelps of glee echoed off the surrounding cliffs in the dark. I hugged myself at the edge, longing to feel the glorious freedom of being naked in water but worrying that a bear might steal our bananas. Four in the water; one onshore. They were too involved with one another to notice if the bear ate me instead. I longed for my brother David. If he were here, he would have brought more bananas. I scooped water into my hands and washed the silent tears from my face.

∼

Three summers later, my brother Richard and I spent our first overnight together on Buckle Island. Richard had a reputation of being distracted and accident-prone. I was often moody and timid. When my mother suggested we have an overnight, I saw her permission as an act of trust and an opportunity for us to become friends.

My parents left us ashore and sailed away. Richard and I brought our bags and food up from the beach to the cabin we had built as a family the summer before. I picked wildflowers, moss, and mussel shells and made an arrangement on the kitchen table. I liked building miniature worlds. I placed the shining shells and small flat stones on the moss as a pathway to the flowers. Beauty was my contribution to the day.

While I washed up after dinner, my brother lit the kerosene lamp and sat down at the kitchen table. Light reflected on his thick glasses as he bent intently over a sheet of paper. I asked what he was drawing, but he refused to tell me. We were not easy companions. I would do as he asked and often said what I thought he wanted to hear, but he still didn't want to play with me. Many years later, he told me that not being true to myself felt manipulative to him. I didn't know that my mother expected Richard to be my caregiver, a role bound to result in feelings of resentment. I only knew that my brother would not let me get close and I wanted his friendship.

I hoped my curiosity would be satisfied in the morning, and went to bed. I slept restlessly and woke with the first rays of light. Richard was already outside the cabin, dragging from the beach a door that we had found a few weeks before. He propped it up against the cabin and came in to see if I was awake.

"Let's have some breakfast and head out to the woods," he said. The night's sleep seemed to have given him a new acceptance of me. I was happy to think he wanted my help. We ate in a hurry, as if someone were waiting for us. The *someone*, for him, was the plan he had conceived. For me, it was curiosity.

Richard picked several pieces of spare lumber from a pile outside the cabin and asked me to bring a hammer and some nails. He led the way, dragging the wood behind him along a trail to the center of the island. I fell into line, in the familiar role of assistant. Being included was more important than knowing what was about to happen. I suspected his goal had something to do with the door we had found.

A few weeks earlier, he and I had rowed from Buckle to a nearby island to dig for clams at low tide. After filling our hod, we noticed an old door from an abandoned fisherman's shack lying on the bank above the beach. With some effort we dragged it over the mud and placed it crosswise onto our dinghy. At the time, neither of us knew what we would do with it, but we agreed it was a treasure. I held it tightly on top of the boat as Richard rowed us back to Buckle.

I was thinking about our former adventure when we reached the darkest part of the woods. The pine trees grew so thickly it was almost impossible to walk off trail. Richard dropped the lumber and told me to leave the hammer and nails.

"What are we going to do?" I was no longer able to suppress my curiosity.

"I want to put the door we found up here."

"You mean you are going to hang it right in these woods?"

"Yup," he answered. "I just need you to help me carry it."

I still did not see the meaning. Then I realized that was the point. I laughed and followed him back to the cabin to retrieve the door. My feet were light.

Mist filtered through the branches as if fairy weavers were fingering filmy threads in and out of the trees. I imagined them living inside dead stumps, padding their houses with soft hairy-cap moss for beds and dragging in mushrooms for chairs.

The door was caked with sea salt. It had faded with the sun to a brownish gray, but the round porcelain doorknob was still like new. All that was needed were two hinges to attach it to the frame we would make. To my astonishment, Richard had already planned for this. He stepped into the cabin and pulled a paper bag from his duffel, producing two brand-new hinges with screws to match. I raised an eyebrow. How could he have kept this a secret? Why hadn't he told me before? I knew the answer and could have sulked, but I was so excited by the prospect of participating in his fanciful mission that I simply stared as he stuffed the hinges and a Phillips-head screwdriver into his back jeans pocket.

We lifted the door together and carried it edgewise along the trail. I could hardly feel the weight for I was already fantasizing the reactions of people who would happen upon it. Would they stop and wonder? Would they feel differently after they stepped through? The woods on the other side were so thick, they would not be able to go around.

We plopped the door next to the lumber and chose two trees on either side of the path that were just the right distance apart to receive our door. Richard took rough measurements with his hands to make sure we weren't making the frame too narrow to allow a proper swing or so wide that it wouldn't latch.

I was quick to help Richard position the frame on each of the trees and hand him nails as he hammered. I was good at making myself useful. This did not quite make up for the desire to be needed or wanted, but it was a good start. I was reminded of other island projects with him, including our pirate's raft built from driftwood and a trimaran he made out of seventy-five wire hangers and orange-painted canvas. Richard was good at thinking outside the box.

After nailing the door frame onto the two chosen trees, we stopped to reflect on our progress. I could hear little whispers of wind in the woods as if the fairies were talking. In my mind's eye I could see them climbing out of their stump houses, cocking their pointy ears as they scampered toward our doorway. They must have helped us lift the door because it seemed lighter now. A warm feeling of hope flushed my face. It occurred to me that it might be possible to make things happen the way you want if you are having enough fun.

The spruce and balsam trees were so dense, I could hardly see ten feet in any direction. We angled the door into the frame and I held it in place while Richard made pencil marks where the screws for the hinges would go. There were eight holes in all—as many as my siblings and parents combined. Was this pure coincidence? My young mind found meaning in numbers. They were a way of making sense of things, of feeling that I belonged.

I held on tight as Richard turned the screws through both hinges. I was determined to be a useful partner, if not a fun playmate. It was cool in the dark woods, but I was sweating. A random breeze tugged at the curls in my hair and I looked over my shoulder. Surely those were little fingers waving. Perhaps the fairies would tell my brother to be friends with me.

Richard let go of the door and we both stood back. Sweat dripped behind his glasses and ran down his freckled face. He smiled at his work, opened the door, and walked through. I followed close behind.

"There's a difference!" I exclaimed.

"What do you mean?" he queried blankly.

"Don't you feel it?" It was as clear as the fairies' houses to me. "The woods and trail before the door are the same as always. But as I step through the opening it feels different, like it's enchanted. From now on let's call these woods the Enchanted Forest."

I doubt whether Richard ever felt the way I did, but he liked the name enough to draw a map of the woods beyond the door for our mother on which he labeled them *The Enchanted Forest*.

It became known among our friends and was discovered by many a shoreward sailor. For over forty years, the door in the woods invited others unknown to us to step across its threshold. Fairy houses have proliferated along the trail sides. Little stones and mussel shells line the paths to their front doors, and on a foggy day you can almost see smoke coming from their chimneys.

Something about a door invites one into the mystery of new possibilities, even friendship. After years of hammering and adjusting, my brother and I are on the same side.

The door in the woods that my brother Richard
and I built on Buckle Island

14.

IT DOESN'T MATTER WHERE
YOU START

I spent most of my childhood scared of making mistakes. I was teased by my siblings, criticized by my mother, and shamed by my father. I can still hear their reproaches: "You're stupid," or "You're too sensitive," and "You don't know *that*?" It was hard to believe I had anything to offer. Feelings were not talked about in my family, and admitting them was considered a weakness. I couldn't help showing my feelings. They were the only things I could trust. The constant rebukes convinced me I must be very weak, as well as stupid. Fears escalated, and I developed a block about learning almost anything except how to read emotions. They were proof I was still alive.

Long before I learned how to read words, I read emotions in my mother. I could tell what she was feeling before she entered the room. I heard it in her tired walk or the way she pushed down just a little too hard on the piano keys. I saw it in the slightest twist of her mouth or the warning wave of her foot dangling over the other leg like a tiger's tail. I learned to dance around her moods and weave in and out of my family's responses to them, like a kitten chasing a ball of twine. It was safer to stay behind the furniture, beyond the radar, but it did not serve my intellectual growth or self-confidence.

I attended two of New York's most prestigious schools: Chapin and Brearley. My sister Peggy and I were driven to school in our parents' chauffeur-driven car and we made sure he let us off two blocks away so we could look like we walked to school, just like the other girls. We were picked up by the same kind Norwegian man, named John Johnson. He taught me songs like "Hans Hagen the Farmer" in Norwegian. I had no trouble learning from him, but school was a different matter. My brain seized up, and my hands perspired constantly from stress. Not wanting others to know, I avoided touching them on their skin, and stopped asking questions after feeling the teacher's disapproval at my daydreaming. Isolated and alone, I was terrified.

In fourth grade I scored a 10 on a history test when 60 was the passing grade. I concluded that the teacher must hate me. Why else would she put such a low mark in red? My stomach jumped into my throat as the tears spilled onto the little blue test book. I was so mortified I couldn't look anyone in the eye. I wanted to die.

My mother recognized the feeling and hired a tutor. This felt like the ultimate disgrace until she told me she hadn't done too well in school, either. She comforted, "Any school who allows a teacher to rub a child's nose in failure is not the right place for education." It was one of the few times I really felt her on my side.

I worked hard to catch up. A year later, I had made only marginal improvement. Neither Chapin nor Brearley had been able to help me, and they defended themselves in letters to my parents saying, based on my test scores, I didn't have the intellectual rigor. To my mother's credit, she recognized I was test-phobic and that this was not the only way to measure intelligence. Unable to help me at home, she shipped me off for seventh grade to a farm and wilderness boarding school. I was twelve.

North Country School was founded in 1937 by a wise man and his wife who became my surrogate parents. Walter and Leo Clark's educational philosophy was based on John Dewey's belief that experience is the best teacher.

The school was situated among the high peaks of Upstate New York's Adirondack Mountains. Flower and vegetable gardens lined the dirt road stretching between the school and horse barn. In the depths of winter, regardless of temperatures that dropped as low as minus thirty degrees or snowdrifts reaching higher than a fifth grader, we walked the quarter-mile road twice a day to feed the animals. Breakfast and dinner were not served until the animals had eaten: a lesson in caring for those who depend on us. Jobs like helping in the kitchen, cleaning the art room, and growing vegetables let us children know we were an important part of the community.

Though the school remained small, with fewer than seventy-five children, working together on the farm expanded my understanding of education. Decades before health food stores sprouted around the country, Walter Clark used the term *organic*. Vegetables grown without pesticides were a staple of the daily diet, and sugar was replaced with local honey and homemade maple syrup. Conservation was taken seriously. We recycled paper, turned off water while brushing our teeth, turned out lights unless essential to a task, and turned down the heat at bedtime. The latter resulted in many blankets, flannel pajamas, and a warm hug good night.

I arrived at North Country School in the fall of 1964. My brother Richard had graduated the previous year. We were the only two to go there. Richard had suffered from facial tics and bullying. His academic scores were no better than mine, but four and a half years at North Country School had transformed him from a floundering student to an intellectual force, going on to Choate, Harvard, and eventually Harvard Medical School to become a family doctor.

I admired Richard's success and hoped for the same myself. I was terrified of leaving home but intrigued by the place that had helped my brother. Like him, I thrived in this environment where animals were part of daily life, math was learned as easily in the garden as in textbooks, art and chemistry were borrowed from the earth's clay and minerals, and sheep's wool found patterns in cloth. I became a weaver at North Country School and the school wove into me the discovery that learning can happen anywhere.

Fear receded as small triumphs were celebrated. In October I won my first grand championship at the school horse show. Riding became a passion that I continue to this day. Blue ribbons gave me courage to wear the fierce persona of Captain Hook during the winter term play of *Peter Pan*. By spring, I gave my first piano recital in front of the whole school. These were not academic successes in the traditional sense, but they were fundamental to gaining self-confidence. In being acknowledged for them, I began to see a different person in the mirror. For the first time I dared to be curious, and in being curious I started to listen. If I did not know something, I could safely ask a question. In not being teased, criticized, or shamed for my ignorance, I grew to love questions as much as answers. I began to start life over again.

15.

PULLING TOGETHER

❧

North Country School's motto was "Ruggedness, Resourcefulness, and Resiliency." I learned ruggedness from the craggy peaks of the ancient Adirondacks, which we climbed even in winter on skis with skins. After pulling myself up the mountain branch by branch and learning to slide down on my bottom while warming my hands with my hot breath, a spelling test seemed less threatening.

I learned resourcefulness from the art studio. Whether weaving a tablecloth, making a pot, or painting scenery for a play, I was encouraged to pull something from inside, to reinvent myself in the reflection of a tree or a mentor. Anything was possible.

Watching a horse recover its stride after it stumbled or seeing a plant revive after watering it taught me about resiliency. A misshaped clay pot could be slapped back on the wheel, a warp thread that snapped could be retied, a paper could be rewritten, and a math problem recalculated. The spirit of resilience was seeded in me. Over time a core of inner strength began to grow alongside the knowledge that I was part of the larger community.

Walter and Leo Clark believed that to get along in the world, you first had to know you belonged. Whatever your strengths, each person has something to offer the larger community.

Of all my experiences at North Country School, the overarching lesson about community had the most impact. One day after lunch at our council meeting, Walter stood up at his usual post in the dining room to announce the afternoon "out time" activities after classes. He often used this interlude to discuss the importance of our choices on the world. That day he described a project that would require the entire school.

Some climbing poles stood outside the front entrance of the school and one of them had become unsafe for children to play on. The partially sawed-off limbs, which we used to climb on, were beginning to rot. Walter wanted to replace the pole with a new spruce he had found in the woods. However, the forest was so dense that the tree he had in mind could not be hauled out by tractor.

"We are going to need all of us to pull it out together." He had the room's attention. Walter went on to describe his plan and I had a feeling he was grateful for the impenetrable woods.

"We will assemble outside the main entrance after classes at three o'clock," he announced. With that he released us to class, leaving just enough unsaid to make us wonder: How big was this tree? How far would we have to walk? How many of us would it take to pull it out?

By three o'clock, I could hardly wait to see what adventure lay ahead. Several teachers carried coiled lengths of rope, thick enough to grasp. It was a cool, early spring day and the pungent scent of pine permeated the air. Clouds lent a kind of "Hogwarts" atmosphere to the woods and mist seeped between the trees. Some children ran ahead, some lingered behind, and there was a happy hum of chatter as we all followed Walter into the woods.

The tree in question had already been cut down and was lying on its side in a little clearing. Its branches had been precut to the right length for climbing. Some children were impatient to try their strength and several attempted to pull it on their own. The tree did not budge. Then several tried together, but to the same effect.

Walter loved to see children stretch themselves, to try out new ideas and work together to succeed. Many adults would have stopped the first child who put his hand on the tree and told us to listen up for the plan. Walter knew better. He wanted as much brawn as brain in gear. This was not a test on paper. It was an opportunity to experiment and discover together.

He waited until we had exhausted our initial excitement before speaking. "Have any of you counted the rings on this tree? How old do you think it is?" Walter was never in a hurry. He milked our curiosity as if it were sap oozing from the branches of our imaginations. Several children who liked numbers bent down and started to count aloud. Others crowded around.

"Sixty-four!" someone shouted.

"How could that be?" I exclaimed. "That's as many as us students!" There was a passionate re-counting as we huddled closer. But it came out again to sixty-four. I felt like some kind of message was about to be conveyed.

Walter asked the final question. "How many of you do you think it will take to move this log?"

Hands shot up. Numbers were shouted out. "Five!" "Eighteen!" "Twenty-three!" "All of us!"

Walter seemed as curious to find out the answer as we were. He asked one of the teachers to tie a rope around the thinner end of the tree, where it had been topped. This way there would be less resistance when we began to pull, for branches tend to have more flexibility downward than up.

Our team got in place: sixty-four students and twenty faculty including Walter and Leo. The rope was long enough for each of us to form two handholds. It was made out of hemp and I still remember the smell, like damp hay. The rough consistency felt good on my bare hands.

Some children angled to be at the front of the rope while others were more excited to be near the tree and see it behind them. I was one of the latter. Being at the tail end felt familiar.

We lined up along the rope with our feet on both sides like a human caterpillar. Our cries pierced the air in anticipation of the big pull. Then, as all 168 hands were placed on the rope, Walter counted to three in as long as it would take to say, "Ruggedness, Resourcefulness, and Resiliency." We pulled together and the tree moved behind us like a giant animal dragging its tail over the forest floor. In that moment we were one.

The following winter, when I was a "senior," in eighth grade, Walter asked me to lead some underclassmen on snowshoes through seven miles of heavy snow. March was fickle. The weather had been teasing us, warming in fits and starts that caused melting and made the snow heavier underfoot. The last few days had tantalized my nose with the first sweet hints of thaw. I wanted to get out in the woods, to smell the scent of earth again, and to explore the winter wilderness for what could be the last time that year.

Walter must have seen the snowshoe trip as an opportunity to advance my leadership skills. He stood at his post in the dining-room hall, tall and lean as a tree, his white hair and mustache reflecting the snow outside. "I want to check on our house at Clifford's Falls, and need some volunteers to go with me. The trip will take most of the day so I need whoever goes to be caught up on all your work." We did not have grades at North Country School, but my teachers' comments let me know that after two years, I had finally met the school's academic standards on my papers and exams. I crossed my fingers that I would be chosen.

"Raise your hands if you feel rugged enough to make the trip." His eyes looked calmly around the room, and came to rest on me. I could hardly put mine up fast enough. I wanted to prove my muscle to this man who had become my surrogate father. "Eileen, I'd like you to lead it with me." I sat up straight and felt like I had just been nominated for president of the United States. No one had ever asked me to be a leader before.

My fourteen-year-old definition of leadership was very narrow: get out in front and keep going, stay ahead and show the way. I hoped the round metal signs on the trees would be clear. The Adirondack Mountain Club put them along all the trails but sometimes a bear or hikers pulled them off. My sense of direction was as dyslexic as my spelling and I did not want to make a fool of myself, but I knew Walter would not set me up to fail.

The day he announced the trip, the temperature climbed high enough to melt some of the snow. That night a blizzard blew in, laying twelve inches of fresh powder over everything. The silent trees were heavy with snow. Even the birds were quiet. We gathered at the start of the trail after breakfast, our backpacks stuffed with snacks and extra clothes. There were no tracks except for the occasional marks of a fleeting squirrel. I tightened the buckles around my boots on the long wooden snowshoes and looked at Walter as if to say, *Am I really up to this?* His white mustache quivered, as it did whenever he was trying to suppress too big a smile.

I don't remember who else was with me, but the other boys and girls fell into line behind me. Walter took up the rear. The cold air made smoke clouds out of my breath. I lifted a foot and slid the snowshoe along the crust of the snow before plunging it down in front of me.

A mile after we started the air had warmed, requiring far more effort to move through the heavy snow. I stopped to strip off my outer layer. How could I have thought I would need more clothes? I was dripping with sweat. I removed my hat and parka, exposing my shirt and long underwear. Others did the same. A clod of snow spilled from a branch above me right down my neck. I heard others behind me yelp and giggle from the same experience. I joined in. Our wet body heat smelled like damp feathers.

Walter spoke from the rear in his slow, steady voice. "Who knows what direction we are going?"

"Toward Clifford's!" I said flippantly. My internal compass had long ago spun out of control. I thought my new challenge as leader was just a physical test. Now he was asking us to use our brains, too. Walter liked to push the edge.

A girl from behind me yelled, "We're going south."

"How do you know that?" Walter probed.

"Because I saw it on a map," the same smarty-pants called.

Apparently, that was not the answer Walter was looking for.

"Right now we have no map or compass. How can you discern what direction is north?"

This caught everyone's attention. Until now, we had been walking blindly, trusting that Walter would tell us if we turned the wrong way. I should have known. Walter did not believe in the concept of being lost. Nor did he miss any opportunity for teaching. What others might define as lost he saw as an opportunity to go a different way, to tread new territory. Right now we were on new ground, both literally and figuratively.

One bright boy shot up his hand. "I know. You look for the moss on the tree trunks. It grows on the north side."

Walter smiled broadly and his eyes sent a beam of warmth around our circle. "Why do you think the moss grows on the north side?" The final piece to this puzzle was easy. Someone blurted out, "Because it's colder?"

"No," I said, remembering my lesson in the woods on our family island in Maine. "Trees have more moss on the north side because there is less light."

We looked at the conifers around us. Sure enough, each one had green moss on the same side, facing north.

"Now you will know which direction we are going." Walter's voice was full of satisfaction for this teaching moment. "And while we are standing here, where is the sun coming from?"

It was hard to tell because the sky was gray. But just then the clouds thinned and the sun shone through the overcast.

"There it is!" I pointed. I felt I had to have the right answer. After all, Walter had asked me to be the leader. Others concurred and the smarty-pants girl beat me to the final answer. "It is in the east because the sun comes up in the east and sets in the west." She was a year younger than I. At least I saw the sun first.

It was time to move on. We had only gone a few miles and, now that we had stopped, we were getting cold again. I wondered how long it would take to get to Clifford's at this pace.

We had a long day ahead. The longest part was between the step and lift of my snowshoes. They grew heavier with every mile. By the time the sun was directly over us, my thighs were beginning to ache. We stopped for snacks a few times. I caught Walter's eye but could not read beyond his smile. I felt that if I let anyone else take the lead, I would have failed at my job. I kept telling myself, *The leader is supposed to be out in front.* How I wished that someone else could take a turn breaking trail. Why had I wanted this responsibility anyway?

Deep inside, I knew the answer. I wanted to learn how to lead. If I didn't try to the point of failure, I would never know. So I kept going until we reached the turnoff to Clifford's Falls. My legs simply wouldn't lift any longer. I fell down and started to cry.

Only then did Walter gently suggest that somebody else take a turn in front. I lay by the side of the unplowed road and watched the group move slowly forward. They formed a relay. Every few yards the person in back moved up to the front. I got up and fell into line. It was so much easier to follow in others' footsteps. I was learning something from this perspective. On the well-trodden path I was able to walk again. I was going to make it after all.

But what of my role as leader? Had I failed Walter by staying in front for only six out of the seven miles? I looked back at him and apologized. "I'm sorry I wasn't a very good leader," I said.

"What do you mean?" he asked gently. "Leadership doesn't only mean being in front. The others need to learn their strength, and you need to pace yourself. Now you are leading by a different kind of example. By seeing how tired you got, they learned the value of taking turns. A good leader leads from behind."

I felt Walter's wise eyes on me. He had been waiting for me to reach this moment. I had not disappointed him after all.

16

MUSIC LESSONS

❧

I grew up in a house filled with piano music. My mother practiced every day for up to two hours and made sure each of us children had piano lessons. Ultimately, David, Neva, and Abby preferred their singing voices, though Abby played cello for years. Peggy tried the violin, and Richard became accomplished on both piano and guitar. I stayed with my mother on the piano. She praised me for practicing and I kept at it.

When I was eight years old, Arthur Rubenstein came to our house in New York City to play Chopin waltzes in our living room. I listened from the stairwell, after bedtime, entranced. Five years later, he came to our house in Tarrytown to hear his protégée Alicia de Larrocha play before a small selected audience. I was so excited to have these two famous pianists in our house that when I shook Rubenstein's hand all I could think to say was, "I play Chopin, too." He kissed me on the cheek and I had a crush on him for months.

My mother and I practiced Bach for dexterity and mental focus. Beethoven stretched our technique and musical cognition, and Chopin and Brahms were emotional candy. During adolescence, I played some of the same Schubert impromptus as she did, and shivered as he took a melody and licked it all the way down the spoon.

I was not aware of feeling competitive until I went away to school. The distance gave me freedom over how long I practiced and what pieces I played. She was clearly ambivalent about her desire for me to progress. She gave me lessons from two of her best teachers, yet when I advanced to her level she told me one day, "Your brother could be a concert pianist if he wanted to. You and I don't have the talent." She called Alicia de Larrocha and had her give Richard two lessons. He balked under the pressure; it was not his choice.

What possessed her to think of saying and doing such things? Why would she pit me against my brother? I came to understand that she had grown up thinking it was okay for a man to do better than a woman ("They make the best chefs too..."), but she did not want me to exceed her. Her father had taught her, "You can do whatever you like but make sure you are the best in something." The mixed messages were confusing.

When my fingers began to run faster over the keys than hers, she ceased her compliments. I was stung. I learned to recognize competitiveness. I offered to play when her friends came for lunch, hoping to gain her approval from recognition by others. She would allow one short piece. Her friends told me my playing was beautiful and they liked my expression. All I could remember afterward were Mum's subtle denigrating words. "Well, she's working hard." So, I worked harder.

I had been practicing up to three hours a day for my senior recital. It was the culminating moment of my years before college and I was proud to be considered the best piano player at Oldfields, the all-girls finishing school in Maryland that I attended after North Country School. I felt embarrassed standing in front of my mother as I bowed to an audience of over a hundred people. It was dangerous to accept praise in her presence. I told myself I would hear their applause later, when I could listen to the recording in the safety of my own room.

As soon as I was alone, I turned the tape player on and listened, amazed by the technical speed and emotion conveyed through my fingers. The end of each piece came. There was a brief rise of clapping and then it clicked off. I pressed PLAY again, thinking there must be some mistake. Each time, the tape cut off before the applause. The experience provoked a memory, worse than a nightmare.

I am ten years old. I have developed a persistent fear that my parents will abandon me. They often go out to dinner parties. One night my loneliness overwhelms me. I lie in bed, crying, and can't stop. My siblings would have kept their sadness inside, but part of me wants my mother to hear how desperate I am, hoping that my tears will evoke understanding and comfort.

It is eleven o'clock when I hear her footsteps walking toward my bedroom. My heart leaps. I will soon be in her arms. She opens the door with a push and her words crack like a whip.

"How dare you cry like that? Stop this behavior at once. I will not have it. I don't want to hear another peep out of you. Do you understand? Now go to sleep."

She turns around and slams the door behind her.

With unsteady fingers, I played the recording one more time. My shoulders heaved and shook and tears poured off my cheeks in waterfalls. I gasped until I threw up. I concluded that my mother must not love me.

I cringe now, thinking back to how much I needed the applause and praise of others. I have learned that my own sense of self-worth is what matters, but part of getting there is feeling that those closest to me are supporting me along the way.

Many years later, after hundreds of hours of reflection in therapy and in the company of sympathetic friends, I have come to realize it was not her love that was missing, but her attention. She was burdened with responsibilities and, in feeling the pressure, she did to my siblings and me what her mother had done to her. It was common in those days for parents of the privileged class to fear praise would swell our heads and make us think we were superior. Mum's insistence that we act no different than anyone else, paradoxically, inferred we *were* above everyone else. We just shouldn't let it show. This created an emotional briar patch. I believe my mother was embarrassed by having married into more privileges than her own siblings or friends. Some part of her felt undeserving and afraid to shine. She tried hard to blend in while maintaining her own unique ways of standing out, succeeding through humor, self-deprecation, and working with her hands, but she did not succeed in caring for herself enough to love her children unconditionally.

I have often confused the loss of attention with the loss of love. Partnering and parenting have helped me understand that love is always there, as surely as the trailing song of a Swainson's thrush, the purple stamen and yellow petals of a flower, or the spurt of juice as I bite into a freshly plucked apple.

Love does not always come in an immediately recognizable form, but it's in the sky above, the earth below, and the air around us. I feel it now when I listen to the Brahms Intermezzo in B-flat Minor, op. 117, no. 2. I can see my mother playing it, sitting at the brown Steinway in the wood-paneled living room in New York. Her belted dress drapes in pleats around her, the hem falling just below her knees. Music fills the room and floats up the red-carpeted spiral staircase. Her thick glasses reflect light from the window overlooking the garden. Her sun-spotted fingers are perfectly arched, capable of strong chords and large stretches. They sprint up and down the keyboard, just like she moved from house to house, and duty to task, until she died from exhaustion. I purse my lips, in concentration, just like she once did. What we take from our mother is not always what we want. Other things, like music, hold us together in a chord. I inhale deeply, accepting myself in ways she couldn't. Her love is the love I've found in me. I hear it flowing from Brahms, sweet as the first song of day.

17.

CULTIVATING LOVE

❧

I remember the first hug so well, I can still see us standing near the entrance from the dining room into the front hall. Dinner was over and I stood with my back to the door, arms outstretched, inviting my mother and father to join me in a circle. As we intertwined our arms, my long blond hair fell partially forward, and I noticed their heads were at least twelve inches higher than mine. With our warm breath turned to the center, I could smell the sweet scent of Palmolive soap on their skin. The safe and unfamiliar feeling of intimacy tightened our little circle of family. This became the first of many hugs. And over time, as the American culture shifted from kissing to hugging, our family expanded its repertoire of affection.

My siblings and I called our mother's emotional outbursts and withdrawals her "black cloud moods." They were later diagnosed as episodic clinical depression. As the youngest, I watched my two brothers and three sisters each try in their own way to protect themselves. Some left home early and found solace in friends, humor, and career paths. Others rebelled and fought back, or used books and intellectual acumen or their natural good looks, clothing, and powerful men as their defense. I studied them to see which if any techniques improved her mood or their relationship with her. Nothing seemed to help.

If my mother's love was the first food, my siblings were a powerful second helping. Part of me wanted to join them as they banded together in self-defense, but I had already made my choice. By the time I was ten they had all left home for boarding school or college. For the next two years I was alone with my parents. I needed to practice my own methods of self-preservation.

My first tactic was to sulk. This was not only unattractive but produced little gratification. I tried being more direct in my demands for attention. The result was only partially successful, though negative attention is better than none. My options were dwindling, so I refined my technique, making my demands more oblique. Instead of saying I'd like them to take a walk with me, I'd ask if they wanted to. Direct statements were criticized. "I really don't think it's appropriate for you to ask." This began a pattern of indirect communication and manipulation. It was the best I knew.

One day, I stumbled on love. Having not been heard, I became the listener, and turned my attention to pleasing them. This translated into being, in my parents' words, *a comfort*. I started listening to their concerns about my older siblings, offering information or ideas I thought might help both sides, or which at the very least would gain *me* some attention. For the two years I was home alone with my parents, I sat with them at the formal dinner table, served by a maid and butler. At these times I often felt the air heavy with my mother's black cloud moods. Despite loving each other deeply, my mother's depression sometimes turned her self-criticism toward my father or me. "I just cannot have you bringing more people home, David. This was the third cocktail party this week. The staff is exhausted." She wouldn't mention herself.

As their sole child present, I looked for ways to cheer her up as a means of avoiding her cutting judgments. After many failed attempts I finally discovered that if I told them nice things about themselves or steered the conversation to happy memories or places they loved, the atmosphere would begin to lift. "Mummy, I really like the gown you are wearing. You look beautiful." I can still see her glistening eyes behind the thick glasses.

One night, when things were going especially well, I told them, "I love you." The whole room blushed, but I felt their appreciation. Up until then, such words had not been spoken in our house, as my parents feared they would swell our heads. I had broken a taboo. There was no going back, but my sense of a deficit of love remained.

The summer after I turned ten I started having trouble going to sleep. One warm night in Maine as I lay in bed, I realized it wasn't the heat that was keeping me awake. My mother had been in a stormy mood all day. Everyone was on alert. I was unable to relax. I lay awake wondering what I could do. The beautiful sound of her playing the piano downstairs drifted up to my room. I knew that the new Brahms intermezzo was not the only thing she was working on. Music calmed her. Learning a new piece provided temporary solace for her sorrowful heart.

With sudden inspiration, I tiptoed downstairs in my pajamas and quietly entered the living room until I was standing beside her. In that moment, I realized with thumping heart that I did not have a plan other than the broad goal of self-preservation and sleep. As I stood beside her an idea came to me. She saw me and stopped playing. Her eyes moved up from the keys and she glared at me, startled, on the verge of anger. I knew

I had only one chance to change her reprimand to love. The former would not help me get to sleep. So I said tenderly, and perhaps with divine channeling, "I just want to tell you, you are a wonderful mother."

Her face shifted from molten anger to a flicker of guilt. Then she melted into the mother she wanted to be.

Turning her upper body toward me, her eyes met mine and filled with tears. As her heart opened, so did her face. She pulled me to her and hugged me. Her voice was quiet as she cooed, "Well, darling. You're a dear girl and I love you very much."

Bingo! I had miraculously touched the right chord. It revealed the need in her to be a wonderful mother and it satisfied my need for love. This wasn't the kind of love I had read about in fairy tales, but it was enough to help me get to sleep.

Thus began an expanded contract between us. I would be my mother's defender, comforter, and supporter in return for her giving me enough love, or at least enough attention, to function. I sacrificed relations with my siblings and became, in effect, an only child. It would take years to heal the consequences of this decision.

I went upstairs to bed with a feeling of triumph. But the feeling didn't stick. It would require endless repetition. Not until years later did I realize there is a difference between love and attention. Attention comes and goes. Love is forever.

My father was less complicated but as unafraid to voice his anger in certain circumstances. My first big crush was on my sailing teacher. Sam was tall, blond, blue-eyed, and handsome, and for me as a fifteen-year-old, he was the most exciting thing on two feet. He was twenty-four, and the nine-year age difference made him a heartthrob. I watched other girls, who were slim and tanned with long legs and straight hair, walk down the dock with hips swaying. They caught Sam's attention and I was jealous. I was not fat but neither was I "slim." My face was freckled and I kept my unruly hair out of my face with a headband. I also had braces. I would have to find more original ways of attracting Sam.

There were lots of white and red jellyfish in the harbor that year. The red ones stung, but the white ones were easy to handle. I flopped down on the dock on my belly and scooped them up when Sam's back was turned. When he wasn't looking, I slipped them down his socks. For some reason he was slow to catch on to the depth of my feelings from this ploy. I spent hours listening to his guitar playing and even feigned interest in Red Sox games. In return, he laughed at my stories and tousled my hair. A few weeks later, he invited me out to my first drive-in movie and gave me my first kiss. I relived that moment every night before I went to sleep for the whole next year.

A week after that kiss, his older sister, Ann, arrived for the weekend with two friends. By then I had practically become an appendage to Sam. We decided to ask my parents if we could sail their old R boat, the *Jack Tar*, down to Buckle Island. They agreed and we left in the early afternoon. The wind was light and my heart was leaping with joy. The five of us talked and laughed as we slipped through the water and put down anchor three hours later. Slim wisps of fog crept toward us, and it dawned on me that we might have trouble getting back. Perhaps we would have to spend the night! I imagined myself wrapped in Sam's arms to stay warm. The idea sent shivers of excitement up my spine.

I showed Sam and his sister and friends around the island. Ann and I decided to have a skinny-dip on the far side, out of sight from the others. I imagined Sam there instead, drying me off as I emerged wet, dripping, and svelte as a mermaid. I could almost feel him holding me in his arms. Ann and I sat on the rocks talking about family and friends, and the fog settled in without us realizing it. It was so dense, we couldn't see any boats offshore.

A loud horn blast tore into our conversation and I jumped. I recognized the abrasive sound. It was the *Dragon Lady*, my uncle Nelson's eighty-foot retired submarine chaser, which he bought at a benefit auction after World War II. It was painted battleship gray and had been dubbed *PT 109* by the summer kids, signifying its likeness to a torpedo boat.

I ran like a bullet to hear my father shouting at Sam, "Get over here right now!" The delicious fantasies I had entertained after swimming evaporated.

I have *never* heard my father yell at anyone before or since.

Dad's face was red as he reprimanded Sam and ordered him aboard. When he saw me, he yelled, "Eileenie. Come here NOW!"

I didn't know my father had such a big voice. I was simultaneously surprised, terrified, and angry that he had spoiled our lovely afternoon. All we were doing was sailing and exploring the island. I wasn't even doing anything with Sam, and what was wrong with getting kissed anyway? Why was he so worked up? Didn't he trust me?

Sam rowed his sister, friends, and me out to the warship. It looked as large as my father's rage. I think I might have collapsed like a jellyfish had I not seen our boatman, Donald, waiting at the railing with my father. His kind eyes told me he was on my side. Dad had brought him along in case the engine died because Donald could fix anything. My dad could barely open a can of beans. Donald had always been our family's hero. He felt like home base. I glued myself to him and sat under his seat as he piloted us home.

We had just left Buckle Harbor, with the *Jack Tar* bobbing in tow, when my father came and stood over me angrily. "Didn't you see the fog? You could have run aground. Sam should have known better. That was a *very* foolish thing for you all to do." I tried to melt into the floor. For the first time, I realized my dad really loved me.

That episode, while embarrassing, was a turning point in my adolescence. I had graduated from North Country School in 1966 and was about to start my junior at a girls' boarding school in Glencoe, Maryland. Oldfields School was founded in 1867 as a finishing school for girls, most of whom went on to two-year colleges.

I appreciated the beauty of the campus, and the fact that I could keep my horse there. However, I felt hemmed in and resentful of the restrictions on exploring the woods and fields. I introduced our headmaster, George S. Nevens Jr., to Walter Clark, hoping he would absorb some of Walter's wisdom. He didn't seem to understand girls or the importance of racial and religious diversity. The student body was all-white and Protestant. I thought a woman would have been a better choice for headmaster, but as we were stuck with Mr. Nevens, I attempted to ingratiate myself to him.

One day during the fall of my senior year, my mother called to invite me for a weekend getaway to the Maryland countryside. This was our first outing together in years. Her ancestors came from Maryland, and her favorite cousin, Bobby Keidel, lived nearby. I enjoyed him but hoped we would have time together, alone.

She arrived on a warm autumn day in a rented car. I checked myself out and grabbed my packed overnight bag. Once on our way, her first words were "Isn't it fun to be on a spree?" The very word *spree* conjured up freedom, adventure, and fun. It also meant we had no idea where we were going. I am more the type to want a plan. She thrived without one. But I was happy just being together, and all the more so because we weren't visiting relatives. We talked about our options as we drove into the countryside. "I have heard there are Amish people living in Maryland," she said. "Let's go see if we can find them." She turned south and we sped along in search of "the old ways."

The Amish held a fascination for us both. We appreciated the simpler, slower pace at which they lived and the virtues of horses over cars as a means of transportation. This allowed us to conveniently ignore the fact that we were in a car going sixty miles an hour.

Before long, we came upon fields being plowed by horses and roadside stands with women and children in dark clothing and white caps selling vegetables. We passed several men driving horses and buggies.

We talked about the disappearance of farmland and the need to preserve it. Perhaps this trip was a foreshadowing of my mother's creation of the American Farmland Trust in 1980 to protect the best American farmland, and especially family farms. I sat in the passenger seat, my eyes glued to the bucolic scenes of pumpkins dotting the fields, horses pulling hooded carriages, women sweeping their doorsteps with homemade brooms, and young boys in dark pants held up by suspenders swinging scythes in the long grass. To my mother and me, this was meaningful work where you could see direct results. I knew that much of her work of managing people, making lists of things to remember, presents to buy, and menus to plan were a drain on her energy. Hers was a life several steps removed from the tangibles. I am sure she did not feel as much accomplishment from training the new butler or entertaining fifty people for cocktails as she did from planting her spring garden or harvesting a row of fresh green peas. She would not have given up the former, but she needed balance.

We were so engrossed in the pastoral scenes that we forgot to think about where we would spend the night until shadows cast their long fingers across the street of a town. I have no memory of where we were.

I only remember that as we began to look for an inn or a B and B, every sign said NO VACANCY. It never occurred to my mother or me that Amish people would have so many enterprising tourist stops or that they would all be full. But we only needed to look at the orange leaves on the trees to realize we were in the peak of leaf season. Autumn in Maryland is not as dramatic as in Vermont, but it still has a change of color, the chirr of late-season crickets, and the scent of drying hay and cooling earth at the close of day.

After passing through several towns without seeing a single vacancy sign, Mum and I began to giggle. Had I been alone I would have been terrified. To my mother this was all like a practical joke. She loved nothing better than when things turned out unexpectedly and forced her to drop all the other plans for the sake of adventure. "If all else fails, we can sleep in the car. It'll be perfectly comfortable," she soothed. We were just beginning to think this was our fate when we saw a small light illuminating a handwritten sign: VISITORS WELCOME.

My mother parked the car by the curb and we walked up to the door and knocked. After a pause, it opened slowly and a bearded face wearing spectacles looked out at us.

Mum was basically shy, and I imagine she was nervous having to ask a stranger if we could stay in his home. But in her distinctive accent, flavored with short *a*'s, she asked, "Would you by chance have a room for my daughter and me to spend the night?"

The man opened the door wider and invited us in. A stout woman in a full-length dress with her hair tied back and a lace cap atop her head was sitting on a couch, crocheting. I noticed that the arms of the couch had crocheted covers. There was a pump organ on our right with a very large Bible laid open on top. To our surprise and slight disappointment, there were electric lamps on either side of the couch and behind the easy chair facing it. The woman stood and, with an impassive expression, led us into their guest room.

We were so relieved to have found a place to sleep that at first all we noticed was the bed, which filled most of the space, and an armoire directly at its foot. There was a table on either side of the bed with electric lamps, and another Bible, significantly smaller, sat on the near side as a reminder that this was a religious house. But its owners were not so observant that they neglected the comforts of life. In addition to electricity, there was a modern bathroom across the hall. We could have been in middle-class suburbia.

We brushed our teeth and came back to the bedroom to change into our pajamas. When I sat down on my side of the bed I spied something very unusual on the bedside table. It was a metal box with a slot in it, just big enough for a quarter. I pointed it out to my mother and asked her what she thought it was. Neither of us had the slightest idea. We had never seen anything like it in other homes or inns. We sat together on the bed and discussed what to do.

There seemed no option but to put a quarter in the slot and see what happened. I dug one out of my purse and slid it in. To our astonishment, the bed began to quiver and shake underneath us. My mother and I were so surprised, we held our hands over our mouths and shook with laughter. We did not want to insult our hosts, whom we could only assume thought that all people from the "outside world" must expect such a modern convenience upon visiting.

We laughed so hard that we kept the bed bouncing for far longer than the quarter's life span. All afternoon we had filled our heads with images of idyllic family connections, the bounty of harvest and community, and a simple life. As I pulled the blanket up over us, I realized we were not the only ones with assumptions.

18.

YOU CAN LEAD THEM
TO THE WATER . . .

～

M y final senior project at Oldfields, in 1970, was a research paper
on the pollution of the Hudson River. I had spent many nights
as a child watching the sun sink behind the Palisades, across the Hudson, but I had never stepped foot on its banks. The river flowed just two
miles from our house as the crow flies.

That spring, a family friend and mentor, Phoebe Milliken, gave me
a book called *The Hudson River: A Natural and Unnatural History*, by
Robert Boyle. I was horrified to read how many chemicals were being
dumped into the water, killing the fish. I was equally dismayed by the
author's opinion that members of my family were to blame. He called
my father and my uncles Laurance and Nelson "cosmetic conservation-
ists." It stung. I decided to drive down to the river to see for myself.

Several sites were within easy driving distance from our home. The
waters were not blue, like I had seen from the distance, but streaked
with rainbows of oil, white plumes of pulp, and yellow, sulfurous

chemicals piped into the water from the other side of the railroad tracks. Nothing could have prepared me for this scale of filth.

A few hundred yards downriver I spied a man fishing and approached him. "Do you eat the fish you catch here?" I asked, somewhat horrified. He answered, nonchalantly, "They aren't bad after I soak 'em overnight." I went home and finished Boyle's book.

Robert Boyle was a fisherman first, an activist second. He had become a major voice in the fight against polluters, including Pennsylvania Central Railroad, Standard Brands, and, most famously, Consolidated Edison's electric generating facility on Storm King Mountain, whose heating had been killing tens of thousands of fish per day through its intake system.

I wrote Mr. Boyle a letter commending him for his research, explaining my project, and saying I hoped he would not think ill of all my family. A few days later, I gathered my courage and called to ask for a meeting. After introducing myself as Eileen Rockefeller, I quickly added that I was not a "cosmetic conservationist," as he claimed my father and two of my uncles to be, and I hoped he could tell me firsthand about some of the problems of pollution in the Hudson so that I might bring them to the attention of my father and uncles. His voice barked on the phone, but he invited me to his house in Croton-on-Hudson.

I was so nervous about meeting him that I backed my parents' station wagon into his wall. Mortified, I opened the car door to be greeted by a strong but friendly hand. He had a good heart. I could see it in the squint of his eyes and the way he looked intensely into mine. He invited me in to meet his family.

The old stone house had been a sheep barn on an experimental farm. It had wide boards nailed laterally across the walls and huge slabs of stone on the floor. A ten-foot-long fish tank with striped and large-mouth bass swimming around in it was a centerpiece of the living room. He explained that these fish came from the river and they would not have lasted long in the waters where he found them. They were caught among medical waste, raw sewage, pulp from paper mills, and industrial chemicals. These fish were the lucky ones. We had a big cleanup job to do.

He showed me slides of at least twenty different kinds of fish living in the Hudson River, including one picture of a net full of baby fish he'd collected by seining for twelve minutes. He could name every species. I was impressed by his knowledge, but he warned how the fish wouldn't grow to adults with this level of pollution flowing into the river.

Bob Boyle was hard driven and strongly opinionated. I suspect he was delighted to have a Rockefeller come interview him, even a naive one. Perhaps he hoped I would be able to get through to the governor. He told me he had discovered two laws called the Rivers and Harbors Acts of 1888 and 1889 that forbade pollution of American waters. He planned to hold the state accountable.

I left with a mission. I was going to invite Uncle Laurance and Uncle Nelson to see the pollution for themselves, in hopes that they could do something about it. This would not be easy. They were busy men, and deeply involved in business and public affairs. I was their youngest niece and had not yet proven my potential. I thought of how Bob Boyle's passion had driven him beyond convention. I picked up the phone, cleared my throat, and got right through.

"Hi, Uncle Laurance. This is your niece Eileen. I'm doing a senior project on the pollution of the Hudson River and I have seen the most *awful* poisons spilling directly into the water. Since I know you are concerned about the environment, I was wondering if I could show you and Uncle Nelson one of the sites? If you say yes, I'm sure he will come with you. And maybe you two can do something about it."

"*Well* . . . yes." He often started his sentences with *well* to give him time to think. I suspect my request surprised him, but he was probably pleased to see one of the youngest members of the next generation taking an interest in his field. "I'm so *glad* to have a new friend in *conservation*. I'll call *Nelson* and see what we can do."

In that moment, Uncle Laurance became my ally. I would later learn of other subjects we held in common, such as the connections between mind, body, and spirit. He called Uncle Nelson and they made a date to come with me to see the Hudson River up close. In the meantime, I told my father about the project and how two of his brothers had accepted my invitation. Dad had recently started chartering a helicopter to make the daily commute to his office in Manhattan. I asked if I could hitch a ride and take pictures from the air after we dropped him off. He was impressed that two of his older brothers were going to join me, and he agreed.

The great bird thundered into view at 8:15 a.m. and landed lightly on our back lawn. We got in and buckled up as the whirling rotors lifted us straight up above the house, turned, and, in perfect imitation of a dragonfly on steroids, fled toward New York City to deliver my father to the Thirty-Fourth Street Heliport.

Not every schoolgirl gets to photograph her project from a helicopter. I was determined to use my unique opportunity to find the worst sites to show the extent of the problem to my uncles. After saying goodbye to my father, we flew north along the Hudson. I took pictures of raw sewage, brown and yellow oil, and white slop pouring from a paper mill. We circled four times around the Consolidated Edison power plant, whose hot water discharges had gained recent public outcry for killing masses of fish. My father was not known for conservation, but he had given me a leg up on what I was about to study.

Two weeks later, I met my uncles at the appointed place on the east side of the river. It was a dismal day, perfect for showing them the worst pollution site I could find. Nelson was then governor of New York State and Laurance was the newly appointed chair of the Citizens' Advisory Committee on Environmental Quality and president of the Palisades Interstate Park Commission. He had also founded the American Conservation Association. If Nelson was too political to be swayed easily by emotion, surely I would have an advocate in his closest brother, Laurance.

I watched with amusement as they climbed out of either side of a chauffeured, black limousine in their tan trench coats. They looked like two detectives at the scene of a crime. I hoped they would see it that way.

My uncles waved hello to me and stepped over the railroad tracks. I kissed them each on the cheek and thanked them for coming. Their noses were already wrinkling with the reek of oil gushing out of a pipe from Penn Central. The stench was so strong, it grabbed our lungs. We found a date, 1929, cast into the pipe, proof of the duration of spillage into the Hudson.

My uncles were satisfactorily horrified. They thanked me for showing them this example of pollution and, as we stepped over several dead fish, agreed something must be done. I had a feeling they could not wait to get back to their car.

I let out a squeal of joy as I got into my Subaru. This was a first for my uncles, who had lived near the Hudson River far longer than I had. I could hardly wait to see if their visit would have an effect.

A few months later, Uncle Nelson sent me a letter announcing his appointment of Henry L. Diamond as New York State's first commissioner of environmental conservation. He said the agency was created to combine all resource management and antipollution programs into the nation's first environmental department. Before Nelson left office as governor, he became chairman of the National Commission on Water Quality, created by the United States Congress to review federal water pollution policy and to recommend a much-needed reform of the Clean Water Act.

I cannot take much credit for these developments, nor were they the sole reason the Hudson River's cleanup gained so much attention. I was a small fish in a very large tributary of political activism, but I did my part when I led my uncles to the water.

Laurance and Nelson Rockefeller near the
headwaters of the Hudson River.

19

ROADBLOCKS

~

My foray into water quality activism might not have been as successful without an impactful experience the previous year, before graduating from Oldfields School. It was 1969, the height of the
civil rights movement. Martin Luther King Jr. had been assassinated
the year before, and his tragic loss and the influence of his message were
felt around the country. Oldfields School had finally joined the growing number of schools wishing to introduce racial and ethnic diversity,
but they mishandled a situation and I found myself in the middle of it.
It haunted me for years.

The spring of my freshman year, 1967, our headmaster, George S.
Nevens Jr., called an unexpected all-school meeting. One hundred and
fifty girls in cranberry red and plaid uniforms filed into the century-
old library and sat in rows on the carpeted floor. The overheated room
filled with the smell of perspiration as Mr. Nevens began. "I want to tell
you of a historic decision made by the board of trustees. We are going to

admit the first Negro students, starting next fall. They are two sisters from Harlem, New York." His bald head flushed as he spoke, uncomfortable in his own skin and, as it turned out, with the board's decision. Then came the request.

"Obviously, I will understand if some of you are uncomfortable, but the girls are going to need roommates." He spoke as if he were talking about aliens. "So, if any of you would be willing, please raise your hand."

I grew up with people from many backgrounds coming to our house. I knew what it was like to feel different, so I was sensitive to prejudice of any kind.

My hand shot up, along with those of six others. I knew from the moment Mr. Nevens saw me that he would pick me. It would probably strengthen his image with the board to say, "Our first black student is rooming with a Rockefeller." It didn't occur to him, or me at the time, to match our interests, habits, and preferences, as is the practice with most roommate situations. He was covering new ground and was clearly uncomfortable. I felt excited to be part of a new trend in admissions that was long overdue.

Toni Cockerham became my roommate the following fall. Toni was admitted from the Ethical Culture Fieldston School in New York City. Karen, her older sister, came from the High School of Music and Art, also in New York. Their father was Reverend Ivy Cockerham, the highly regarded first African American minister of the Chambers Memorial Baptist Church, in East Harlem. Their mother, Thelma Cockerham, a respected community organizer and activist for education reform, was executive director of the Harlem Education Program. When the opportunity arose for Toni and Karen to be pioneers of integration in a small girls' school in Maryland, they accepted the challenge.

I liked Toni from the moment I saw her warm smile. She was a serious student with a great sense of humor. Her robust laugh could be heard from far down the hall. She was a star in field hockey and a conscientious and brilliant student. Her older sister, Karen, then a junior, was more reserved, but equally intellectual and thoughtful.

Toni and I became friends, but our work habits eventually caused a strain in our relationship. She was a night owl. I was an early bird. By December we decided to trade roommates. I was happy I had been the first to welcome my new friend.

My reputation as a leader and catalyst was growing. By the end of freshman year I had led a successful campaign against the antediluvian practices of hazing, and during the fall of sophomore year I started my first organization, the Outing Club, to get off campus and explore the countryside. It soon became the largest and most popular club in the school, enrolling 80 percent of the students. In May of my junior year, elections for various student offices were held for next year's senior class. The two most powerful posts for incoming seniors were head of the student council and president of the school, an alias for the student body. The president of the school was the only position voted on by all students and faculty. I was elected president of the school. I was on top of the world.

The feeling did not last long. One week before graduation, Mr. Nevens called Toni and Karen into his office and admonished them for "acting too black." Karen had worn a dashiki to school after spring vacation and let her relaxed hair grow out in its natural curls. I can only conclude from what followed that Mr. Nevens was threatened by Karen's display of identity and saw Toni as her accomplice.

But who among us trying to grow up doesn't experiment? The quest for discovering who we are is a necessary part of our journey to belonging.

I still remember Karen's ocher-and-black dashiki. To me she looked exotic and beautiful. She had become a leader, too, elected to the student council and leader of the Dubious Dozen singing group. Why couldn't Mr. Nevens see her example as a learning opportunity for the whole school? Instead, he remonstrated, "There is no such thing as black culture or the black experience."

As he carried on his tirade, both sisters rose silently from their seats and walked down the hallway back to their dorm rooms. In short order they received a final message from Mr. Nevens: "You two have forty minutes to pack up and get out."

A school meeting was called after their abrupt departure. Mr. Nevens' face looked pale as he stood before us and reported, "Karen and Toni were not expelled, but they withdrew." There was a stunned silence. Several of us raised our hands with questions. "We are not taking any questions at this time."

I was outraged and heartsick, and pondered what to do. I felt I might have some influence because of my new position and because a distant cousin, descending from the William A. Rockefeller branch, was chairman of the board. I talked with Mr. Nevens and asked if there had been some mistake. "This is between me and the board. You really don't have to concern yourself with it," he said stiffly. I left his office feeling patronized and angry.

On commencement day a week later, all hell broke loose. The graduates, in long white dresses, gathered at the top of the hill while the rest of the students lined up behind them. As the newly elected school president, I stood in front of the graduating class. From this vantage point, I was first to see an unfamiliar yellow school bus drive up the main road and park just below the ceremony site. I watched as the bus doors opened and out came Karen, Toni, their parents, and forty other black men and women. Karen and her supporters stood silently at the foot of the hill.

Mr. Nevens walked rapidly toward me, puffing a cigarette. His hands were shaking and he was breathing hard. I thought to myself, *Doesn't he see that he's setting an example of drugs by smoking?* Rumor had it he was also an alcoholic. His normally rosy nose and cheeks were drained of color as he took me aside and spoke in a strained, raspy voice: "Eileen, as president of the school you have an obligation to be on my side. I want you to do everything in your power to keep order." In a flash Mr. Nevens was down the hill, smoke trailing in the air behind him, fumes of anger.

What the hell did he mean? Was he telling me I couldn't have my own opinion? I didn't like conflict any more than he did, but I admired those girls for coming back and I thought he should have listened to them in the first place. I stood mute.

The music began and the seniors, guided by decades of Oldfields tradition, marched down the hill, laying bouquets of flowers on the ground before the "May Queen," the girl voted prettiest in her class. Some students, in silent protest, placed flowers at Karen's feet instead, as if to say, "I'm with you."

I could see Mr. Nevens and his board chair arguing out of earshot with Toni's parents, no doubt trying to intimidate the unwelcome group. No one budged. Karen and Toni stood between their father and another male supporter with tears running down their cheeks. I hoped Mr. Nevens would relent and allow Karen into the ceremony. She had been accepted to Middlebury College, but would she be able to attend if Oldfields refused to issue her high school diploma? This seemed the height of cruelty. I stood behind the seniors and cried.

I lost contact with Toni and Karen until Barack Obama was first elected president.

For years I had wondered about her and her sister. Where were they? What had become of them? I still felt sad after all these years that I hadn't been able to help them. I tracked Toni down through the Fieldston alumni association and wrote her a letter. A year later she wrote back. She was eager to get in touch but had been caring for her ill mother. I waited three more years. As I wrote my own story, I needed to know where their lives had taken them. My husband, Paul, helped me find the 1969 *New York Times* stories, written directly after the graduation. They reported that Karen's diploma was still under negotiation. What had happened? When Paul located Toni's phone number, I had to call. "Is this the Toni from Oldfields?"

"Yes," said a deep woman's voice.

"This is Eileen Rockefeller." Shrieks emanated from both of us.

The following week, Paul and I met Toni and Karen at a restaurant in New York City. Forty-three years had elapsed since we'd laid eyes on each other. Toni's dark, Nilotic features set off her black, curly hair against a crimson dress. Karen still wore the close-cropped hairstyle that I had admired, highlighting her bright, almond-shaped eyes. As adult women we hardly recognized each other, but after multiple hugs we cried, laughed, and slapped high fives. Karen and Toni sat down across the table from Paul and me. Toni and I shared pictures of family. We caught up on jobs, friends, and losses of parents. They asked Paul about his life and how we met. Finally, I asked Karen to describe what had happened after the day she should have graduated.

Karen took a deep breath, the memory still painful. "Oldfields did not give me a diploma, but Middlebury College accepted me anyway.

After a year I transferred to Fordham University. Toni returned to Fieldston for her senior year and then went to Wellesley College."

Karen stopped to wipe a tear from her eye. Toni squeezed her hand with the familiarity of a longtime supporter. "In 2001 I told my story to the chair of the board of the social welfare agency where I work. To my great surprise, he knew the head of Oldfields at the time and went down to the school to tell her about our experience." Karen looked down before continuing, to collect herself. "The Oldfields headmistress, Kathleen Jameson, came by train to New York and hosted a ceremony to give me my diploma. It had been thirty-two years."

We all dabbed our eyes. Paul and I reached across the table to clasp Toni's and Karen's free hands. Despite the loud chatter in the restaurant there was a moment of silence within our circle.

Finally I asked them both, "When you look back on your life, what are you most proud of?" After a long and thoughtful pause, Karen spoke first. "I guess I'm most proud of my family, for sticking together and helping each other."

We waited while Toni found her words. "I'm proud of never giving up."

20

GRAPHIC

GRADUATING

I was ready to leave Oldfields. I had discovered my role as a leader, and had improved my grades enough to welcome the challenge of college. The primitive almonds in the medial temporal lobes of my brain still got triggered by test anxiety, but I had learned to compensate. When Miss McPherson, the college adviser, tried to tell me I was only two-year-college material, I defied her condescension and applied only to Middlebury, an esteemed four-year institution. I got in, early decision.

The fall of my freshman year, I fell in love with geography. This was a surprise, as I have no sense of direction. But maybe that was why. Today I know it was more than that. Geography was about seeing the whole, a subject that demands perspective with the knowledge of a generalist.

At Middlebury, I became a weaver of natural science and writing. I worked hard, made many friends, built rafts to race in the spring swells of river flow, and initiated the first crafts fair for students and faculty. My senior thesis brought me back to my old stomping grounds near

North Country School. I analyzed the methodology of the Adirondack Park's land use plan.

When the time came to graduate, the ceremony held special meaning to me. It marked the culmination of many tears and sweat, and the painful, uphill battle to believe in my abilities, despite average grades. Social and emotional skills got me the help I needed, but confidence was still hard won. At times I was unsure if I would do well enough to graduate. I did.

A month before the Middlebury commencement, I learned my father was going to be given an honorary degree at the ceremony. I was proud of his many successes, but I felt overshadowed by his fame and didn't want him to upstage my own accomplishments on graduation day. The work I had done to succeed academically and to compete in family debates suddenly felt invisible. I had a narcissistic need but a justifiable one, given how hard I had worked, to have my own day in the light. My father had often been away on my birthday and had never been able to come to my class plays or piano recitals. The only event I remember him attending was my eighth grade graduation. How dare he get an honorary degree when he hadn't even worked for it? I called my mother.

Had I thought more clearly before reaching for the phone, I might have remembered her own distress at not being allowed to attend college when her parents were too proud to let her accept a full scholarship to Bennington College after losing much of their money in the Great Crash of 1929. My plea unleashed years of suppressed regret and humiliation. Her words sizzled over the phone. "How dare you talk like that? You have no right to object. This is selfish and spoiled behavior and I don't ever want to hear you talk this way again." A cold tingling emanated from the pit of my stomach upwards. I put down the phone and shook. Her words stuck like cuts from a hundred lashings.

Perhaps I gave my mother an opportunity to express the rage and sorrow she had bottled up so many years ago when her own parents probably talked to her in the same manner. From her vantage point she would gladly have shared the stage with her father had he only let her go to college. Unresolved pain repeats itself.

A strange event happened shortly thereafter, which marked the beginning of my belief in God. On May 20, 1974, ten days after the excruciating phone call with my mother, my father slipped on a recently washed terrazzo floor of a hotel lobby in Taiwan. His hip snapped. He was fifty-nine years old and it was the first bone he had ever broken. Tests later showed he was beginning to get osteoporosis. The result was that he could not attend my graduation. I would have my hard-earned moment in the spotlight after all.

I was asked to give an acceptance speech for my dad's honorary degree on his behalf. I spoke about his collection of beetles as a way of humanizing the man who could get his telephone call returned personally from practically any leader in the world.

What were the chances of his breaking his hip just before the culmination of my years of painful, though ultimately successful, academic training? I said a prayer of thanks and asked God to heal my father's hip fast. Just in case there was a glimmer of truth in my mother's diatribe, I also asked Him to forgive me for my selfishness. I felt God answer my call for forgiveness as I remembered the words engraved on the wide silver bowl I had received upon graduating from Oldfields: COURAGE, HUMILITY, AND LARGENESS OF HEART. It was their highest honor for character. Whenever I feel myself doubting my own worth, I remember the bowl and how its wide rim opens like the shape of acceptance.

21

GIFTS GIVEN

G ift giving is an art no matter whom you are giving to. It is more challenging if you fear the recipient already has everything. When my parents received an invitation to visit the king of Morocco in the early 1980s, they thought hard about what kind of gift to give him. They had less than one month to prepare and my mother wanted to make a good impression.

My mother's sense of humor was tinged with irreverence, and when it came to thinking up an original gift for a prominent person, no one could match her. She turned her mind to thinking about what she and the king might have in common. She knew he liked rugs but decided a rug would be redundant in a country known for them. He was a king and probably liked to be in control. What better symbol for power than a bull? She did not have a statue or painting of a bull, but she did have some live ones.

My mother was in her farming phase. At the age of sixty, when I, as her last child, left home, she decided to raise Simmental cattle. She took a course on artificial insemination from the University of Pennsylvania and was so successful in improving her breeding stock that she had recently been given an honorary degree. This offset her regret of not having attended college. Her top breeding stock had begun to win "best of breed" at shows around the country.

Giving a bull to anyone is not easy to arrange. When it is someone living across the Atlantic Ocean on the northern tip of Africa who happens to be a king, it adds layers of complication. My father, whose faith in my mother's taste in presents was unfailing, was willing to foot the bill for transportation.

The king was about to dispatch three jets to the United States to get spare parts for his fleet. When word reached him that my parents were sending him a bull, he diverted one from Georgia to Stewart Air Force Base in New York. My mother and her farm manager, Don Homer, were waiting with the bull. They had built a special crate to forklift him into the plane. In the end, they had to jettison a spare engine that one of the king's men was waiting for, just to be able to fit the bull and his crate on the plane.

The king might have had everything a man could want, but my mother's present was probably in the top one percent of his most unusual gifts.

I admire my mother's art of giving. It is one of her many talents that helped me to recognize generosity in other women and to learn from them. My male mentors have given me tangible advice. They introduced me to people and ideas, instructed me on the kind of man I should look for in a husband, and helped me launch my first career. I learned more subtle lessons from women. Those lessons have turned out to be every bit as important.

I have had four influential women in my life besides my mother. The first was our nurse of fourteen years. Gibby was known as "our other mother." She was from Scotland. Her real name was Miss Rae Gibb, but we called her Gibby. Originally hired to care for my oldest three siblings, her kind and gentle nature was like a soft rain. My mother depended upon her heavily, and by the time Gibby made the transition to caring for the youngest three children, she was tired. This did not stop her from giving. One day, when I was no older than five, I saw that my sister Peggy was being given many presents. I cried because I had none.

"Eileen, dear, it's only because it's Peggy's birthday," she explained, rolling her r's. A few minutes later, she returned with a leather-bound book of poetry by Robert Burns, which she gave to me. I knew this was a treasure from her bookshelf, as well as her own country. I never again asked for a present on someone else's birthday.

Gibby gave so much of herself that she eventually gave out. I saw it happen the summer I was nine. She was sitting in her room, next to mine in our house in Maine, playing cards. I walked in to join her and was stopped halfway by a strange look in her eyes. The usual trust and love had been replaced by fear. She mumbled, "I think someone has taken my cards. Now who do ya think woulda done that?"

"I promise it was not me, Gibby," I pleaded.

A dark cloud descended. I would later learn to recognize it as paranoia.

I told my mother. She took one look at Gibby, put her in the car, and took her to the hospital. Gibby's days as a nurse were over. She had had a nervous breakdown. Even shock treatment couldn't bring her back to her former self.

I learned from Gibby that you have to take care of yourself or you could end up going mad and be put in an institution. I did not want shock treatment, but I have come to see that I had a version of it the day I saw her drive away.

A year later, a much younger woman arrived to live with my parents and me. Florence Hammond had been looking for a room to rent in New York City while she studied piano. She was a few years out of college and had met my parents through a cousin of ours. My mother saw the advantage of having a younger companion for me and invited her to live with us. Flossie stayed for two years, until I went to boarding school. She became the older sister, and almost mother, I had always dreamed of having. Her natural fondness for people fit in well with my parents' social schedule. She was the perfect dinner partner when an extra woman was needed, but most of all she was my loyal friend and champion.

Flossie was the first person to appreciate my emotional intelligence. She told me I had an unusual capacity for empathy and for understanding people "beyond your years," she would say. I doubted her at first, fearing I had nothing to offer.

"But you must see, Eileenski, that not everyone your age, or even older, has the depth of insight about people that you do. It's a gift." She was the only person who ever called me Eileenski. Until then, I had thought my intuition was just a way of surviving in a big family, but Flossie expounded. "These qualities are not only worthy, they're hallmarks of your personality, angel." I liked being called "angel." I began to see myself through a new lens.

"But," I still protested, "others judge my sensitivity as moody and needy."

She defended me. "Your sensitivity is what helps you understand others. Your needs are justified, Eileenski. Everyone deserves to be seen for who they *are*, not for what they are supposed to be."

I breathed a sigh of relief. She confided in me about men she loved

Family Portrait of John D. Sr. with John D. Jr., Abby Aldrich Rockefeller, and their six children. Back row: John D. Jr. Middle row: John D. III, David, Abby Aldrich Rockefeller, John D. Sr., Abby. Front row: Laurance, Nelson, Winthrop.

Aerial shot of John D. Jr.'s family homestead, including Kykuit, the Playhouse, and the former Abeyton Lodge, where my father grew up. *(Photo by my cousin, Mary Louise Pierson)*

Portrait of my father,
David, with his
grandfather.

Abby Aldrich Rockefeller, front center, with the immigrant women
at a Bayway Joint Conference, 1920.

My mother's parents:
Neva Van Smith and
Sims McGrath.

Family portrait with my dad at age two. From left to right: Abby, John, Nelson, Laurance, Winthrop, and David.

My family portrait when I was two. From left to right: David, Abby, Neva, Peggy, Richard, and me.

With my siblings in the living room of our home in Manhattan.

Me at age two.

Dressed for church:
Richard and me with our
nurse, Gibby, circa 1957.

Family portrait on my parents' first
sailboat, Jack Tar, circa 1958.

My brother Richard and me at the
JY Ranch in Wyoming, 1958.

My dad with his beetles.

My dad's beetle man,
Freddie Solana, with
Abby and her friend,
Peggy, and Neva.

Me, surrounded by Hanse the deer and other friends, age six.

ABOVE: Sailing together—happiest times for my parents.

RIGHT: My mother at the helm of Jack Tar II.

The cabin we built on Buckle Island and called "Buckle Botel."

Richard on the raft that Peggy, her friend Gloria, and I helped him build.

Inside our home on St. Barths with my parents and M. Genet.

The best of times with my mother and me, age eight.

A family bike trip through France, 1961.

My piano teacher, Don Rand, teaching me at North Country School, 1964.

Me (center) as President of the School with Student Council, Oldfields, 1970.

The Sudanese refugee, Ariat, holding the tapestry we made together in Gambella, Ethiopia, 1972.

Me with a lion cub, Surma, Ethiopia, 1972.

My parents and me, age twenty-five, in Seal Harbor.

My mother with her bulls, one of which became a gift to the King of Morocco.

With Walter Clark, 1978.

Norman Cousins
and me, 1979.

Harold Hochschild taking
Paul and me with some
friends for a boat ride
on Blue Mountain
Lake, Adirondacks,
New York, 1980.

Florence Hammond
and me, later in life.

The early years: Paul and me, 1980.

Science Advisors of the Institute for the Advancement of Health including Laurance and Mary Rockefeller and my parents and Paul. From left to right from back: Laurance Rockefeller, Mary Rockefeller, T George Harris, Steven E. Locke, M.D., Halstead R. Holman, M.D., Rachel Naomi Remen, M.D., Barry Flint (executive director), Kenneth R. Pelletier, Ph.D., Bernard H. Fox, Ph.D., David Rockefeller, Marion Miller, Carole Rae (a friend), Joel Elkes, M.D., Leisha Heyden (board member), Norman Cousins, Neal E. Miller, Ph.D., Martin L. Rossman, M.D., Audrey Flint (Barry's daughter), Jimmie C. B. Holland, M.D., Peggy Rockefeller, Eileen, and Paul.

Family wedding portrait: My father, mother, me, Paul and
his parents, Ursula and Bert Growald, 1981.

Just married: Paul and me in my grandmother's garden, 1981.

Me with Adam, four, and Danny, two, at the time we first taught them "heart talks."

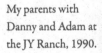

My parents with Danny and Adam at the JY Ranch, 1990.

My parents at their island house in Maine, shortly before my mother died, 1995.

At Abby's farm house. From left to right: Richard, Abby, Dad, Peggy, Neva, Eileen, David, 2003.

My Uncle Laurance and me, in his last year, age ninety-four.

Me with my dad at age ninety-five, in Maine.

Dad driving a pair of horses at his 95th birthday in front of the Playhouse in Tarrytown, NY, 2010.
(Photo by Bob Eddy)

Celebrating my dad's 95th in the living room of the Playhouse.
(Photo by Bob Eddy)

In the Fish River Canyon, Namibia. From left to right:
Richard, Nancy, Peggy, me, and Paul, 2008.

Paul and me at the former
JY Ranch with Phelps Lake
and the Tetons in the
background, 2010.

With my dad in Maine at Christmas
2012. Clockwise from my dad:
me, Danny, Adam, and Paul.

and her fears of playing piano in front of others. I saw her vulnerability mirrored in mine, and through her example I began to accept myself.

The following year, I was seated in the dining room of North Country School with co-founder Leonora Clark the day she told me about her near-death experience. "Leo" was mostly deaf from multiple infections as a child. She wore hearing aids that whined, and her teeth clacked as she talked. I think it was her way of relieving stress. On bad days her strong jaw looked as if it could crush you in two. Leo often frightened me, for she was, like my mother, prone to depression and anger, but she shared my mother's magnetism. When she told stories, she drew a crowd.

As she told this story, her mouth softened. She reflected on the time she had had such a bad infection that they had to perform an operation.

"The next thing I knew," Leo recounted, "I was running toward the light through a tunnel. Everything was beautiful and I couldn't wait to get there."

Leo's pupils enlarged as she looked around at each one of us. I tucked my feet around the rung below my wooden seat and propped my elbows on the pine tabletop. No one had ever talked to me about death before. I was mesmerized. She continued.

"Just as I was in reach of a beautiful field, flooded with light, I heard someone calling my name. They seemed far away, but they were calling, 'Leo! Come back! Leo! Come back!' I did not want to come back, but then I felt a lot of pressure on my chest, as if someone was pumping it. The beautiful field started to fade and I felt myself return to the voice and the pressure. I had been rescued from the brink of death."

Leo's teeth clacked again. I shuddered. Her voice was certain and comforting as she added, "Now I know death is not a place to fear."

Leo's story gave me goose bumps. I still fear the suffering that might precede my death, but I am no longer afraid of opening new doors along the way. Leo awakened in me a curiosity about the mysteries of life and whatever comes after.

Four years later, when I met another mother figure in Phoebe Milliken, I was wondering about the meaning of life. I asked her, "If life can get snuffed out so fast, why are we attracted to danger?" I told her how my mother went sailing single-handed in forty-mile-an-hour winds, and how I sometimes looked over a cliff and wondered what would happen if I jumped.

Phoebe's hair had turned white when she was very young. I puzzled over what had prompted the change or whether it was just genetic. She looked at me with her bluebird-colored eyes and smiled. I knew my questions were welcome. We were sitting together on a wooden bench, overlooking the ocean. She answered, "But *don't* you think that is exactly *why* we cherish our lives so much? *Just* because they can end so *fast*?"

Her voice undulated with emphasis and certainty, precise in its New England pronunciation of the short *a* in *fast* and the *h* in *why*. I liked the way she answered my questions with questions of her own. It leveled the playing field. She was only three years younger than my parents, but she never told me what to do or how to do it. She simply listened.

Phoebe has lived into her nineties and has a deep, abiding faith in God. She starts each day with prayers of gratitude and expresses her thoughts in dozens of handwritten notes and e-mails to young and old. I have been the lucky recipient of many. She has found the gift of giving without attachment and writes even if I don't always answer. We have made a point to get together at least once a year since we first met over forty years ago. When we are together, she appears to have no other desire than to be with me in that moment. I have learned from Phoebe the blessing of being present to life.

22.

LEARNING RESILIENCE

❧

Adversity opens the door to resilience. I am grateful to the females in my life who have modeled it. Among them are two tribal women I met in Ethiopia during 1972 when I was twenty. One was from the Anuak tribe, in a small southwestern town called Gambella. The other was a Nuer woman who fled to Gambella as a refugee from the Sudanese civil war. Nuers and Anuaks have a long history as enemies, resulting in mortal conflict, but these two women forged a friendship through weaving. They met through my friend Anna Parr, a Peace Corps volunteer, who built a shop in Gambella to help them earn a living by weaving and selling their tapestries. I spent three of my six weeks' winter term there from Middlebury, as an apprentice.

I met Anna and her then husband, Peter, my senior year at Oldfields School, when they gave a slide show about their life in Ethiopia. I had dreamed of going to Africa since I was five, after someone read me "Androcles and the Lion." Something about the authenticity of an ancient land, the imagined protection from lions, and my fascination with different customs called me. Two years after meeting the Parrs, I was on my way. My parents were understandably nervous. The letters back and forth are evidence, but there was no stopping my first adventure into the wider world.

The first week was spent with the son and family of the head Christian missionary in Ethiopia. They were building a school in an outpost west of Addis Ababa, for the Surma people, a subsistence tribe that had lost their cattle in a drought fifteen years before. The Surmas have a click language. The men carried spears and wore nothing more than skins draped over their backs. The women adorned themselves with earrings and round lip-plates, up to fifteen inches wide. I was enthralled and fascinated, but otherwise very comfortable with these friendly, naked people. Two orphaned lion cubs, the size of Labrador puppies, held equal fascination. The missionary family had found them near their encampment. I played with them and felt like the famous naturalist Joy Adamson.

On my last day in Surma, the crowned princess of Emperor Haile Selassie arrived by plane on a dirt airstrip to pay a state visit. She looked visibly shaken when the Surma men ran toward the extended stairway, naked but for designs painted with ash on their bodies, clasping spears and shields, as they sang and danced their welcome. She did not know that this was their way of greeting a powerful person.

I thought of how my father had made a similar misjudgment when he met the emperor a few years before. Haile Selassie had two pet lions, which sat on either side of the entrance to his chambers. In contrast to the ones I played with, these were full grown. When my father entered, he tried to pat one of them and it roared. I felt a bond growing between Dad and me. I wished he had seen it that way. Years later, he admitted,

"When you went to Africa I felt you were deserting the family." I was shocked. Did he not understand that I had to leave home to appreciate it?

I flew to Gambella in a four-seater bush plane and moved into a tin-roofed house with Peter and Anna to begin work with the weaving shop. I had been weaving since fourth grade. Anna set me up next to the An-uak woman, named Ariat. We sat side by side on the same bench and fingered handspun woolen yarns in and out of cotton warp threads on the upright loom, following the picture she had drawn in crayon and pinned under the warp. Her scene showed brightly colored ostriches and turtles surrounding a sun. I wondered, as I gathered red, yellow, and blue yarns from the basket behind us, whether she had contemplated the symbolism of these animals. Both had the capacity to hide from them-selves, even in broad daylight. Was there any meaning to the fact that she wove the sun from coarse goat's hair? She was the one who had fled from atrocities, across the border. Perhaps the sun would never again be bright for her. I wished I could ask her but she spoke no English.

Ariat had a short, slight build with quick hands and a soft voice. She hummed as she worked, in a light singsong voice, sometimes accompa-nied by words. Periodically, she would call to her colleague, Naikir, across the room. Naikir was a tall, robust Ethiopian Nuer. Her muscu-lar body and high cheekbones looked strong enough to withstand al-most anything. Her people were known for their aggression. Naikir often overtook Ariat's singing with boisterous laughter, bellowing from behind us. Her white teeth gleamed against her night-black skin. If Ariat's singing was light as the moon, Naikir's was bold as the sun. She greeted us each day with a wide grin followed by loud exclamations.

The two women talked and sang together like old friends, sharing stories in their own languages about challenges at home with their families and husbands. I did not know the tragedy of their lives at the time. I only saw their demeanor and response to events of the night before.

Naikir was usually the first one to the shop. The morning she didn't show up we all got gooseflesh. Warfare between the tribes continued. Anna asked Ariat if she knew what happened. Ariat shook her head silently and kept on weaving. Her fingers worked extra fast, as if competing with her mind.

Naikir was two hours late. The moment she entered the room I could tell she had had a rough night. Her right eye was swollen shut and surrounded by purple bruises. Ariat took a quick look and turned back to her work. She seemed to understand the importance of timing. Some kinds of pain need space before the story can be told. We waited and wove in silence.

Half an hour later Naikir started humming, softly at first. Gradually she turned up the volume and added words. Suddenly, her singing exploded into laughter. We jumped at her thunderous voice. I could no longer keep from staring. She was now ready to tell us, through pantomime and rapid-fire words, what had happened to her.

Naikir tipped her head back, cupping her hands to her mouth, and swallowed loudly and often, to pantomime drinking. Her movements faltered, as if she were inebriated. Anna whispered to me, "It was her husband." Naikir showed us how he punched her repeatedly, and she spat out shrieks of laughter as she dramatized herself fighting back. Hysteria moved up her body in waves of high-pitched ululation.

I was stunned. I had never seen anyone make fun of something so painful. Anna told me, "This is not the first time Naikir's husband has stolen her money, gone drinking, and beaten her. It happens a lot here."

I bought the tapestry that Ariat and I had made together and came home with a new perspective on suffering. Today it hangs on my office wall as a reminder of how, in the face of adversity, laughter is a strong thread of resilience.

∽

A few times in my life I have heard someone speak who leaves an indelible mark in my heart. One such occasion was when Archbishop Desmond Tutu came to speak to the Global Philanthropy Forum in Redwood City, California. I had heard about the great leader from South Africa who had won the Nobel Peace Prize, in 1984, as a unifying leader in the campaign against apartheid, but I had never had the privilege of hearing him speak. The group of six hundred people had gathered to learn and share their work about the global state of human rights and social justice. I was a neophyte, and I sat at a round table close to the podium with my knitting on my lap. Sometimes I am able to concentrate better if I have something to do with my hands. At least I can see the progress of my knitting if I feel inadequate in my ability to contribute.

As the archbishop was introduced, we were told he was not feeling well and would have to curtail his remarks. He walked up onto the stage with surprising vigor. His clerical robes floated behind him as his smile stilled the audience. In that moment he appeared larger than life.

I tried to figure out what it was that made his relatively small body seem so big. Then my eyes met his and I felt his love—love that came from a source so deep it had no boundaries or biases. His love of humanity filled the room like helium. I felt tears—of forgiveness, gratitude, and acceptance—even as he said, "Good morning."

When the audience did not respond with full gusto to his salutation, he humored us in a louder voice, saying, "Let's try this again.

GOOD MORNING!" This time the audience responded in kind. We knew he meant what he said. His "good morning" was a blessing on us all, on the day, and on people everywhere in the world who were suffering. I could feel his passion. It bubbled up in his bright eyes, like glistening marbles, and spread in ripples from his smile. He was totally present to our group and he demanded the same from us. The room seemed smaller and we drew closer, as happens in the presence of love. I stopped my knitting and looked up at his laughing, loving eyes.

Once he had our attention, the archbishop began to draw us into the problems of crimes against humanity. On this morning he chose to talk about Darfur. He and Nelson Mandela were among a group who traveled to Darfur, dubbing themselves "the Elders." They wanted to witness for themselves the atrocities against hundreds of thousands of innocent human beings in hopes of broadening awareness and inciting action. I was prepared for descriptions of genocide, but the archbishop surprised us. He did not take the path of horror to stir us. We would have plenty of opportunity to learn about that throughout the next few days. Instead, he painted a different kind of picture, which in its simplicity gave even greater weight to the current genocide.

He began by telling us how he had just come from Washington State, where he had been on a panel with the Dalai Lama discussing the importance of emotional intelligence. The two men have apparently been on many panels together and he said they would inevitably start laughing, no matter what the topic of the meeting. "Finally," he told us, with a twinkle in his eye, "I had to say to the Dalai Lama, 'Your Holiness, there are many press photographers taking our pictures. We cannot keep laughing like this. It does not look very holy.'"

The audience roared. We were now ready for anything. He started to describe his visit to Darfur. But once again we were surprised as he reflected, saying, "It's so simple. I saw a father take a baby on his lap, even though he had no chair to sit on and only a tarp with no walls for his house. The father drew the baby to him and he smiled. You see, it's so simple."

I wondered what he was getting at. He went on. "I saw a woman emerge from her partial shelter to the first rays of sunlight, and as she looked up, she smiled." He paused and repeated in a penetrating voice, "It's so simple." His ability to see the light through the crack of an otherwise endless wall of human suffering softened my fear that it was all too big for us to make a difference. He had widened the circle of hope. I felt a shift in the room.

Archbishop Tutu never did report on the atrocities directly. But like a good poem that conveys its essence without saying what it is, he gave us a glimpse into what it means to survive even in the presence of malnourishment, starvation, brutality, and death. He provided us with pictures of survival through the act of love and the presence of beauty. Beauty is the fastest way to access love. Where there is beauty, there is hope. We don't have to change the world to improve one life, but in improving one life, we help change the world. *"It's so simple."*

His refrain has become my meditation. It reminds me to look for beauty, care for a loved one, talk gently to strangers, and walk lightly on the earth.

23.

GEORGIA O'KEEFFE SPEAKS

~

> They could tell you how they painted *their* landscape but they couldn't tell me to paint *mine*.
>
> —*Georgia O'Keeffe, age 92*

Georgia O'Keeffe was, like my mother, a woman of her own making. She gave me the courage to blaze my own trail in life. When I was twenty-five, I watched a PBS television special about her and was so inspired that I wrote a poem in her voice. I was looking for female mentors and I tried her on for size. Two years later, I was given the opportunity to read my poem to her in person.

I had met oil magnate Robert O. Anderson and his wife, Barbara, at my parents' house in Maine. The Andersons were neighbors of Georgia O'Keeffe's in New Mexico. I shared my poem with them and Bob invited me to visit them and read the poem aloud to her. I could think of nothing else until I arrived.

Bob picked me up at the airport and drove me to their ranch. Several of the Anderson family had arrived to join us for lunch. They came out on the terrace with their mother to greet me. We were served iced tea on silver platters as we waited for Miss O'Keeffe to arrive in one of Mr. Anderson's small planes. At exactly twelve thirty it landed in front of the house. Georgia O'Keeffe stepped down the stairs, into a halo of dust. She was dressed in her signature flowing black dress with a scarf tied around her head. She used a cane and would not accept help from anyone, even at the age of ninety-two.

I shook hands with her. She was nearly blind but she could still hear well. Bob told her I had written a poem about her and would like to read it to her after lunch.

"Well, I'll have to have a rest first," she barked. Bob told her he had her room all ready. I was intimidated by her directness and her peevish response, but I admired how she asked for what she needed.

An hour after lunch, Barbara took me upstairs to the room where Georgia O'Keeffe had been napping, and knocked.

"Come in," Miss O'Keeffe croaked. She was sitting on a chair in a darkened room, her cane by her side. She was expecting me.

I sat down on a chair opposite her and read my poem to her. I was nervous the whole way through. When I finished, all she said was, "Why don't you write a poem about yourself? I should think that would be more interesting to you."

I didn't know whether to be complemented or crushed. After thirty years, I see that the poem was as much about me as it was about her. Georgia O'Keeffe's example and wisdom have guided my life. Though she had an austere, masculine demeanor, her paintings are feminine to the last flower and bone.

Eventually I found the courage to move back to the country, look into my heart, and paint my life with words.

Georgia O'Keeffe Speaks

So what if you walk on the knife's edge?
So what if you fall off?
I'd rather be doing something I wanted to do.
And I have walked along those ridges,
those black spines of hills
casting shadows down the valleys.
Even the wind didn't stop me.
I've often worked in wind so strong
it would have swept my chair away
had I stood up.
Somehow, I managed to hold on
to my canvas.

I always wanted to paint landscapes.
I thought someone could tell me how
but they couldn't.
Why try to paint like others anyway?
You can never be better than they.
You can only be what you are
so why not practice that instead?
When I was twenty, I'd painted a picture
for everyone I knew . . . to please them.
I was fed up with painting for others
so I thought why not please myself,
and I went to the country.

There were no flowers in the desert
when I got there,
but I had to take something back.
There were a lot of bones
so I took them in a barrel.
All winter I painted bones
with a blue sky behind them.
After a while I thought I'd had enough of blue
so I painted a red bone
with yellow sky.

I don't think bones represent death.
They outlast death
and I like painting them.
When the flowers bloomed
I painted them big
to get people to look.
I like their shapes.
I can see shapes.
There are a few I repeated,
Like the evening star.

My sister and I often took a walk
at sunset time.
She would throw bottles into the air
and shoot them.
I liked to look at the evening star.
It amazed me
so I painted it.

I've done things because I've wanted to.
I didn't mind so much about the money,
only Alfred would hold on to my paintings so
(for he hated to let one go)
that I said to him finally,
"It would be nice if
I could make my living this year!"

He didn't let me go
to the country. I just went
because I had to go.
I knew I would live there someday.
It's the only place for me, really—
where I can grow my own vegetables
instead of driving to town through the heat
to get a wilted thing.

Yes, it was hot in the summers,
very hot and no shade
except for my car,
but I went out at seven
and often didn't get back 'til five.
I did it because it felt good
and it still feels good
to walk the knife edge in the heat . . .

24.

MALE MENTORS

I think of poems and dreams as my underwater life and daily experience as my terrestrial. In this way I navigate learning with one eye submerged and one eye above. I have more control about what's above water, but I am often more intrigued by what surfaces from the deep.

One dream, in my mid-twenties, has guided my life. Harold Hochschild, whom I met when I was a senior at Middlebury College, was central to this dream. He had written the definitive, two-volume history of the Adirondacks and my thesis would not be complete without meeting him. I made a phone call that was the start of a seven-year friendship lasting until his death at eighty-nine, in 1981.

Harold became one of my mentors. He loved people of all ages and I visited him twice a year for house parties at his rambling wooden Adirondack lodge, Eagle's Nest. He would send his Piper Cub floatplane to pick me up in Vermont, where I was living and working, to spend the weekend with up to twenty other people.

We rode Tennessee walking horses in the morning, played tennis or hiked in the afternoon, and always joined him at exactly six fifteen each evening for a swim in the lake. He wore thin black bathing shoes, little white goggles, and a pair of tan, loose-fitted trunks. I watched as he slowly lowered his short, hunched body down the ladder at the end of the dock. A man in a mahogany-hulled Chris-Craft motorboat waited to accompany him and any others fit enough to follow, as he swam a quarter mile to the other shore, and back.

Harold was a good listener. He was also a generous philanthropist to many causes and an enduring friend. I was living in San Francisco when he died. He left me $15,000 in his will to do with what I wished. I had never before been given money from anyone other than my family. His bequest became the seed money for a research fund at the Institute for the Advancement of Health, which I founded, in 1983, to promote scientific understanding of mind/body relationships in health and disease. Out of Harold's fund we gave the seminal grant to one of our scientific advisers, Dr. Dean Ornish, who has since become internationally known for his research and practice to reverse heart disease through diet, exercise, and social support. Harold was not only on my side, he was still by my side.

Harold's ability to assert himself at strategic times in my life in loving and supportive ways was perhaps why he became the subject of an important dream.

A few years before his death, I dreamed I saw Harold lying on his bed in a large natural-wood room of his beloved Eagle's Nest. He was on his back with his mouth open, dead. I knelt by his side to pay my last respects.

Next to him was a basket of turkey feathers. I was supposed to take one as an offering. I saw the feathers as a symbol of the gentle side of his personality and the mysterious winged journey ahead.

Holding the feather, I bent over to kiss him good-bye. To my surprise, his eyes opened. He looked at me and began mouthing a word, but no sound came out of him. I looked up and saw a woman standing on a balcony. Dressed like a nurse in a white uniform, she appeared to be an angel of death. I whispered to her, "What is Harold saying?" I was sure it was very important.

The nurse/angel spoke from the balcony.

"He is telling you that love is the most important thing."

When I woke up, I knew that Harold had become a messenger from the deep.

Norman Cousins was an even more impactful mentor. He opened my eyes to new worlds, both personally and professionally. I first met him in Colonial Williamsburg, Virginia, in 1979. My father invited me to join him at the Dartmouth Conference, which he co-chaired with Norman. Leaders from the former Soviet Union and the United States came together in hopes of thawing the Cold War. I felt a connection with Norman the moment our eyes met. It was clear he liked women but, more than that, his playful and searching eyes drew me out of my shyness into conversation. Norman asked what I did. I told him I was living on a farm estate in Vermont, teaching children agricultural and environmental conservation, weaving and writing poetry in my spare time. I gave poetry-writing workshops to children, the elderly, and battered women. The children had won statewide prizes, the elderly wrote about times gone by, and the battered women found community through their shared words.

"I'd like to see one of your poems," he pressed.

"I'm not a published writer." I was embarrassed, for I had just learned he was editor in chief of the *Saturday Review of Literature*, a widely read and highly respected weekly magazine on arts and public affairs, which I had read only a few times; the Cold War was foreign to me, and I was afraid of making a fool of myself. He persisted. I went back to my hotel room and thumbed through my titles for a small selection.

How could a man as brilliant and articulate as he was be interested in seeing something I had written? His talk to the group of Russians and Americans that afternoon had been the most inspiring I'd ever heard. I was magnetized, and I wanted to learn everything I could from him. It was the beginning of a mentorship that would last until his death eleven years later.

That night, I co-hosted a dinner with my father on the grounds of his parents' home in Colonial Williamsburg. Grandmother and Grandfather had built Colonial Williamsburg to preserve the founding values of our country. A white tent was set up on their back lawn and I stood at the entrance with my father to welcome people to dinner. My dad made a gracious toast, recounting his parents' desire for mutual understanding among nations and his own hopes for this conference. Norman spoke about the obligation to do all we can as individuals to keep nations at peace.

I was an unworldly twenty-seven-year-old, but I could feel the growing warmth from the Russians in the room, who were mostly men in their fifties and sixties. They appreciated being received with such respect by my father and Norman, and having me there, as the daughter of David Rockefeller. Norman told me, "It would be good for people to hear from the younger generation. It will give them hope."

The mostly male audience looked drawn and tired, but when I stood and tapped my glass, I saw a spark of surprise and curiosity. All eyes turned to me as I tuned in to the desire for hope and channeled my grandmother.

"I hadn't planned to give a toast, nor has my father asked me to. But you have inspired me. I can feel the presence of my grandparents here tonight and I believe they would be tapping a glass to join me in toasting your efforts to maintain peace between these important nations."

My heart opened. I decided to read the poem I had brought for Norman. I didn't realize then that people take years to translate poetry, and when I asked the translator if she could interpret for me, her face went ashen as she attempted the first line: "Winter's last licks chill our too-soon gloveless fingers . . ."

There was a pause. I looked at the words and laughed at myself for being so naive. "I'm so sorry. I see that this poem would be too hard for simultaneous translation." Everyone but the translator laughed. She was still quivering when someone from the audience shouted, "Just read it in English." She slumped into her chair with relief. I continued.

A Promise of Spring

Winter's last licks chill
our too-soon gloveless fingers,
impatient to plant.

Like crusted snowflakes
seeds fall to earth from packets
and farmers' hope chests
take root in the cold.

The green stalks' bold survival
is everyone's hope,

like the pasqueflower
bursting from its breaking ground.

Such struggling beauty
passing death to life
lifts the wearied leaves aside
in silent promise.

The audience cheered and gave a hearty round of applause. I later learned that Russians have a hunger for literature and nostalgia. They appreciate the sound of a poem, even if they don't understand its words.

People crowded around me afterward and Norman pushed his way to the front.

"Who wrote that poem?" he demanded.

"I did," I said with my heart in my throat.

"I want a copy." His brown eyes penetrated me.

I felt like I had just won the Nobel Prize. This was the beginning of a mentorship that would teach me about writing, relationships, and my own potential.

Norman invited me to assist him later that year at the third Soviet-American Writers' Conference in Batumi, Russia. I was intimidated by Pulitzer Prize–winning writers like poet Stanley Kunitz; journalist Harrison Salisbury; and novelist Francine du Plessix Gray. All I had done was fill copious journals since the age of eight and write as-yet-unpublished poetry. I wondered how I could be helpful to Norman and the group. Would I have value beyond my last name?

September found me sitting next to Norman in Batumi. Twenty of the most prominent writers and journalists from the United States and

Russia sat shoulder to shoulder around a large table in a windowless room. They took turns talking for almost an hour each, including translation. I exchanged notes with Norman. "How can I live up to all the talent here?"

He responded during one of the Russian translations with the following note:

Anyone who can look within as honestly and intelligently as you have done in your little blue book has already succeeded. Success is not just a matter of fame or validated achievement. Success is one's ability to avoid self-deception and to make the most of what one is.

Your dad's "be the best" and your mother's "don't push" are not really opposed to what you believe about yourself. There's no point in trying to succeed in ways that don't suit you or that are beyond you. But you have an obligation not to live under your capacities. This doesn't mean you should strive to be the best poet or the best weaver or the best musician who ever lived. What it does mean is that you are justified in developing and pursuing your talents. Success is represented by the pursuit—not the arrival.

You should take a proper amount of satisfaction and pride in the fact that you possess genuine creative abilities, even though your development of them may not lead to fame in conventional terms. It will lead to self-fulfillment and to a great deal of honest joy and satisfaction by others.

You have a magnificent heritage and you are right when you say you want to be able to do something for your world. Few people I know are in a better position to do so.

My loving prescription: Don't dwell on possible failure. Failure is a matter of context. Concentrate on the context of your life and on creating situations in which good things can happen.

Yes, I have confidence in you—not to be the greatest or the best,
but to live a useful, creative, and rewarding life and to help bring
out the best in other people.

Norman's words filled me with optimism. His prescription for my life
gave me hope that perhaps I did have something to offer, even if I was
once again the youngest in the room. His confidence in me was firm
but encouraging. I began to relax and listen to the luminaries around
the table.

Kalmyk poet David Kugultinov expounded on the value of individual thought in a world fraught with constrictions. I loved his slanted
eyes and dark, imposing eyebrows. His broad Mongolian face was mel-
ancholy, like the bleak landscape he came from, and he looked at me as
he addressed the issues facing his heavy heart. He later inscribed a book
of his poetry to me.

Stanley Kunitz read some of his poems and talked about the necessary braid of human hearts, minds, and souls around the world. He
agreed to read some of my poetry and gave me pointers about images
and authenticity. I was thrilled to be learning from the masters.

A warmhearted Russian woman, Isabella Zorina, drew me in to the
conversation, making reference to my poem "A Promise of Spring,"
which I had shared with her before the meeting. Her archetypal figure
of a nurturing mother—round cheeks and belly, soft blue eyes, generous
waves of blond hair, and inviting smile—comforted me in the midst of
so many accomplished writers. She was editor of the country's most prestigious literary magazine and was excited that a member of the Rockefeller family had joined this illustrious group. Out of gratitude for her
kindness, upon my return I wove her a mohair shawl, and seventeen
years later (the same year my mother died), Isabella sent me a book of my

poems she had selected and had translated into Russian. It was my first published book of poetry.

The meeting was not always stimulating. People talked too long and it was hard to concentrate with translations, but Norman was a master at fending off boredom. One afternoon, when we were all hot and drowsy, he passed me a little note on a piece of scratch paper. It said something like: "Urgent. Immediately after this meeting I need you to . . ." and the rest was illegible. I read it over three times, my anxiety mounting for fear that I could not live up to my mentor's expectations. I passed the note back, on which I scribbled, *to do what?* He wrote his request all over again, but the most important directive was still illegible.

I felt my blood pressure mounting and tears welling up; I had failed him already. How could I possibly live up to the job of being his assistant if I couldn't even read correctly? I wiped my eyes just in time to find another note: *Just kidding.* He had purposely scribbled illegibly as a prank to wake us both up from boredom! I could have smacked him, but I suppressed a giggle and tried to keep a straight face.

Another time, he made spitballs from leftover notes and flicked them from under the table with thumb and forefinger, straight up in the air. One fell on the bald scalp of our Russian leader, Nikolai Fedorenko, editor in chief of *Foreign Literature* magazine and the Soviet representative of the United Nations Security Council. He reached up to scratch his head, thinking a fly had just landed. Next time a little ball swatted the cheek of James Reed, who had organized the conference. His quiet demeanor was temporarily disturbed as his cheek twitched. Norman tapped my foot with his but didn't change expression. He was a poker player on the surface and a mentor of both work and play. He would influence me for the rest of my life.

25

DREAMING MY HUSBAND

❧

The year after we had been to Russia together, Norman told me, "You need to find a man from California and you should live out here." I was twenty-eight. I wonder, looking back, if I would have dared to take notice of Paul when he visited the place I worked in Vermont, had I not remembered Norman's advice.

I had a dream soon thereafter in which Norman and I were walking through an airplane museum. He was a young man with dark wavy hair. We held hands as we looked at the history of flight. I woke up realizing I was ready to take off. I just needed a copilot.

Six months after the dream, Paul Growald walked into my life. He was a young man of thirty-two with dark hair and a mustache, fine features, and big dreams. His slender, wiry build hinted at an active man capable of running hard toward his goal. I would soon learn just how big he could dream.

Paul had flown from his home in San Francisco to spend a few months trying to understand how to influence presidential primaries in New Hampshire. This was not an average thirty-two-year-old's aspiration.

I had recently created my checklist for a life partner. I wanted to be married before the age of thirty and I was already twenty-eight. I also wanted a man who cared about the larger world, loved the outdoors, and who had had a near-death experience. The latter grew out of Norman's brush with mortality from an autoimmune disease called ankylosing spondylitis. He had discovered several important things through his successful recovery. I wanted my future mate to be introspective and I figured that a brush with death would encourage it. I also hoped it would help him realize the value of love.

Paul had heard about the nonprofit for which I worked from a public television broadcast of Keith Jarrett playing jazz on the porch of its mansion overlooking Lake Champlain. He was captivated by the natural beauty in the background and decided to visit it on his next trip east. He sent a brief bio and asked for a tour.

As the organization's director of communication and development, it was my job to determine who might have useful skills and experience for building our programs. Paul's background sounded interesting. In the 1970s he had worked for Stanford University population biologist Paul Ehrlich; had created the first large-scale emergency food bank for groups serving poor people in California, which led to his appointment to the California State Board of Food and Agriculture; and had raised rabbits as part of an effort to engage urban dwellers in backyard farming. He had also been a special correspondent for the *Washington Post* and had created a news service called the Fourth Estate Alternative to report on positive change in the world. His seed grant had, ironically, come from my generation's Rockefeller Family Fund. I made a date for him to visit. I was eager to find out if he'd had a near-death experience.

It was about five o'clock on a snowy Washington's Birthday when Paul walked into my office. Optimism and self-confidence poured from every word as his hazel eyes danced with enthusiasm. Somewhere in the conversation he told me how he'd almost died on a cross-country ski trip in the High Sierras.

I was scheduled to meet my co-directors in half an hour. I told them I would check Paul out. If he was interesting enough, I would bring him to the meeting. Otherwise, I would get rid of him and be right there.

Two hours later, after giving him a tour of the massive buildings and farmland studded with Brown Swiss cows, and stopping to admire the breathtaking views of Lake Champlain and the Adirondack Mountains of New York State beyond, I brought Paul to meet my co-workers, Alec and Marilyn. For the next few hours we discussed our backgrounds and philosophies of life. Paul repeated his life-threatening experience and said he had decided two things as a result. First, he was going to make a financial nest egg so he could help save the environment. Second, he was going to get married in the next two years. Without thinking I said, "Oh! You, too? Well join the club!" Later, he teased me for proposing to him at our first meeting.

A bell was ringing in the back of my mind. Hadn't Norman said I needed to find someone from California? I could hardly wait to introduce him to Paul.

Our first date was nearly a disaster. Paul was consulting for the Sierra Club in New York City the following month. I fabricated an excuse to go there, on the pretext of needing to do some research at the Foundation Center Library. I did not reach Paul by phone but left a message for him to call me back. Phone calls were more expensive then.

Had I known he had a minimal income, I might have been better prepared for what happened.

He called me back collect. We had our first argument over the
phone. "Why did you call me collect?" I asked, tartly. *Was he going to
take advantage of my money? Did he have no manners?* My antennae
were up.

"You said you were coming down for work so I assumed this was a
business call." Paul had blown my cover. I admitted that although I had
work to do, I was also hoping to spend time with him. I did not tell him
until much later that I had contrived the entire trip as a means of getting to know him better.

Paul was an hour late to the library, which almost cost us our relationship. This was our first date. I did not know his temperament
enough to understand how easily he got derailed, but the dozen yellow
roses in his arms were irresistible.

My parents both happened to be home that evening. I took Paul to
meet them for cocktails, not realizing that the family lawyer would be
there, too. It was trial by fire. To my delight, Paul discovered several unusual interests in common with my parents, including insect collecting
and a love of farming. We said good-bye after a glass of wine, and Paul
made me dinner at a friend's apartment. Roses and good food made by
my date were enough to ease my irritation at the collect call and his late
arrival.

A month later, when he had returned to the West Coast, I flew out
to join him and we drove from San Francisco to Los Angeles to meet
Norman Cousins and his wife, Ellen.

I could tell from the start that Norman approved. He took one look
at Paul and walked into a back room to retrieve a photograph taken

when he was Paul's age. It depicted Norman with a mustache and wavy hair. They both had fine noses and high foreheads. Their similar appearance was not unlike my image in the dream six months before. The stars were beginning to line up.

Paul and I continued to see each other once a month, traveling back and forth between coasts. In June I brought him to meet my two other mentors.

Walter Clark was suffering from pneumonia after heart surgery and was unable to talk when we visited him at his home, but I could tell from the smile in his eyes that he approved. It was the last time I saw him.

Harold Hochschild, who was then eighty-eight and had a broken leg, insisted on meeting the man of my dreams. He picked us up in a limousine in New York City to take us to Lutèce, one of New York's finest restaurants, followed by the Broadway musical *Morning's at Seven*. The play takes place in Kalamazoo, Michigan, where Paul grew up. This coincidence added to the evening's romance. Harold took us home and, as Paul got out of the car, Harold leaned over to me and whispered in his husky voice, "He's a good choice, Eileen. I like him."

Paul had passed muster with my three mentors. The final test was to meet my siblings. On June 12, we all gathered for my father's sixty-fifth birthday. He had recently retired and was beginning to turn his attention more in the direction of family.

The dinner table hummed with conversation. Paul had grown up as an only child. I wondered how he would cope with my numerous and diverse siblings, all talking at once. To my surprise and delight, he seemed to enjoy the evening. I was ready for "the ask."

In the fifth month after meeting Paul, I invited him to my uncle Laurance's ranch in Wyoming. My oldest brother and father would be there for a small family reunion. The JY Ranch had a long history of romance. My maternal grandparents had taken their honeymoon there when it was a dude ranch. My own parents had made the same choice, after my grandfather acquired it. I hoped that Paul would feel the vibe and choose this place to ask my hand in marriage.

We have different opinions as to how it all happened. I say he took an insufferably long time, waiting until the last day to drag me up a tall mountain without a lunch stop. He says that it wasn't the last day, but when he hadn't asked me, I threatened to jump into the icy lake from a boat.

On the way up the mountain, called Static Peak, we discussed our common values stemming from different traditions. He prayed in a synagogue. I prayed in nature. He liked structure. I defied it. In fact, we both resisted it; he just knew he needed it more. Traditions and rituals were important to both of us. We even talked about where might be a good place to be married. On this point I wouldn't negotiate. It had to be in my grandmother's East Asian, English garden in Maine. I had dreamed about it since I was ten. The garden was the one place where I felt my grandmother's spirit close to me.

He walked ahead of me, carrying the backpack. He insisted we reach the summit before we had lunch. By now it was four o'clock. We had hiked twelve miles. I was still following him, scrambling up the final steep incline along loose granite scree, when I sat down in a panic. "I am afraid of heights!" I screamed at him. "I am not going any farther! And I don't want to die!"

Paul's plans were not going well. He surrendered to my fear and found a place with a view of Phelps Lake just below the mountaintop. He pulled out a sleeping pad for us to sit on and handed me a sandwich. We had had nothing to eat since breakfast.

My temper was placated once I had something in my stomach. I took in the view. Snowcapped mountains surrounded us. The lake below was glacier-made, dark, and deep, and the musky smell of sage lifted from the distant prairies to the chatter of a chipmunk in a nearby tree.

Paul fell silent. I felt a tingling rise through my body, as if something was about to happen. Paul reached for my left hand and held it in his. His fingers felt cold. He looked me in the eye and took a deep breath. "If you take my last name, your initials will spell 'ERG,' which is a special unit of energy. Will you move to San Francisco and marry me?"

I had been waiting for this question for five months, yet his words took me by surprise. They bounced off the canyon walls and reverberated in my ears. My heart was pounding hard. I said yes before I could catch my breath.

In the next moment everything became clear. Paul reached into the backpack and pulled out a glass and a half bottle of well-traveled champagne. We drank to our future, to the beauty around us, and to our love.

My dream had come true.

26

THE FIRST YEARS

❧

Halloween is an all-city party in San Francisco. On October 31, 1980, I signed the deed to buy my farmhouse in Vermont and flew to California to live with Paul. I was sad to say good-bye to my house, my land, and my friends, but the pull to be with Paul was stronger. Norman's advice, to find a man from California and live there, was still ringing in my ears, and Paul promised to find a way for us to return to Vermont every summer and several additional times each year. I had spent two years working for the not-for-profit, helping them to set up their education programs and working as their first development and public relations director. I was eager to find a new job and start planning our wedding and our life together.

I had watched other family members move in and out of marriages. I did not want our marriage to be corrupted by the pull of the Rockefeller name, or the pressure to join family events. Saying no would have been much harder had we lived within easy commute from New York.

I knew I was making the right choice, even though it was hard to be three thousand miles away from my family.

I bought a white felt mask for my arrival on Halloween. It had a red smiling mouth with a blue tear rolling down its cheek and a yellow lightbulb glowing from its forehead. It personified for me the bright idea to join Paul and start a new life, coupled with the sorrow at leaving my new home. I planned to wear it when I got off the plane and see if Paul recognized me.

I had a layover at Kennedy Airport before the six-hour flight to San Francisco. A middle-aged couple was sitting across from me in the waiting area. The man was holding his head in pain and his wife was telling him he should have brought an Advil. The conversation escalated and was beginning to give me a headache. I found an Advil in my purse and offered it to the man. This ended their arguing and we struck up a conversation.

Morrie and Ruth Kadish were in their early sixties. They were native San Franciscans. Morrie was a short, athletic-looking man who had just run the New York City Marathon. Ruth was not the running type but was his self-proclaimed cheerleader.

I shared my recent engagement and told them Paul would be meeting me at the airport. They said they had a son about my age who was picking them up. I hoped I could introduce Paul to my newfound friends, even if they did argue in public. Their banter made them real. I enjoyed the fact that they were willing to be themselves instead of hiding behind masks of equanimity. This was not the world I had been raised in, but it was refreshing.

Ruth and Morrie flew first class. I was in coach, but in those days you could visit someone in first class if they invited you. Ruth brought me to their seat and we visited for an hour or more. I showed them my mask and told them how I planned to surprise Paul. I asked if they would be willing to walk off the plane on either side of me to make my identification more difficult. They readily agreed.

When the plane pulled up to the gate I put on my felt mask, and Ruth and Morrie flanked me as we walked into the waiting area. In front of us was a small crowd including Ruth and Morrie's son standing next to two men. One of them was wearing a bear mask. No one else wore a costume. The man in the mask was hiding yellow roses behind his back.

I took a chance and hugged the bear. He handed me the roses. My white Vermont farmhouse seemed small and far away.

This was my first step toward marriage, and the first of our many shared bright ideas. Paul wrapped me in his arms and kissed my lightbulb. I was home.

August 16, 1981, we were married under an evergreen tree in my grandparents' East Asian, English garden in Maine. Fog dripped through the branches onto flowers in a symphony of color. One hundred fifty people gathered to witness our vows. We honeymooned in Switzerland at a friend's château, climbing mountains among wildflowers by day and dipping bread into fondue by candlelight at night. The first five years were about discovering our similarities and starting our own organizations. Over the next fifteen years, while Paul amassed his own nest egg through the cable television company he built from scratch, I started my first nonprofit organization and gave birth to our two sons.

We rented a small apartment overlooking Mountain Lake Park in San Francisco, discovered common tastes in old houses, antiques, and Le Creuset pots and pans. Items we owned individually either matched or were the same brand. We even had many of the same obscure record albums, like Keith Jarrett's *Nude Ants* and the same recording of African drumming. We enjoyed eclectic music and new ideas. Conversation was never dull.

Outdoors, we shared a love of hiking, running, biking, and cross-country and downhill skiing. Paul taught me to fly-fish. I taught him to ride horseback and we rode my parents' horses whenever we visited back East. On weekends we went to a neighborhood green grocer for our weekly food shopping, having mock competitions over who could come closest to guessing the total cost. We took a cheese course together and packed Bucheron Chèvre and Vermont Cheddar in our backpack along with fresh bread and wine for picnics to Point Reyes. As we walked, we dreamed about places we would like to visit. We wanted to see the world before it changed too much, and we made a must-see list of shifting cultures that interested us. They included Africa, China, India, and Peru. Africa appeared on the horizon as we entered our fourth year of marriage.

We discussed our shared values around the importance of family, a unified base of religion, and balancing fun with work in the world. We had clear goals to do something that would outlast us and spent hours developing our vocational missions. Mine was connecting people and ideas for a better world. Paul's was inspiring people to see and protect the beauty and diversity of life. Paul started a business to build his own financial nest egg so he could make a contribution to protecting the environment. I founded an organization to help build the mind/body health field.

We decided to wait five years before having children, just to be sure this really was the match made in heaven that we thought it was. An astrologer who looked at our horoscopes said he had never seen two people's charts so aligned.

It was time to take our last vacation before starting a family. We planned a trip to East Africa.

27

GORILLA ON MY SHOULDER

❧

"D on't look them in the eye. And don't smile. It's a sign of aggression." The guide's advice about gorillas ran contrary to our social training, but we followed him up the faint trail without a murmur. Our group of six was eager to go before the moist heat of the day melted us in our boots. We brushed under a canopy of overhanging cecropia leaves and plunged through a fringe of bamboo. He turned to us with a final warning. "And one more thing. If they touch you, just sit still." I imagined a five-hundred-pound gorilla coming up to me and patting me on the back. *Still* was not an image that came easily.

Paul and I had looked forward to this expedition as the highlight of our three-week trip to Kenya, Tanzania, and Rwanda to look at wildlife. It was 1984, and Rwanda's Virunga National Park was still relatively peaceful and abounding with gorillas.

I thought back to the only other time I had visited gorillas. My parents brought Peggy, Richard, and me to Europe when I was nine. Our driver was a friend of the London zookeeper and had arranged for us to have a backroom tour of the gorilla cages. Peggy was a budding adolescent of thirteen. She had long brown hair and behind her tortoiseshell glasses her brown eyes were wide open to the world. The zookeeper led the way, with Peggy following at his heels. Richard and I were close behind.

When we reached the gorilla's cage the keeper opened the door. A male gorilla, larger than the three of us put together, lumbered onto a table in the feeding hall. He had silver hair on his back, which we were told was typical of a mature male. In that moment I was glad to be at the back of the line. The silverback seated himself comfortably. His eyes fixed on Peggy and he leaned forward, inviting her into his space. Trusting her instinct, she moved close enough to smell his breath. His long, hairy arm reached out with fingers extended to touch her cheek. He was surprisingly gentle. His fingers had dark nails and wrinkles around the joints. They looked almost human.

With his right index finger he carefully opened her mouth and examined each tooth with the care of a sensitive dentist. Then he moved his finger up to her nostrils and, with the same gentleness, opened each one. He was really seeing her. Had he not been dressed in black fur, I might have thought we were at our family physician for an annual exam. I was envious of all the attention on my sister. My nine-year-old self already felt in her shadow, seeing how my father favored her, while my mother preferred my brother. I wanted someone to favor me. Even a gorilla. I pushed closer, hoping to divert the large hairy beast's attention and redeem myself as special.

It was hopeless. The gorilla would not take his eyes off Peggy. To make matters worse, he leaned closer to her and very carefully kissed her on her cheek. Now I was really jealous. I suspect my brother was, too, for he would not let me get in front of him. We jostled for position and finally both of us squeezed closer, shoulder to shoulder, making ourselves so obvious that the gorilla could no longer ignore us. With a sigh, the large animal momentarily turned his eyes from Peggy and gave each of us a perfunctory pat on the head before turning back to his newfound love. No amount of antics, wishing, or demanding could draw him away from her. This was an all too familiar story.

Twenty-three years later, I was still plagued by memories of being last, unseen, and unsure of how or whether I belonged. My mother had faced similar doubts and had coped by escaping to the sea during gale-force winds. The tumultuous sea brought her back to herself, forcing her to stay present and forget everything but survival. Through her I learned to equate the natural elements and adventure with self-discovery and hope.

I felt the heartbeat of this ancient land. I reflected once again on "Androcles and the Lion," about a boy who is protected between the paws of a lion after removing a thorn from its paw. It gave me an image of myself as part of a larger family where people and animals are interconnected.

The steep trail up the side of the volcano was choked with stinging nettles and vines that made progress difficult. I left Paul's side and worked my way up to the front of the line behind our Rwandan guide. He was dressed in a dark green uniform and carried a rusty Lee-Enfield rifle at his side in case poachers threatened us. He walked with quick, accurate strides, avoiding sticks and curled-up leaves whose cracks and crunches might signal our presence. He stopped every so often to look up at the trees while we waited for the last person in our group to catch up. The lagging man wore a prosthetic leg and was missing an arm. He needed a cane to walk. Even more than for the rest of us, this trip was a life's dream. We willingly moved at his pace.

It seemed like hours before the first sign of gorillas appeared. We were tired and muddy. Our guide had warned us that it might take most of the day to find them and we would have to be as quiet and patient as possible. I kept close to him, hoping to get the first sighting. I imagined a thick black hand reaching out from behind a tree. Instead, our first glimpse was a shiver of leaves in the distant canopy. I would not have recognized the movement as a sign of gorillas, but our guide put his hand up to stop. He crouched down and slinked along the trail on fingers and toes until he came within throwing distance of the gorilla-occupied trees. He determined they had accepted our presence and beckoned us forward. We sat down in a circle with our backs toward the gorillas and lowered our heads to communicate peace and nonaggression. I could hear my heart drumming in my ears. Time expanded. I reminded myself to breathe.

There was scrambling in the trees. To my right I saw what looked like a two-year-old swinging from branch to branch as it made its way to the ground. It bounced in our direction like a curious child. I kept my head turned at a forty-five-degree angle, careful not to look at it directly.

A silverback male emerged from behind the base of the same tree and followed the baby. I curled myself in a tighter ball and peered out from under my elbow. He was an impressive animal with a prominent head and shoulders, expansive chest, and long hairy arms. He easily weighed six hundred pounds. His presence must have relayed a message to the mother and other members of the troop, for they stayed up in the trees.

I prayed the baby would come close to me. I also prayed that the father would not. This was not the back corridor of a zoo. It was the real deal and we were guests in their playground and dining room. I was glad gorillas were vegetarians.

It took all my willpower to sit still and not stare right at them or smile dumbly in a way that might communicate aggression. I was glad Paul was next me. His hand found mine and squeezed tightly. We were soaked with sweat. A fly circled my face. Here in the jungle, with the grunts of gorillas around us, I felt a sense of kinship stretching back to a time when my ancestors had very few words. In the curve of the gorillas' foreheads, I saw the horizon of time. My tears flowed.

A flash of fur darted behind me. No sooner did my heart leap than I felt something warm and furry climb up my back. It smelled of sweat and leaves and its little, hairless fingers grabbed at my right shoulder as it jumped down. Goose bumps rose over my body. I might have shouted for joy had I not been aware of the male gorilla lumbering behind the baby. When he reached a distance of ten feet from my left side, he stopped and watched. I hid my eyes. This simple form of hide-and-seek must have attracted the baby, for it climbed back on my right shoulder, snuffling and pulling my ear. I imagined that playing with my own children might feel like this.

Curiosity, play, and exploration: I had observed this in humans, dogs, cats, horses, lions, and elephants, and now with gorillas in the wild. This time I was the subject of fascination. The little one somersaulted off my back and nibbled my right knee. I wished he were my brother.

28.

TIME FOR BEING

❧

Paul is an only child of a German immigrant mother and her first-generation American husband. His parents were affiliated Jews. Paul's Jewish ritual and practice fills his mind and heart, but it has also served another purpose—to help maintain his own identity in the presence of my family's prominence and size. His background is very different from mine. I come from a large Protestant family and I grew up in a house like Grand Central Station; he comes from a small, middle-class Jewish family that rarely entertained.

Ironically, at the start of our marriage, Paul's minimal experience in social settings worked to his advantage. He often didn't notice if he offended someone by moving too close or turning his back while talking to another family member. Part of me envied the way he let others' opinions roll off his back, but at the same time I was embarrassed and wished I could change him. My wish for sameness stemmed from years of yearning for a close brother or sister. But he was my husband.

His attention deficit disorder did not help matters, either. The first time we drove to the San Francisco Zen Center's Tassajara Hot Springs for a weekend retreat, I was deep into telling a story about my family when he blurted out, "Look at that beautiful hawk on the telephone wire!" I enjoy birds, too, and enjoyed its flaring red tail, but I was offended that he interrupted me at the climax of my story. An hour later, when we had turned onto the last paved road before climbing up the twisting dirt route to the sanctuary, he jammed on the brakes and started backing up. Our conversation was once again interrupted.

"What are you doing? And why are you interrupting me?" Paul was so focused on what he had seen that it was hard for him to speak.

"I hope I didn't run over them," he muttered.

"What?" I probed, getting exasperated.

"Weasels," he said.

Now I *really* wondered who this man was I had married, but I was curious to see the weasels.

We jumped out of the car and ran around back.

"They're *perfect* roadkill," Paul exclaimed, as excited as if he had just won the lottery. "Look! It's a mother and her baby. They must have just been killed because they're still warm." He was already picking them up and reaching in the car for a garbage bag to put them in.

"What on *earth* are you going to do with them?" I asked, my jaw hanging wide.

"They will be beautiful stuffed."

"But where will we put them?" For once I was being the practical one.

"Oh! I don't know. We'll find a place, or give them to a school. Feel how soft their fur is." I stroked the long white-furred animals and touched the black tips on their tails. I had to admit they were very soft and cute. I was sorry they were dead.

"But Paul, we can't take them with us," I protested. "We're spending the weekend at the Zen Center."

"That's no problem," said the eternal optimist. "We'll just keep them in their freezer."

"Well, *you'll* have to ask them."

He did, but not having been trained to set context, all he said at the kitchen was, "Do you mind if I keep my weasels in your freezer?" The cook looked at him quizzically and said, "Well, no, but we *are* vegetarian here."

"Oh! I know," responded Paul. "I don't plan to eat them. I just want to stuff them." As if that explained everything. The man shook his head and put the bag in the freezer.

It took two years before Paul got around to finding a taxidermist. We had to keep a sign on our freezer for guests when they stayed at our house. It read: PLEASE DON'T EAT THE WEASELS.

What annoyed me about Paul also amused me. It's hard to compete with roadkill, but when I really need Paul's attention, he's always there for me. I attribute his generosity of spirit not only to his love for me but to his parents' deep interest in him and to the values he inherited from Judaism. Love of family and nature and caring for others and the wider world are his signature strengths.

Paul grew up with Sabbath rituals, celebrating the start of the Sabbath on Friday night at home and going to Friday evening and Saturday morning services at his parents' synagogue. He invited me to join in the Shabbat ritual at his parents' home in Palo Alto the first time I met them.

Paul's mother, Ursula Speier Growald, escaped Germany at the age of ten with her younger sister, Eva, and their parents, soon after Hitler's rise. They came to the United States via Amsterdam. Ursula won a scholarship to Johns Hopkins University and became a special education teacher. Her father, Max Speier, had been managing director of a private bank in Cologne. When the Nazis came to power, his bank moved its money to Switzerland for safekeeping, but after a major Nazi setback the bank returned the assets to Germany. Soon thereafter, the Nazis burned the Parliament building and took total control. They froze all Jewish assets and eventually stole them, including the life savings that many of Max's friends had entrusted to him in his bank.

Max never forgave himself for what he felt was betraying his clients' and friends' trust. He got his immediate family out in time. But other relatives, and many associates, died in concentration camps. Max brought his family to America and took the only jobs he could find as a Jew, first selling men's ties in offices, and later Fuller Brushes door-to-door. After he was widowed, he lived with Paul and his parents. They all called him Daddy, and Paul developed a deep bond with him. But Max never fully recovered from the trauma of all that he had lost. He died a broken spirit when Paul was five.

Paul's father, Bert Growald, grew up in a very poor family on the Lower East Side of Manhattan. His parents had emigrated from Austria and Prussia. Two of his six siblings died on the *General Slocum* excursion boat that sank in the East River in 1904, and one was run over by a fire truck in front of their Second Avenue tenement. When Bert was five, his father died in the 1919 flu pandemic, leaving him without a male role model. Miraculously, his mother was fifty-five when he was born and his three remaining sisters were much older. Yet the tragedy of his childhood did not deter him. He was the only member of his family to attend college, which he did over ten years of night school. He became a successful chemist, but his job necessitated moving his family every few years. This made it hard for Paul to win friends because he was always the new kid on the block. It didn't help that he was slight of frame and Jewish, and that his father didn't know how to throw a ball. Paul was occasionally bullied. He turned to nature, friends, and his synagogue for comfort. Nature is one of the places where Paul and I connect spiritually.

When we moved back to Vermont in 1997, Paul became a beekeeper. He founded the Pollinator Partnership to protect the health of pollinators, which are responsible for one third of the food on our tables. He has spent part of his career protecting bees, birds, bats, and butterflies. I see a connection between the loss of many of his ancestors in the gas chambers and his desire to protect the diversity of life and the traditions that honor them. I like Judaism's connection to natural cycles and references to nature's beauty and sustenance.

I was one of the first in my family to marry a Jew. Paul and I bought a silver goblet to use for our matrimonial cup of wine, and for Shabbat dinners forevermore. We had it inscribed with our names and the date of our wedding. Below these two lines are etched the following words: TO HONOR, CHERISH, SUPPORT, AND MAINTAIN.

When others join us at our table for the first time in three months or more, for holidays, or when we eat the first of any vegetable or fruit of the season from our garden, we hold hands and say a special blessing. "Blessed art thou, O Lord our God, Creator of the Universe, who sustains us, preserves us, and allows us to reach this special occasion." The beauty of ritual, like that of the seasons, is its return.

I'm not always comfortable with religious rituals, but Shabbat holds special meaning for me. It honors the role of the feminine in reflecting upon and balancing our lives. It is considered by many to be the most important Jewish holiday.

Paul introduced Shabbat into our household after we were married.

He showed me how to say blessings to the Eternal for giving us light, granting us the fruit of the vine, and providing the seeds of Earth that sustain us. The prayers remind us to set aside time for being and reflecting in the midst of so much doing. I breathe in my love of life and praise God for gifts of family, friends, nature, and food.

Paul's devotion and desire to raise our children in his tradition eventually influenced my decision to "expand" to Judaism. I was initially uncomfortable joining any organized religion, and I didn't want to give up the beautiful hymns at church or my own family's tradition of a Christmas tree. Paul was not altogether comfortable, but he agreed to my having a Christmas tree. His acceptance helped me to embrace both traditions with an emphasis on Judaism.

When I told my parents I was going to convert to Judaism, my mother said, "You will never be Jewish." I think she meant I would never feel I belonged. I suspect she was still struggling to feel at home as a Rockefeller. My father was sorry I had rejected Christianity but glad I was adopting a faith. In truth, I neither rejected nor converted. I expanded. I have a foot in two rivers of faith, but they both run into the same sea.

Judaism reinforces Paul's and my reverence for the natural world. I like that the holidays are timed to cycles of the moon and that they begin the night before, at sundown. Nature is a shared bridge with my family of origin.

Both my parents' families were Protestant. If my mother had a religion, she found it in nature. She was uncomfortable with structure and ritual, but she lived her values of caring for people, land, and animals and passed them down to us, along with a strong sense of right and wrong. She raised us on *please* and *thank-you* and insisted we shake hands and look people in the eyes.

My father was introduced to religion as a daily ritual. His father read the Bible to his family every morning, and they said prayers before meals and at bedtime. Sunday was their Sabbath. They went to church and took walks in nature but were forbidden to work.

My father gave up most of these rituals when he married my mother, but he shared her love of nature and beauty as well her insistence on manners. He continued going to his family's Union Church of Pocantico Hills, built by his father. I occasionally join him, even though I didn't like going there as a child. It makes him happy to have my company.

Church is a time for quiet reflection, but the ritual Dad loves most is having our whole family eat together around the dining-room table. He was once the youngest, but now he is the elder. I watch him at his place at the end of the table, his face glowing as he dings his wineglass for a toast. We stop our conversations and listen to his familiar words.

"I just want to say how pleased I am to have you all here tonight. You each have found your own way to make a difference in the world, and I'm so proud of you. Family is the most important thing, but when one has a nice family it is a really good thing."

I feel his love fill the room as we lift our glasses of wine and join him.

When I sip the ceremonial cup with Paul, I am reminded of my father. As I light the Sabbath candles, I often think of my grandmother, Abby Aldrich Rockefeller. Though she was a churchgoing Protestant, I share her broader custom of honoring family and the sanctity of home. I emulate her efforts to welcome immigrants and to give objects of beauty from all cultures a place of honor. The welcoming opens my heart to the wonder and diversity of life, which I call sacred. Shabbat is one of the portals.

Our sons were introduced to Shabbat as soon as they were in my arms. Every Friday night, just before dinner, Paul would put on his yarmulke, or skullcap, and place smaller ones on Adam's and Danny's heads. They joined us in the Hebrew prayers and songs as they grew.

One night when Adam and Danny had reached the ages of seven and five, they surprised me by adding their own innovation to our ritual. I had set the table with special china from my father's collection to honor the start of the Sabbath. I put our ceremonial goblet in front of Paul and placed the silver kiddush cups, given to each of our sons at birth, in front of their places.

The four of us took our seats and, as is customary, I began the ceremony by lighting both the regular and ceremonial candles. I was relieved that for once there was no argument over which boy was going to blow out the match. I sang the blessings over the Shabbat candles while drawing my outstretched fingers to my face three times to bring the light inside. I then read the prayer in English from the prayer book and passed it around the table to Paul. He lifted up our kiddush cup, partially full of wine, and blessed the fruit of the vine.

Paul said the prayer with the same love of family that my father would make a toast. The boys and I joined him in the singing part and he passed the cup around the table. Adam and Danny were allowed a sip from our family chalice in addition to the grape juice in their own kiddush cups. Paul said the blessing over the bread, and we sang more songs.

It was time for the blessings of the children. There is a separate prayer for sons and for daughters, another one for the mother, and a fourth prayer taught to the children to bless the parents and our love for one another.

Paul asked Adam and Danny to stand on either side of him so he could give them their special blessing first. He laid his hands gently on top of their heads, his fingers spreading like tributaries of love, and read from the words in the prayer book: "May God bless you and keep you and make His face to shine upon you . . . and may He make you like Ephraim and Manasseh" (two brothers who loved each other). He pointed to the blessing in the book for one's parents and they read: "May God bless our love for one another." We hugged them and they returned to their seats.

Paul turned the page to the blessing for the mother from Proverbs, chapter 31. I appreciate how he modeled to our boys his love of me and his honoring of the feminine. I also feel uncomfortable being in the limelight, but on this night I sit at my end of the table, as I had on many Friday nights, while Paul read the blessing: ". . . her children rise up, and call her blessed; and her husband also, and he praises her."

Just as Paul said, "Her children rise up . . ." both boys jumped to their feet and joined their father in reciting "Blessed."

A new ritual had been created. It has continued to this day, whenever they are home. I have added another tradition, of wiping my eyes.

The end of the Sabbath, at sundown on Saturday, is called havdalah. It is intended to bless all the five senses. We hear the blessings, taste the wine, smell the sweet spices, see the flame of the four-stranded candle, and feel its heat.

The mystics say we gain an extra soul during Shabbat and that it flees when we resume our regular work. The blessing of this moment, at the end of Shabbat, is as soothing to me as the final purple hue across the evening sky.

Havdalah means "to divide." The ceremony marks the end of the Sabbath and ushers in a new week by separating the special holy day from other days of the week.

We gather again at the dining-room table just as darkness descends on the day. Paul takes a sip of wine from our silver marriage cup and passes it around. "The wine symbolizes the joy in our hearts after a day of rest," he explains. "The spirit of wine is supposed to help us to see beyond the misery in the world while inspiring us to help in whatever way we can." I think to myself, *This is one of the ways values get passed on.*

Next, Paul lifts the ceremonial spice box and sniffs the sweet bay leaves, spicy cinnamon, and cloves. He passes the perforated silver box around, saying, "The sages tell us that smelling the spices refreshes our souls."

I take a deep breath through my nose. Sweetness abounds. Adam and Danny turn off the lights and strike a match in the dark to kindle the four-stranded havdalah candle. We read together by its dancing light: *"The havdalah candle, unlike other candles, is composed of four intertwined strands. By itself, each strand would make only a little light, but the four burning together make a great flame."*

The four of us draw close around the candle. I feel the warmth of the flame, like our family.

Paul takes the candle and douses it in a plate with 100-proof vodka. The dance of light begins.

No one speaks. We watch the playful flame diminish as it evaporates the alcohol. It invites us into silence, like the last birdsong at the end of day. The flame sputters, kicks, twirls, takes a bow, and expires. We say in unison: "Bye, bye, Shabbat," and for a moment longer, we savor the stillness.

Slack Tide

I hold your hand and you hold mine
like clamshells, closed on each other's half.
Still, still as the slack tide's spine
near where I sat at dusk (too tired to laugh),
and watched saltwater lick the shore,
tonguing without advance or retreat.
Even the clouds seemed to snore.
A face appears, supine and sweet,
"Slow down" are the only words I hear,
between interruptions of worry,
and the last warbling songbird
settling on its branch, without hurry

like you and me nesting here, still as death,
the only movement, our breath.

29

LAUNCHING THE MIND/
BODY FIELD

～

Whatever you can do, or you think you can, begin
it. Boldness has genius, power and magic in it.

—*Goethe*

I discovered the relationship between mind and body as a young
child. Even before I was old enough for school, the unsmiling substitute nurse who came on Wednesdays gave me a headache. I wanted to
tell my mother but she wasn't there. She didn't have a formal job, but
her life was filled with luncheons, board meetings, and obligations.
When she arrived home, she fixed me "a nice cup of tea," assuring me it
would help. It did. Tea is nice, but a mother's love is the real elixir.
Sometimes I felt better before the water even boiled. Later my fear of
school often made me sick. If I spiked a fever, the family doctor came
to visit. Most times all Dr. Anderson did was smile and ask me what
was wrong. Sometimes I jumped out of bed to wrestle with him. Invariably, I felt better the next day. I've had an intuitive understanding
of mind/body interactions ever since.

Two decades later, in the 1970s, the Canadian endocrinologist Hans
Selye proved the harmful impact of stress on the body and coined the

term *eustress* to describe the healing effect of positive emotions on the body. My mentor, Norman Cousins, read Selye's work and popularized the concept in his best-selling book *Anatomy of an Illness as Perceived by the Patient*. It was published in 1979, the year I met him. Cousins recounted his own recovery from a life-threatening disease through the use of laughter and Vitamin C. He equated laughter with internal jogging, for it releases endorphins critical to the body's recovery.

Norman's experience revived memories of my childhood headaches. I was looking for something to do after the start of my married life. Paul was recruiting investors to build a cable TV system in Vermont. I thought if I could build on Norman's theories and prove that the mind and body are linked, it could improve health care in America and put the patient back in the driver's seat. I hired a consultant, Barry Flint, to help scope the mind/body field and its key players.

We discovered there was no field. One visionary organization, the Institute of Noetic Sciences, had begun doing research on the mind's effect on body and spirit, but the founders of psychopharmacology, psychoneuroimmunology, and biofeedback, and researchers and practitioners using meditation, relaxation, hypnosis, and transpersonal therapy to bring the body and mind into balance were alone in the tangled wood of medicine. They had all suffered criticism and ridicule from the medical establishment. If they were going to be taken seriously, they needed to work together.

In 1983, I founded the Institute for the Advancement of Health to further scientific understanding of mind/body interactions in health and disease. Had I known what a big job I was creating for myself, I might not have dared. Family connections and naïveté were on my side.

I called up the president of Rockefeller University, the Nobel laureate Joshua Lederberg, and asked for a meeting to describe my new institute. My great-grandfather had founded the university and my father had chaired the board for thirty-five years, or I probably would have been turned down. Dr. Lederberg invited Paul and me to his home for dessert with his psychiatrist wife, Marguerite.

Joshua Lederberg was a molecular biologist and geneticist. He had not yet thought much about how the mind could influence the body. He greeted us at the door, his handshake and no-nonsense glare as large as his reputation. "Come in," he said, still barely smiling. This was going to be a hard sell.

Paul and I sat together with his wife, eating chocolate cake from small plates on our laps. At the appropriate moment, I told Dr. Lederberg what I had come to talk about. He listened patiently to my strategy of finding science advisers across a broad spectrum of the psychosomatic field, in hopes of proving its credibility. When I was done, he sat back and rested his hands on his paunch. I could tell by his stiff back that he did not approve. "You really are wasting your time," he said. "Why don't you look into real science?"

I was prepared for skepticism but not for his patronizing words. I took a deep breath and said in my most innocent voice, "Well, just in case I was to be so foolish as to persist in my exploration, who do you think I should involve?" The sly fox finds a small hole into the chicken coop. This turned out to be the right question.

"I suppose," he allowed, "if you got Neal Miller, the founder of biofeedback here at Rockefeller, or Jimmie Holland, chief of psychiatry at Memorial Sloan-Kettering, or Lewis Thomas, the chancellor of Memorial . . . if any one of them signed on, I would take this idea more seriously."

I thanked him and, feeling like I had just begun to scratch at the door, told him I would keep him posted. I made appointments with all three luminaries, telling all of them that Dr. Lederberg said he would take the subject more seriously if they joined. I added that if each of them said yes, the other two would as well.

My strategy worked. Within a month, all three had become members of my science advisory board. They were some of the most prestigious names in the emerging mind/body health field and would be a good balance to Norman. Their presence attracted an impressive roster of scientists, researchers, practitioners, and media experts.

I sent Dr. Lederberg my list. He had become my barometer for opening the minds of skeptics. A year after I founded the Institute, Dr. Lederberg started sending me clippings related to mind/body interactions. Each one had the parts relevant to my subject matter meticulously highlighted with yellow pen. He was paying attention. I was gaining ground.

Paul encouraged me to host the meetings on my family's estate in Tarrytown, New York. He and Barry Flint, who had become the founding director, said the presence of my family would add a layer of seriousness to my intent. At first I was hesitant. My older cousins were embarrassed by the opulence and grandeur of my grandfather's former mansion, Kykuit, today a historic site of the National Trust for Historic Preservation, managed by the Rockefeller Brother's Fund. It housed dignitaries from around the world during my uncle Nelson's tenure there, and has continued to do so during the fund's meetings today. Its location, overlooking the Hudson River and the Palisades cliffs, provided a grand setting for bold ideas, a gracious setting in which to hold my Institute's founding dinner. Our two-day meetings would be held in the rambling Tudor-style "Playhouse" on the estate grounds. Until then the Playhouse, which my grandfather built in 1927, was the exclusive gathering place for family and friends or an occasional private party. The meetings of the Institute for the Advancement of Health were the first time a member of my family used the estate and its buildings for nonprofit work.

My uncle Laurance was a big proponent of mind/body connections and he owned several guesthouses on the estate. I obtained his permission to invite the group to stay in them during the two full days of meetings. He and my parents helped me host the first dinner at Kykuit. When my father saw the list of people I had convened, he perked up. "Eileen, this is really very impressive." From then on he stopped calling me Eileenie. My mother acted proud, and on one level she probably was, but I could still see the strain of competition in her tight jaw. Nevertheless, they both attended the dinner.

Uncle Laurance gave an inspirational toast in which he read his and my favorite quote by Goethe: "Whatever you can do, or think you can, begin it. Boldness has genius, power and magic in it." Just as he finished speaking, the sun's last rays bathed a bronze Buddha in the circular parlor where we were going to have dinner. We all took notice of the auspicious beginning.

I treated my science advisers and board members as both family and royal guests. They were the most interesting and intelligent group of people I had ever gathered. I was humbled by their acceptance of my invitation and told them so. I acknowledged each of them for their courageous and visionary work. In turn, they felt validated by my family's support. Dr. Miller asked me if I knew what I was doing. "Eileen, you know this is going to be something big. Are you ready for it?" This was like asking a full-term pregnant woman if she is ready for her first baby. I said yes and, like a new mother, I had no idea what challenges I was giving birth to.

We met twice a year after that seminal gathering. Members of the science advisory board shared their work and the obstacles they encountered in efforts to be taken seriously. They were skeptical of one another at first, and had differences about strategy and priorities, but I used my inclusive style of convening, and my love of each individual, to nurture a culture of collaboration over competition. Fear gave way to trust by the end of the first meeting. The science advisers listened with rapt attention to each other. We had 100 percent attendance twice a year, for seven years. Their community of like-minded pioneers had become a family.

The Institute published the first journal in mind/body health, called *Advances*, which was unique not only in its content but in its accessibility to both scientists and laypersons. We developed a speakers' series in major cities to educate the public about ways to employ the mind in healing our bodies. Our audiences outpaced the medical establishment in their interest and knowledge. They and my family gave generously to our cause and amplified the drumbeat of their desire for mind/body practices to be included in standard medical practice.

At every fund-raising event people told me personal stories. I was surprised and moved by their openness and eagerness to be understood. A young woman in New York City described how she had used imagery and biofeedback to help her cope with chemotherapy in her struggle to overcome breast cancer. A doctor in Palo Alto explained the startling discovery of how rheumatoid arthritis patients who sought weekly social support did better than those who exercised and took their medicine but did not join a group. A mother in Chicago shared how she believed that if her daughter had had better support from her doctors in treating her mind as well as her body, she would not have committed suicide.

I felt like I had removed a big thumb from the dike of the human heart. The need for people to share their stories and to be listened to carried the subject of mind/body health into the domain of preventive medicine and improved doctor/patient relationships. I was surprised by how great the need was across the country for people to be heard. Listening became the most important part of my work. I spoke at small and large gatherings of my own experiences and let the stories flow from others. Companionship and comfort were the themes most commonly expressed. I had found my purpose as a catalyst and connector of people and ideas.

Public interest and pressure enabled more and more credible research. The swelling numbers of scientific articles, along with anecdotes told by patients about themselves, their families, and their friends, forced the medical establishment to take notice.

Thirty years later, the circle of mavericks who accepted my invitation has expanded to help make the connection between mind, body, and spirit as accepted as the family doctor of my childhood. Modern medicine is rediscovering wisdom in ancient knowledge. A supportive community can forestall or even heal an illness. Love accelerates the healing process. A headache is not just a headache. It's often a symptom of stress. The Institute for the Advancement of Health brought the scientific understanding of mind/body interactions in health and disease to a new level of acceptance. Like a good cup of tea, it brewed a new definition of healing and health.

30

AT THE FOOT
OF THE LADDER

❧

The Institute years were fertile ones. In addition to hatching my first nonprofit organization and field of endeavor, I gave birth to my two sons. By the time they were three and five, I could no longer bear the pull of the organizational and fund-raising demands against their needs and my desire to be with them. Nothing seemed more important, but I didn't know how to make the transition. My psyche and body turned out to be my teachers.

In my dream, one of my science advisers, Joan Borysenko, beckons to me from the top of a very tall ladder. "You really should come up here, Eileen. The view out the window is spectacular." I look up to where she is balancing on a rung, high above the rafters of the cavernous barn. Light streams through a window at the peak of the roof. I admire her multicolored, stylish clothing that adorns her enviable body. Unlike me, she is unafraid of heights. She seems to have it all.

Good job, handsome husband, renowned research, beautiful figure and face. It is tempting to climb up there, away from the family I have begun. I think hard about all I would have to give up in each case. Something tugs me from within and I hear myself say no. When I wake up, I realize I have begun a new chapter in my life.

Some dreams hit you square in the face. I had led the Institute for the Advancement of Health for seven years and was grappling with whether and how to end my term as president. There was so much dazzle in meeting brilliant scientists, Nobel laureates, appreciative lay leaders, foundation heads, and wealthy philanthropists. At thirty-two, I was featured in the *New York Times Magazine* as "one of the leaders of the Cousins' generation of my family." I founded IAH before I was pregnant with our first son. But after the second one, I was no longer able to annually raise a million dollars and two sons simultaneously. At thirty-nine, I needed to choose where to spend my time.

The woman in my dream did not have children of her own, and she beckoned me toward the light and glamour of a career outside the home. No one was standing with me at the base of the ladder. Who stands with mothers? Something very old and instinctive that was wiser than glamour kept me on the ground.

I made my choice, but it was not without challenge.

Feelings of guilt, panic, and desperation had been mounting since the time I held my first baby at my breast while making fund-raising calls. I would wake by six in San Francisco and bring him into bed. No sooner had he latched on to one side than I was dialing the East Coast in hopes of raising money for the Institute. The challenge doubled when my second son came along. By July of the Institute's seventh year, when I was almost forty, I developed bilateral ear infections and bronchial pneumonia. My body was telling me to listen and slow down. I was once again experiencing unhealthy mind/body connections. Something had to change.

It had already been a difficult year. My mother-in-law died from cancer in June. Paul and I had spent months driving an hour to and from Ursula's bedside with our two small boys in tow. The stress of her loss most likely played a role in my illness. In July my family of origin held a first-ever reunion in Wyoming. We had a good time, but old tensions came back to life. My brother Richard had commented, "Eileen, why do you act as if the Institute is the most important thing in the world? There are many good causes, you know." It was true. I had exaggerated our accomplishments to impress my brother. He was the family's only M.D., and I thought this would be our point of connection. It didn't bring Richard closer, but my passionate belief in the Institute's importance helped me raise the money needed to keep IAH alive.

Within days I got sick. My illness felt like a manifestation of the suffering we continued to feel as a family. Ironically, it was my brother Richard, the family doctor, who diagnosed my symptoms as walking pneumonia. He told me to see a doctor as soon as I got to Maine, where I was given the directive to stay in bed at my parents' house for a week and take a vacation from the Institute and mothering. Paul took a more active role as father to our sons and I was grateful for his skill and devotion.

The time alone helped me accept the choice already evident in my dream. I had a lot to figure out. Closing the door on my involvement with the Institute was like ending a marriage. For the next four months I worked with a philanthropic adviser to plan the succession. We found a home for our journal, *Advances*, with our largest donor, the Fetzer Institute. After many meetings, the three largest foundations that had supported us decided to take full ownership of our work. The Mac-Arthur and Cummings Foundations joined hands with the Fetzer Institute in creating the Center for Advancing Health in Washington, DC, as a policy advocate for the field. It was a dream come true.

My last responsibility was to help the board and science advisers to accept that they would no longer come together for meetings. I knew separation would not be easy. As one science adviser said, I was their mother. Some people felt betrayed, but most were genuinely sad. The community I had built would miss the twice-yearly meetings on our family estate in Tarrytown, New York. They would have to find other ways of getting together and supporting one another. I had two young sons who needed coaching for the lives they would one day enter, and my commitment was to them.

At the end of November, after our final meeting had taken place and good-byes were said, there was one more good-bye I had not expected. Norman Cousins died. Norman had inspired the Institute and had played a major role in creating it. More important to me, he had stood by my decisions, including the need to move the Institute on to other hands. He celebrated my every success and bolstered me in times of doubt.

One week after Norman died I received a letter he had written only hours before his heart attack. It was dated and sent on the day of his death, November 30, 1990. Despite having a twenty-one-cent stamp when twenty-five was the going rate, it arrived intact. He was my champion to the end:

Dear Eileen,

Your November 9th letter, which has finally caught up with me, is E.R.G. at her best. It is beautifully sensitive, compelling and persuasive. The tone, characteristically, is one connected to new beginnings and new prospects rather than to history. I've never been prouder of you than while reading your letter.

Love, Norman

I stood at the foot of the ladder and had no regrets.

31.

IN THE FIRE

❦

Paul and I did not fight openly until we had been married for nearly ten years. Sure, we got angry, but we didn't let our sons see our raw emotions and mostly kept them to ourselves. Adam and Danny were little and we wanted to create an ideal, safe, and happy family, different from those in which we had grown up. I had been raised in a family where anger went underground, like fire, and popped up somewhere else unexpectedly. Paul's mother snapped and criticized his father and Paul hated it. No one had taught us how to express or deal with feelings, or how to get to the source of them, so we kept them under wraps. Most of the time we got along anyway, so why burden our boys with occasional outbursts? The problem was that little sparks become larger and larger flames when left unattended. Something had to change.

The transition to full-time motherhood, after having formed such a close community of highly intelligent and empathic people, was initially wrenching. I had to reinvent my identity in a culture where mothering gets a third-class seat. It was a whole new life. I kept my housekeeper but let the nanny go and leapt into managing the children and house. Paul was commuting nine times a year between San Francisco and Vermont to oversee his growing cable television business. He spent more time on the road than with the boys and me and we missed him. I wasn't ready for any of this.

Paul tried to make up for his absence and my homesickness for Vermont by taking us on ski vacations in California and by spending summers back East. That just didn't cut it. I missed Vermont in *all* its seasons: the sound of peepers in springtime, the smell of hay, scarlet leaves, frost in my nostrils, and the smooth worn granite of the ancient Adirondacks and Green Mountains. I couldn't find a single rock to sit on in California that wasn't angular, sharp, or crumbly.

"Why can't we live back East?" I pleaded. "Everything out here is unfamiliar. Even the rocks are jagged and uncomfortable to sit on." My "rock rant" was a recurrent theme, a displacement for all the things that were wrong in my marriage (or in my past that I had not yet discovered). I did not know my way around the city. I was as unfamiliar with my sons' maturation as the Hebrew letters at synagogue. I didn't like Paul telling me what to do or how to do it any more than I had tolerated it from my brothers, sisters, or parents. I begged Paul to move back East, but he would not hear of it. He was still establishing himself and was not ready to live near my family. I wasn't sure I was either, but I missed them anyway. Our conversations escalated until I saw red. I wanted out.

I blamed Paul for failing to be the father and brother I wanted but didn't have. I saw the face of my mother in his anxiety and perfectionism. His compulsive interruptions and directives—"Not that pot, use this one. Be sure you turn the blue jeans inside out before you dry them"—reminded me all too much of my siblings telling me what to do. I grew increasingly angry and looked for an escape. I was having an identity crisis. The contrast between my work with the Institute—and its accompanying positive attention and appreciation—and the lack of support for mothering was all too stark. My days were filled with laundry, shopping, cooking, and caring for two very bright and demanding children. In retrospect I see that my sons' needs were natural and age appropriate, but at the time I felt triggered by my own unmet needs when I was their age, and I resented them and my husband.

I sought relief in an infatuation with the adviser who had helped transition me away from the Institute. He became my protector and problem-solver, a stand-in for my father. I could talk openly with him and we laughed for hours. I escaped into fantasy. He was brilliant like Paul, and he had an irresistible sense of humor with a tantalizing barrier between his mind and heart. I attempted to slay the dragon that kept him, or at least me, from his innermost secrets, in hopes of sculpting my image of the perfect male. He inspired a period of intense creativity, augmented energy, and, ultimately, anguished disenchantment over the impossibility of an unattainable man. I turned away reluctantly and faced my husband.

Adam and Danny were six and four at the time, too young to understand Paul's and my arguments but old enough to feel the tension. Nothing Paul did could live up to the father figure of my obsessions. I moved forward doggedly, head down, shoulders hunched, blind to the consequences.

Paul gave me Harville and Gaye Hendrix's book *Getting the Love You Want* and insisted we read and do the exercises together. I resisted but later agreed it was healthier to model to our sons the expression of feelings, even when they weren't pretty. The rule was we had to stop short of hurting each other physically. We learned to argue, but too often it turned into blame. Our sons were terrified by the tone of our anger. Adam developed a facial twitch.

I looked for support. Many of my friends with young children were having similar problems, and all but one of my five siblings had already been divorced. Statistics about the stability of marriage in our culture were not encouraging.

I waited until Paul and I were out to dinner together on a sultry June evening in Vermont. The main course had just been served. Then I told him: "I'm not sure I want to stay married to you." There was a moment of stunned silence.

"I have to go pee" was all he said.

Forty-five minutes later, when he returned, the food on our plates sat uneaten and cold. My cheeks were tear-stained and when I looked up I saw his eyes were red and swollen.

"Where were you all this time?" was all I could ask. I had thought of calling someone to bring me home.

"I went to pee in Lake Champlain," he said curtly. For years afterward we would joke that he took the longest pee on record. In fact, he needed the time to plan his response.

"I'm not leaving until we figure this out. If you quit now you will make the same mistake with the next man."

"*My* mistake!" I said testily. "*You* are the mistake." My words were sharp as a butcher's knife, but to my surprise and relief, he did not use the same ammunition. He simply repeated, "I'm not leaving until we get to the bottom of this."

Paul called our therapist in San Francisco the next day and arranged for a three-way conversation. I felt ganged up against. At one point, when the therapist was prodding me to open up to Paul, I said, "You may think you are close to the hearth of my heart, but I imagine my heart as a woodstove with a glass door in front. I don't want you any closer and I won't open the door." All I could think about was the man who *had* opened the door to my longing. It is so much easier to look outside than to see the image of ourselves mirrored in those closest to us. I was not ready to open any door.

Two days later, Paul packed up his bag and flew west. He went to visit old friends and his closest cousin to decide on the best strategy for saving our marriage. One thing was clear. I had not married a quitter. I had felt a shift in him ever since he attended a men's weekend workshop six weeks before, the ManKind Project's New Warrior Training Adventure. Something told me a separation was not going to be easy. Nor was he going to back down from my angry words. He was gone three weeks. I had a lot to think about.

I don't remember what Paul told the boys before he left. My head was spinning. I looked at the worried faces of our sons and said something like, "Daddy needs to have some alone time and he's going to visit friends."

Adam protested. "But he won't have alone time if he's with friends. Why doesn't he just go for a walk in the woods here?" I explained that his daddy would probably do a lot of walking in the woods. He was just staying with friends.

My comfort felt shallow. Danny spun in circles, pretending he wasn't listening. Adam went outside and climbed a tree. Separation makes no sense to children.

I was on my own. I did not know then how important self-knowledge, self-care, and emotional skills are to sustaining a marriage or any relationship. These subjects were not taught in school, nor were they mentioned in my family. My guilt was already taller than both of our boys combined. I suggested we go for a swim in the lake.

Each night at bedtime they asked me all over again, "When is Daddy coming home?"

"Soon," I would say. "Now go to sleep." I heard my mother's refrain like when I had asked her about owls. My heart ached for them, and me. I dreaded the time ahead.

August is the month we always go to Maine to be with my family by the ocean. We drove over in our Chevrolet Suburban soon after Paul returned. As spacious as it was, I could hardly breathe. I hoped that when he came back we would decide on the timing for our separation.

Paul seemed to have gained clarity and strength while away. The three weeks apart had transformed him. I could hardly believe this was the same man I had watched double over with embarrassed laughter a few months before when I pointed out that he was as uncomfortable talking about emotions as I was talking about money. He had joined a men's group and there was no looking back. My abrupt demand for separation had further catalyzed his incentive for personal growth. Whatever his friends and family had told him reinforced his initial resolve to get to the bottom of our issues.

It felt too late to me. I spoke to each member of my family. No one tried to stop me from pursuing divorce, not even my parents, who had been married fifty-one years. My father said, "Well, dear, I never did think he was up to you." I thought to myself, *If they aren't willing to support me, what other option do I have?* Paul and I had explicitly asked everyone at our wedding for support if times got rough. No one came forward. We were on our own.

For some reason, we were still sleeping in the same bed. It was a white-painted, Victorian-era double bed with brass balls on the posts. They looked like doorknobs. The boys had been asleep for hours. At 2:00 a.m. I told Paul I wanted him to open the door and leave. "Now!" I used my nastiest voice. He didn't budge. I tried again. "Get out of bed and GO!" I roared.

Paul moved to the foot of the bed and held on to one of the brass balls. I tried to unclasp his fist and push him away. The scene was not unlike a kindergarten playground where an argument escalates in force until one child pushes the other onto the ground or a teacher intervenes. But we had no referee.

I felt younger than a kindergartener. The anger I had held in me since I could first remember started to rise like hot lava. "I hate you. Your company is a joke. You keep leaving us, and you depend too much on my money." Flames of anger distorted my face as visions of my father welled up inside me.

Paul didn't budge. "I won't go until we get to the bottom of this." This had become his mantra. "Otherwise, we'll repeat the pattern in a subsequent marriage."

I showed him my worst side, hoping I could control him. This was a test of wills. "If you don't leave now, I'm going to roar." I spewed, with all the volcanic fury of a lifetime. "Get out, get out, GET OUT!" I was blinded by rage. It went on for hours and hours. By three in the morning, my will finally broke. Paul was still there, waiting at the foot of the bed. I crumpled into a tsunami of sobs.

I cried so much, I used up a whole box of Kleenex and three of Paul's white handkerchiefs. All I could think was: *No one in his right mind would want to be married to someone as fickle, nasty, and angry as me. No self-respecting man would stoop so low. Paul must not be deserving of my love.* The mirror then flipped: *I have nothing to give.*

I heard my mother: "I have nothing left but the scraps."

I was not deserving of love. Not worth the effort. No one would ever love me. Who said that? Who was speaking inside my head? How long had they been talking that way?

I struggled to make sense of the voices, like waking from a bad dream—a very bad dream. I had trouble breathing. The victim was calling. I did not know then that she had inhabited me all of my life. She dominated my internal dialogue and shaped my external habits, infatuations, and actions. She was the scullery maid, meant to scrub floors and pass hors d'oeuvres. Happiness was out of bounds for her. How dare Eileen go against the rules?

There was not enough love to go around.

She should have removed herself from the competition. She had gone her own way, and now she would pay for it.

Paul held me tight until my tears subsided. I still wasn't sure which reality I was living in, but one thing was clear. More than being disappointed in Paul, I was angry with the victim in me who had tried to sabotage my relationship. My new identity as a mother after leaving the Institute for the Advancement of Health and losing my mentor had rocked my confidence. In my confusion I had fallen for a romanticized hero and become blind to the reasons I married Paul.

That night changed everything. I finally agreed to do all the exercises from *Getting the Love You Want* and attended a weekend workshop called Marriage Encounter. We also had a daylong session with two of my cousins, renowned family therapists, and found an unconventional counselor in Vermont with whom we practiced the art of loving.

Our work will never be done, but we have faced many mirrors since then, unveiling hidden wounds as we go. Each one opens images like a secret door to a deeper level in the mystery of love.

❧

Secrets revealed bring awareness to life. I like unearthing metaphors. When I'm in a forest in Maine, I hunt for chanterelle mushrooms. Certain patches are reliable, year after year, peeking out of the moss and from under pine branches, just like my willingness to be vulnerable. Others crop up in unexpected places, poking through the side of an earthen cliff, as if forming their own clubs, like the anger from my victim that ganged up against me.

I have stumbled upon many secret clubs in life. Some of them I belong to. Others I will never join. They include the mystery of birth; the time, place, and person with whom we had our first kiss; the best friend club; the onset of menstruation or menopause; the relationship or marriage clubs; the divorce club; the single child or parent club; the death of a parent and of the last parent club. Finally, there is the old age club—until death pulls us back to earth and we become members of the last of the secret clubs. Clubs are most meaningful when we realize we belong and we can share our membership with another.

What I shared with Paul on that seminal night in Maine changed our relationship forever. I joined the club of commitment. It helped me admit to my vulnerability.

"Shortly after our thirtieth wedding anniversary I joined a new club," I confessed to Paul in bed one night. "I really need your love."

Even though we have worked through tough issues that could have blown us apart, I had never admitted this to myself or him. It was like joining the club of vulnerability. It's easy for me to be vulnerable to anger. It's another thing to be vulnerable to love. That's where the real mystery begins.

I was still shivering two days later, even though Paul reassured me he was not going to leave and was not scared, surprised, or repelled by the truth of my disclosure.

In the early morning, as the pink sun was waving its hand through our window, I asked him again, "Do you *really* feel okay when I tell you I need your love?"

My childhood had taught me that direct statements of need were signs of weakness. I still remembered my mother's admonishment, "How dare you cry like that!" and my three sisters maligning me: "Crybaby." I took my deepest needs underground, like mushroom spores, and turned them into barbs that popped up unpredictably.

On this morning, I let in the warmth of Paul's arms. He wrapped them tightly around me, snug as earth around a toadstool.

"Of course," he comforted. "You will have my love forever."

My head rested on his shoulder. I took in a deep, slow breath, like smelling sweet earth for the first time.

"Do you need my love, too?" I wondered aloud.

"Yes," he said simply.

I exhaled the past. "You will have mine forever, too."

The smile spreading across his face tickled my forehead as he added, "I believe we said this to each other about thirty years ago." Some secrets bear unearthing more than once, just like the chanterelles I depend on year after year. I never know where they will turn up next.

32.

DANCING AMONG THE STARS

~

One must have chaos in oneself in order to give
birth to a dancing star.

—*Friedrich Nietzsche*

Two years before I turned forty I stepped into a sunlit room resounding with the beat of African drums. The scene was Anna Halprin's dance studio on Mount Tamalpais, twenty minutes north of San Francisco. Floor-to-ceiling windows filled one side of the room. There were life-size self-portraits hanging on the wall opposite that took my breath away. They seemed almost psychedelic in their design and colors. Though in the midst of a major metropolis, the wooden floor joined a wide outside deck surrounded by redwood trees that gave the studio the feeling of a jungle oasis. I had come here to discover the wisdom of my body.

Anna was a little over seventy. She and Martha Graham had worked together, but Anna moved west after World War II to develop her own style and following. By the time I met her in 1990, she was famous for her use of dance to heal her acute intestinal cancer two decades earlier. She told me how she had gathered friends as witnesses while she performed an hour-long Dance to Life. X-rays taken weeks later revealed no trace of her tumor. The cancer never returned. Some call it spontaneous remission, the power of mind over body—or a miracle. She called it a time for change and refocused her dance practice, teaching large workshops and classes to help people with AIDS, cancer, and other forms of illness heal themselves. She kept a few slots open for others to attend. Twice a week I joined her class, called Dance for Life, with fourteen other women and men.

We began with a warm-up ritual on the floor, moving our bodies in a spiral. I felt like a prehistoric chambered nautilus. As the primitive dancer emerged in me, my fingers and arms stretched in circles above my head like kelp swirling in the ocean. My feet and legs followed, mirroring the movement of my hands. Within twenty minutes, thoughts had vanished and my body became the leader.

Anna could see when we had dropped into our bodies. She invited us to sit quietly on the floor to draw and write with crayons and paper. My body steered my mind to unexpected places.

Sun, moon, stars, and sky
I'm goin' to let the old ways die.
Sun, moon, stars, and sky
I'm goin' to change me by and by.
Water, fire, earth, and air,
I'm goin' to do what I didn't dare.
Water, fire, earth, and air,
Hey who's the new woman I see there?

Sometimes Anna would have us join with a partner to dance our poem or drawing to each other. On one occasion she asked us to draw four self-portraits—physical, intellectual, emotional, and spiritual—one minute per portrait. Mine were a blur of blue and orange lines, quick strokes that emanated from my body/mind. I did not think about them. I just drew whatever came through my fingers. With my partner watching, I took each drawing, one by one, and danced what I saw. My partner danced hers for me. We were then asked to switch drawings and dance each other's. Our interpretations were stunningly different. Where I found closed doors, she saw windows. I could see from her face that mine did the same for her. We did the entire exercise without saying a single word. This practice was so powerful, I decided to try it on my own at home.

One night at our house in San Francisco, after I had put our sons to bed, I decided to entertain myself by dancing impressions of different animals. Paul was at his men's group for the evening, and I was curious to see whether I could find wisdom through my body without the direction of someone else.

My closet was full of colored clothes, perfect for dress-up. I turned up my jungle music, pulled on some black body tights, and became a jaguar. The music intensified with shakers, rattles, and drums. I slinked and growled and pranced around the room (making sure the shades were drawn from my neighbors), and soon I found myself releasing anger. This was unexpected and frightening. I returned to my closet and found a feather boa, transforming myself into an ostrich. The music softened; pulling my head downward between my legs, I hid and rested until I was ready to go on.

I recovered from my ostrich state, set aside my boa, and was ready for more. In my black body tights I was a spider weaving her web to ensnare a fly. My hands and feet danced lightly over the floor, lifting high and fast as if they were eight. I spun threads and wove them in and out of each other with my body to the rhythm of ethereal "spider music." With the web complete, I was poised to pounce on my prey. This pose was uncomfortable and left me short of breath. A leopard frog hopped out of me. I put on a long green dress with black polka dots and changed the music back to jungle sounds. Drumbeats rained on my body, moving me in a trance. I leapt and ate the spider.

Suddenly, I felt violently nauseous. I hopped to the bathroom just in time to throw up. Relieved, I saw that the spider was my mother. I had swallowed her to try to rid myself of our co-dependence. Eating was my habit of self-protection. A message came up from my belly, saying, *You can't just swallow the relationship as it has been. Eating will not get rid of it. You need to transform it.* I saw how I had been hiding behind her, afraid to come out in the world by myself. We were joined in an unhealthy way.

I crawled back to my bedroom and removed my leopard frog dress. Naked before my mirror, I felt an urge to put on gold and be a star.

As I was slipping on my star clothes—a gold-colored skirt and top— the voices of judgment whispered in my ear: *There you go again, wanting to be the center of attention. Why do you always need to be a star? Can't you just accept your place as last in the family?*

I wanted to take off my star clothes and shrink into the floor. But the music was calling me. I changed the CD to something brilliant and strong. It helped me find courage to explore this image. *After all*, I told myself, *what if I do want to be a star. Better to see and face it.*

The music soared. I danced out of orbit, out of mind, spinning around and around the room in my gold costume. My hands and fingers fluttered like twinkling stars. Joyful tears wet my face as my body twirled and my gold skirt floated stardust all around me. I trusted my body. It was light as stardust and just as beautiful. I was dancing my truth. My wish was not to be a famous star with paparazzi following my every move, or a brilliant nova alone in the sky. All I wanted was to belong to something larger than myself, one small star among many.

33.

PRIMAL PARENTING

~

She is a long, sleek animal, lean in body, alert in mind. Her numerous spots look like paw prints—two or three black dots surrounding a brown center—on pale fur. She barks a low warning as one of her two cubs climbs down the tree, her eyes constantly moving from one to the other in the fiercely protective way a mother looks after her children when on the edge of danger. This is Lagadena, the leopard (pronounced with an *h* for the *g*), as those who view her in the wilds of Botswana have dubbed her. She is my soul-mother.

I did not come to Botswana expecting to find her. I came because my father invited his family on safari for his ninety-third birthday. Sadly, this did not include my eighteen- and twenty-year-old sons, as they were both working. I wish they could have met Lagadena.

My initial concern was making sure Dad was safe as he climbed in and out of the Land Rover multiple times each day. I was also curious to see the place I had camped at, in 1974, when I was twenty-two.

I remember setting up my tent by the Savuti River with a team of biologists and game scouts. I had accompanied them to investigate the effects of foot-and-mouth disease transmitted by cattle and tsetse flies to Cape Buffalo. Now, thirty-four years later, what I was about to see was a remarkable example of natural biological change in my lifetime.

Ironically, the tsetse fly was responsible for our having a safari in the upper reaches of the Okavango delta, the only inland delta in the world. Some years after the study I had participated in was completed, people living in the Okavango moved out due to the infestation of the tsetse fly and its accompanying sleeping sickness. People sought higher and drier ground. Now, the megafauna that once drank from the Savuti River near where I had camped, walk on a dried-up riverbed turned into grassland.

We have come to watch the animals move along the former river path to nearby pans of water. Elephants lumber among the mopani trees and papyrus grass, swiping branches and roots with their long trunks. Giraffes crop leaves from the tops of acacias, and lions lie in the tall grass until hunger moves them in the direction of their next meal. There is such diversity among the animals that at first glance it might seem like a Garden of Eden.

The constant movement of earth, animals, and plant life is what makes the Okavango so richly diverse. Water, oozing from the Zambezi and the Linyanti Rivers, dictates the flow of flora and fauna filling depressions of earth that become watering holes and transient flood plains that migrate up to seven inches a day, depending on the rains. Huge flocks of birds and herds of animals frequent the water holes, each taking their turn, each aware of the other in relation to their survival. Life is ephemeral. Nothing is wasted. A Cape Buffalo taken down by a pride of lions is finished off by hyenas, marabou storks, vultures, and finally beetles, flies, and termites. What goes in one end for food comes out the other as fertilizer for the ground and an incubator for beetle larvae. Like all healthy ecosystems, the cycle of life is about survival of those who prosper as part of the whole.

On the last morning of our trip we came across Lagadena, stretched along a tree trunk high above us. She is unruffled by the noise of our Land Rover. She is busy licking the head of one cub while watching the other chew the remains of an impala carcass. Her son has slung it over a branch and is holding it down with his left front paw. Her daughter is eyeing him, waiting for her turn at their catch. When her brother has had his fill, he rises, licks his chops, and scampers down the tree to the ground. His mother barks a warning not to stray too far. She watches as his sister crawls to the same branch and picks up where he left off. Lagadena takes this opportunity of her daughter being occupied to climb down the tree and pee. She also can keep closer watch on her son, who shows a penchant for wandering off.

I am reminded of my two sons when they were young, especially when walking through an airport. I picture myself thirteen years ago at the check-in counter with Adam and Danny at ages seven and five. Paul hands the tickets over the counter with our identification and we get the boys to help us put the baggage on the scale. Invariably one of them decides he has to lift the big bag all by himself. A squabble ensues. I distract them with my backpack.

"Danny, would you carry this while Adam helps with the luggage? It's getting too heavy for me." I commit a small deviation from the truth. If he feels important, too, he will not need to compete with Adam. Mercifully, he takes up the challenge. We are at the front of a long line and the Chicago airport is as crowded as herds of wildebeest on the African plains. I make the boys hold my hands as soon as theirs are free. Paul gives me back my driver's license and ticket. I put it in my pocket while keeping one eye on my sons. It would only take a second for them to disappear or for someone to lure them away.

We walk through the crowds toward the gate. I let the boys run in front of us but they are never out of sight. My ears are alert to their tone of voice with each other, to the shift from happy chatter to competitive challenge or intrigue with a forgotten box of gum that slipped behind a chair. I tell them to leave it. Danny turns from the gum, his eyes twinkling with feigned rebellion. He takes his right hand and flicks his right ear repeatedly, as if he were a rabbit scratching with its hind leg. I laugh until the tears run down my cheeks, partially from embarrassment, and hurry him along. Adam is asking Paul how long the flight will take. He seeks his father's hand for reassurance and connection.

When I see Lagadena placing her paw on top of her daughter and later licking her son with her front legs wrapped around him, I am reminded of when I used to hold my boys on my lap and stroke their heads or give them back rubs. I let out a deep sigh. Tears trace the memory down my face. I miss them. Lagadena watches her cubs, her light green eyes ever moving in their direction. She has reason to be concerned. We found hyena tracks following in hers as they led us to the tree. In watching her, I recognize something primal inside of me.

This is not about animal versus human behavior. It is not about wilderness survival versus human survival. I am feeling one of the most primitive instincts in the world: maternal protectiveness. Whether conscious or not, it comes from an ancient place, as deep as her bark, as present as my tears. Her instinct is the same as mine despite her four legs and my two, her spots on fur and my freckles on skin. We both have green eyes, though hers are lighter. We are intent on the safety and survival of our young. Though our eyes never meet during that hour, my heart beats as if it were hers. Mothers are the same everywhere. New life depends on us.

༒

I remember when my sons were even younger I needed new tools for resolving conflict. A gift arrived in the form of a red velvet heart with a rainbow stitched across the front, given by a teacher at a conference I sponsored to advance social and emotional learning in the classroom. The teacher told me it was stuffed with seeds as a metaphor for peace and healing. She used it with her students as a kind of "talking stick," adapted from Native American ceremonies, to help her students resolve conflict in the classroom or on the playground.

The rules were simple. Whoever had been hurt got to hold the heart first. They were asked to tell only two things: what they did not like and what they would have preferred. Then the heart was given to the other person with the same instructions. She was amazed at how creative the kids were when given the tools to resolve their own conflicts. They paid better attention in class and became so used to heart talks that they often requested one if they were having difficulty resolving conflicts.

I liked the idea of engaging each person directly without taking sides and giving them tools for resolution.

No sooner had I opened the kitchen door than my older son, Adam, came running to greet me. He had urgency written all over his face.

"Mummy, Danny bit me today. Look at my arm." Adam was four. I crouched down to see the slight red mark still outlined on his slender forearm. Instead of making assumptions, or sending one or both to their room while planning some punishment, I said, "That must have hurt, Adam. Let's find Danny and Daddy and have a talk in your room. I have something that might help."

I couldn't believe the timing. Paul and I had been struggling as relatively new parents to find the right balance of accountability and resolution. Too often, in the midst of conflict, we defaulted to doing what had been done to us. We were committed to learning how to be better parents. I pulled the red velvet heart out of my bag and called Paul. We found Danny hiding in his closet. He knew he had done something wrong and had to be coaxed out. I told him I had a new toy. Being a two-year-old, his curiosity got the better of him and he came with me. We sat down in Adam's room on giant pillows in the reading corner. When the boys got settled, I opened my hands and showed them my new heart.

I explained having met a teacher who taught me a new way to help children solve arguments. Paul said we wanted to be fair and it was important that we find better ways to work things out. It occurred to me that this technique might benefit *us*, too.

I took a deep breath. I could see anticipation rising in our sons' eyes. Danny, who loved anything soft, immediately wanted the heart. I explained that the one who was hurt got to hold this heart first. Each of them would have a turn as they told each other two things: what they did not like about what had happened and what they would have preferred.

I looked at Danny, wondering if this new method was fair to a boy who had just turned two years old and had begun to talk in full sentences only a few weeks before. The alternative was to resort to old practices that I knew didn't work. I took the risk and handed the heart to Adam.

Adam had said his first word when he was five months old. He continued to surprise me with his command of language. He clutched the heart against his red jumpsuit and, with all the seriousness of his four-year-old self, turned to his brother.

"Danny, I didn't like it when you bit me today. It hurt and I was scared."

Wow! He even added how it made him feel. Paul and I looked at each other, amazed by his clarity. Not only did Adam think to tell Danny how he felt, he knew *what* he felt.

I was curious to see how Danny would respond. But first Adam needed to tell Danny what he would have preferred. With barely a pause he said, "And next time I would prefer you scream!"

Paul and I were so surprised by Adam's age-appropriate solution that it took every ounce of self-control not to laugh. After squeezing my giggle into a smile, I thanked Adam and asked him to give the heart to Danny.

Danny sat cross-legged in his tiny boy blue jeans and T-shirt fingering the soft velvet heart in his little hands like it was a furry animal. He straightened himself up, as if the heart had given him courage, and responded with all the grandeur of a two-year-old. "Adam, I didn't like when you pushed me off spring horse. I was angry and scared."

Our jaws dropped. Not only did we learn what had provoked his behavior, we learned that he, too, knew what he felt. I had been offering the vocabulary of feelings to them from the beginning, but I had no idea how much they had absorbed until that moment.

He looked his brother straight in the eye and added, "Adam, I sorry I bit you. Next time I will scream LOUD!"

We could no longer contain our laughter. We thanked them both for their clear communication and told them how proud we were of them.

This was the first of many heart talks we would have while the boys were growing up. Danny never bit Adam again. And for years, whenever he was angry with him, he screamed. *Loud*.

34.

A Good Christmas

‿

I can still hear my granddaddy, Mum's father, reading *The Night Before Christmas* to my whole family. We gathered around him in the library, the fire roaring while he opened the book on his lap. His white mustache danced above his mouth in cadence with his resonant voice, a song of words. He held a monocle up to his eye as he began: "'Twas the night before Christmas, and all through the house, not a creature was stirring, not even a mouse." It was hard to think of Granddaddy as short because, even though his feet barely touched the floor from the overstuffed chair, his deep voice filled the room. My brother David and my son Adam have inherited it.

Granddaddy died on September 14, 1959, when I was seven. My father, who was dyslexic, was too embarrassed to read aloud, so my mother took Granddaddy's place. After the reading we galloped upstairs ahead of her, to her bedroom, and waited for her to open her dresser drawer, spilling out a stash of her mother's real silk hand-me-down stockings onto the floor. They came in black, white, and tan, each retired with runs. She let us choose from the designated pile and hang ours with a tack to the edge of the wooden fireplace mantel, opposite my parents' bed. Below it, on the hearth, I got to place a cup of milk and a plate with one cookie on it for Santa. By morning only a bite would be taken and most of the milk would be gone.

In our house Santa only brought stocking presents. The other gifts were from our parents to each of us siblings, plus a few aunts and uncles, nannies, and close family friends.

My mother said Santa must have been in an awful hurry. She was, too. Christmas during my childhood was the only day of the year when my family put aside all other distractions and obligations to be together. I first learned how to tell time on Christmas morning by watching the little hand at the bottom of the clock by my bedside as it landed on the six, a year more than my age, just as the big hand covered the twelve. This was the earliest I was allowed to wake my five older siblings. It was also the only day they did not get mad at me for waking them up.

I ran upstairs in my flannel pajamas to my oldest sisters, Abby and Neva, chanting, "Merry Christmas," as I kissed them each on their cheeks. They took the longest time to rise. I woke Peggy next. She slept in the room next to mine, and David and Richard shared a room across the hall, next to my parents. I skipped from one room to another like a town crier, bidding everyone awake. "Merry Christmas! Time to get up!" Even in their sleepy stupor they answered back the same, and David drew me over for a kiss. It seemed like hours before we finally gathered outside my parents' bedroom. Abby counted to three, and we burst through their door, bounced on their bed, and woke them with kisses and wishes for a Merry Christmas. This was the moment I had waited for all year.

My parents sat up, wiping "sleepies" from their eyes, as my siblings and I dragged our silk stockings from the mantel onto their double bed. There was barely enough room for all of us and the little windup toys, knickknacks, and tissue paper that flew out of the tiny gifts. The next half hour was the best part of the day. There was no pressure to thank anyone, no fear of doing it right, no demands other than "please don't sit on my feet" as the eight of us angled for dwindling space on their bed.

As much as my parents loved abundance in beautiful artwork, furniture, and porcelain, they were strikingly modest in personal tastes, such as the small size of their bed or my mother's use of hand-me-downs for stockings. My mother not only bought the presents herself, she made each package a work of art. As I grew older I was often her helper, laying them out on the guest room beds for wrapping. She kept the ones for me carefully hidden and turned on her own version of Christmas carols: Dietrich Fischer-Dieskau singing German lieder, or Kiri Te Kanawa singing arias. The music helped boost her mood. Hours each day were spent cutting paper to fit exactly, and making double bows with luxurious ribbons. She instructed me to hand her small pieces of Scotch tape to hold the paper in place, and, "Now, be a good girl and put your finger on the knot," while she tied bow after bow. By the end of each day she was weary.

After a Christmas breakfast of scrambled eggs and sausage, we children donned our party clothes and lined up impatiently outside the living-room doors to receive our main gifts. My favorite Christmas was when I was eight. The year after Granddaddy died, we were in Tarrytown, and instead of lining up at the living-room door, as we usually did in New York, my mother told me my main present was waiting in the front hall. I walked around the corner to find a little black pony with a red ribbon around his neck. His name was Tiny Tim. I shrieked and jumped up and down for joy. He let me hug him round his neck and that's how we became friends. I rode and drove him in a basket cart every weekend until I went away to school. He even lay down if I tapped his front knees, so I could pretend to shoot over his back as if I were a cowboy. To this day riding and driving horses are my passion.

Christmas was the only time in the year I was allowed to be first. Usually we were in the city. My parents opened the door to our forty-foot-long chestnut-paneled living room with a large crystal chandelier hanging from the ceiling. There were three seating areas. My parents sat on the gold-upholstered couch straight ahead under a Cézanne portrait of a young man and piled the chairs on either side with presents marked for them. Gifts for each of us were stacked on different chairs. I was proud to get the couch by the fireplace under the Bonnard because it was bigger than the chairs. Peggy was assigned one green armchair opposite me and Richard had the other. David, Abby, and Neva were seated at the far end of the room by a Signac portrait of sailboats. My mother had put a white pad and pencil by each sitting area for us to write down who gave us what, so we would write thank-you letters later.

We ran to our chairs and tore open our presents. I was bubbling with excitement, but I also felt mounting anxiety. What if I didn't like some of my gifts? I was supposed to pretend I did. I could tell when my parents pretended. They sounded wildly enthusiastic but were quick to move on.

I began with the box of books. At least I knew what was in there. Every year a few weeks before Christmas, my father took me to the Charles Scribner's Sons bookstore on Fifth Avenue. I held new hopes each year that I was going to get the books I wanted. Someone always recognized my dad the moment he walked into the store. He addressed the nearest salesperson, saying, "Good morning. I'm looking for some books for my daughter for Christmas. Perhaps you could show us to the classics."

My heart sank. I wanted my own copy of *A Wrinkle in Time*. I'd even prefer the Hardy Boys to *The Last of the Mohicans*, *Treasure Island*, and *Kidnapped*. These were books he remembered loving as a boy and he thought I should love them, too. But I was a girl. I didn't like war or piracy and I was terrified of being kidnapped. I tried to tell him without hurting his feelings, but he bought the books anyway. My private revenge was not to read them. This year had been no different. I felt a little sick inside, but I went to thank him anyway. We were well trained.

Pretty soon the wrappings were piled higher than the couch. The butler came and went periodically, removing whole hampers of torn paper and boxes.

Finally, the time came to give my parents their present. My heart leaped. I was ten and I had made them a clay-fired teapot at Brearley. My mother always said that handmade presents were best. It was shaped like a brown-speckled chicken with a hollow spout, just like their Meissen figure on the side table downstairs. The tail was its handle and the yellow chick on top was removable. Water even poured out of its beak. My parents looked excited while opening it. I was sure it would rank among their favorite treasures. I hoped I did, too. "Why, darling, thank you *very* much," my mother exclaimed, as she and my dad kissed me on my cheek.

"See the chick on top?" I pleaded. "And it really pours water, too."

"Yes. I *see*, darling." My mother's voice trailed off as she put the chicken down, scribbled the item on her pad, and went on to the next present. I went back to my couch and picked at the hem of my velvet party dress. It unraveled in jerks, just like my tears.

Each year I hoped Christmas would be happier, but it wasn't. When Paul and I had children, we decided to place less emphasis on presents and more on more ways of being together. One year, after Adam and Danny had just entered their teens and were old enough to understand the stories of hope behind Hanukkah and Christmas, we decided to devote part of Christmas Day to others. We spent the morning as usual at my parents' house in New York City with the rest of my family. After lunch and a nap, the four of us took the subway downtown to a homeless shelter to help serve Christmas dinner.

The gated door opened to a room lit by fluorescent lights. People of all ages sat at long tables, looking expectantly at the empty space before them, waiting for a hot meal. Their plastic bags and worn suitcases lined the walls behind them. Smells of turkey, mashed potatoes, and candied yams wafted from the kitchen beyond.

We angled our way through the crowd to help serve the meal. I felt uncomfortable saying "Merry Christmas" after my own champagne lunch, but most people were quick to smile. They seemed grateful for conversation.

The woman in charge in the kitchen thanked us for coming and gave us our assignments. We picked up utensils and napkins and set a hundred places at the tables. Dinner was not quite ready. We ventured together through the crowded room to hear stories of how people came to be there. Their obvious hunger made food a natural topic of conversation.

One man wearing a suit and necktie had set up an easel in a corner of the room. He was painting scenes of flowers and tropical landscapes from his homeland of Jamaica. He told Danny he used to sell his paintings, but after hard economic times in the 1980s he couldn't make enough to pay the rent. He showed us his portfolio, filled with color and joyful scenes of people—such a contrast to the grimy streets where he now lived.

Adam talked with another man who told him he had a PhD in history and had been a college professor. We were amazed. How could a man with a good education and a valuable job be allowed to end up here?

Dinner was ready. All hands had to be washed before receiving food. We walked back to the kitchen to help fill and serve the plates. Paul, Adam, Danny, and I placed Christmas dinner before each person. Their gratitude was genuine. No pad or letter was necessary. I poured them water and imagined it was from the spout of my chicken.

35.

WORKING WITH
EMOTIONAL INTELLIGENCE

~

I feel compassion for children who test poorly in school, having been one of them myself. In 1991, eight years after Howard Gardner's *Frames of Mind: The Theory of Multiple Intelligences* was published, I delighted in discovering that there are many kinds of intelligence. Mine was outside the traditional framework of cognitive academia, in the domain of *inter-* and *intra*personal intelligence. I also had dyslexia and hoped my sons did not inherit it.

I was thick into carpooling our boys when Daniel Goleman, then a *New York Times* correspondent, asked to meet with me. I appreciated the story he had written a few years before about the Institute for the Advancement of Health, and invited him to my office. His small frame packed a lot of intensity as he leaned forward and asked, "What do you think the next field will be?"

I thought back to the red velvet heart I was given the previous year at our final Institute workshop on mind/body interactions in education. I said, with certainty, "Emotional literacy. I believe schools should educate both the mind and the heart. My vision is a world where all children are included in the realm of learning, and every mind is accepted for its unique cognitive ability."

Dan had read Howard Gardner's book, too. He was interested, and he spent the next few years researching the best scientists and practitioners of the field. He asked if I would help him convene some of the people. In 1992, we organized two meetings, one at the Carnegie Corporation, with help from its president, David Hamburg, M.D.; the other at Commonweal, in Bolinas, California, funded jointly by the Fetzer Institute in Kalamazoo, Michigan, and me. I had learned my lesson, from founding the Institute for the Advancement of Health, that a true collaborative must share the load from the beginning. Our purpose was to bring together scientists who had been studying the biology of emotions, educational researchers, as well as teachers who used social and emotional skills as tools in reducing conflict, building empathy, and lengthening attention spans in the classroom.

The first afternoon at Commonweal we were shown their sand tray, originally built for cancer patients to objectify their feelings and find meaning in their illness. A sand tray is often used by Jungian analysts to evoke the unconscious mind. An individual or group chooses from many available figures, symbols, and objects from nature and places them wherever they are moved to do so in the sand.

Our aim was to use it to create a collective vision for educating the heart as well as the mind. Trees, buildings, playgrounds, and all kinds of people were placed in the sand. I put in a bridge between two hills and looked around at the group in the room. Dave Sluyter of the Fetzer Institute stood next to Timothy Shriver, the president of Special Olympics. To his right were Dan Goleman and Mark Greenberg, director of the Prevention Research Center for the Promotion of Human Development at Pennsylvania State University. I stood next to Linda Lantieri, a pioneer in conflict resolution. Something about Linda's sense of humor gave me courage to be bold.

"Look! There's a castle on top of the hill beyond the bridge. Perhaps, if this becomes a new organization, we'll name it Castle."

"We can't name it Castle," said Tim, always the practical one. He smiled with a twinkle in his eyes as Linda broke in.

Linda's dark, shoulder-length hair fluttered as she exclaimed to Dan, "Wow! Perhaps this book you are going to write, Dan, might be this bridge that Eileen is talking about and this is showing us that it is going to open up a lot and lead to something very big—because look at that castle."

On the second afternoon we split the participants into four small groups and asked them to prepare a vision for a new model in American education. We listed obstacles and opportunities. Our facilitator encouraged us to be as creative as we liked.

My group included the University of California psychologist Paul Ekman, considered one of the most eminent behavioral scientists of the twentieth century known for mapping corollaries of emotions in facial muscles. We were joined by Linda, Dave, and a few others.

I challenged our group to consider how schools could train parents and teachers to have better social and emotional skills. Could this be part of every classroom on top of an already overloaded and underfunded curriculum? Would life skills such as these have to be an added program, or could teachers train students as well as parents? We agreed that social and emotional skills had been the missing piece in schools. The magnitude of the work ahead was daunting.

Paper, pens, and markers were passed around. The others in my group made careful notes. I felt more daring in the presence of Linda Lantieri. She enjoyed new and diverse perspectives. I credit her, and the creative dance classes I took with Anna Halprin, for my being drawn to try something other than the written word.

Our individual time was up. I let the others share first. Linda posted newsprint to include everyone's comments next to hers. She compiled a list of ways to change the face of education in one column and wrote OBSTACLES beside it.

It was my turn to talk. All I had to show was a piece of paper with a wavy black line drawn through the middle. Clearly, this was not going to explain very much. I decided to act out my ideas. I tossed my paper aside and plopped down on the floor on my back. Everyone's head turned in my direction. I caught a fleeting glance from Paul Ekman, not unlike the shocked response from a dinner partner when a glass of wine is knocked into his lap. I squeezed my eyes shut, hoping my courage would stay within, and pushed my fists up above my chest as if I were trying to force my way up through pavement. I groaned and squirmed under the weight, trying to find an imaginary crack. It would take more strength than mine alone to create an opening for a new way of educating children. The audience clapped and Dr. Ekman broke into appreciative laughter. We all agreed that progress would be difficult and it would require collaboration.

A year later, and many conference calls later, which Tim asked his colleague, Mary Schwab-Stone, from the Yale Child Study Center, to organize the first year of conference calls and meetings. I hosted one at my parents' house in Tarrytown. It was the same small group who had stood around the sand tray, and two others. Tim invited his former colleague from Yale, Roger Weissberg, to join our group, and he was joined by Maurice Elias, a psychology professor from Rutgers University. By now, the others felt like old friends. The group had identified the need for an organization that would monitor the quality and training of programs in schools. Eventually, our conversation wound up discussing a name.

"Remember that castle?" I suggested, just for fun. The others remembered the sand tray and smiled. I urged them to think outside the box. Having dyslexia can be helpful because there are many creative ways to spell a word. Why should "castle" be spelled conventionally? Maybe it could be an acronym. Before long we had co-created the Collaborative for Academic, Social, and Emotional Learning. It's acronym is CASEL.

Today CASEL's collective efforts, led by its president, Roger Weissberg, and its board chair, Timothy Shriver, is the leading organization behind social and emotional learning. Social and emotional learning (SEL) is in public schools in every state in America and in seventeen countries around the world. Each year, we widen the crack in the pavement a little further and more kinds of minds and hearts are understood.

36.

I WOULDN'T ADMIT IT
IF I WERE YOU

v

Every family has its dark horse. The summer Paul and I took Danny on a roots trip to western New York State, we found more than a dark horse. We discovered my ancestor had been stealing them.

It started out as a perfectly innocent family excursion. I read *The Secret Life of Bees* out loud from the backseat as we whizzed by the countryside, headed toward Richford and Moravia, New York. My great-grandfather, John D. Rockefeller Sr., was born in Richford in 1839. We took pictures of the sign erected there to memorialize his birthplace and headed west to Moravia in search of his childhood house.

It was the year 2000, and Danny was twelve at the time. He and Paul listened attentively to the book, occasionally interrupting me to point out a red-tailed hawk on a telephone wire or a giant windmill being installed in a field. I wished Adam were with us, too, but he was at a canoe camp.

We arrived in Moravia on a hot and hazy afternoon. It was a sleepy

town, not much traffic, people sitting on chairs outside their stores waiting for business or conversation. I had no idea how we were going to find
my ancestral home, but Paul has a gift for such things. He parked the car
near a hardware store on the main street and asked a retirement-age
storekeeper for directions to the town hall. The man wore green khakis
and a short-sleeved seersucker shirt. He looked eager for conversation.

"Right around the corner" was his immediate answer, as if he had
been placed there just for this purpose. "Where are you folks from?" He
wanted to engage us, but we were on a mission. We answered politely and
walked around the corner to find a building the size of a large closet.
We walked inside. A man wearing a baseball cap was standing behind
a counter reading the day's paper. Paul asked him if this was the
town hall.

"Yup," he answered, "and I'm the mayor. What can I do for you?"

I had to admit he did not look like my image of a mayor, but what
did I know? Maybe all mayors in this part of the world wore baseball caps.

Paul very rarely tells people my family name because he knows it
embarrasses me, but in this case he couldn't resist making me a local
celebrity.

"My wife is the great-granddaughter of John D. Rockefeller and we are
looking for the house he grew up in. Could you tell us how to get there?"

I was already blushing. Usually people want to shake my hand or, if
they are old enough, they occasionally tell me how they once received a
dime from my great-grandfather as he passed them on the beach. I was
not prepared for the mayor's response.

"I wouldn't admit it if I were you," he said, turning serious. He
leaned closer over the counter. "His father stole horses. Big Bill isn't
liked much around these parts. I've heard it told he used to steal them

by night, corral them into a cave below the road by his house, and paint them a different color."

This was not the image I'd grown up with. But there was more. "The next day he'd take them off to market, never to be seen again. And he sold snake oil, too. Couldn't trust that man . . . there's been a book written about him. You might want to ask the neighbors. It was their family who exposed his ways."

I didn't know whether to laugh or run out of the building before he ran me out of town. He talked about my ancestor as if he were still committing crimes. Somehow, Paul got the directions from him and we drove a few miles north in a trail of dust. There have been many books written about my family, but I had never heard I was related to a horse thief. This was getting colorful.

We were still giggling when we found Rockefeller Road and pulled up to a plain white plank house. It sat on a ridgeline facing a hay field across the road with views of Owasco Lake in the valley below. A stocky oak tree stood in the front yard with a sign in front of it that read: BOY-HOOD HOME OF JOHN D. ROCKEFELLER.

We took pictures and walked around. The house was vacant. I was just beginning to imagine my great-grandfather playing on the lawn when a man pulled up in a truck. I froze. Had he already heard the news? Would we be run out of town?

Luckily, he was friendly. "May I help you?" he asked. Paul repeated the story about my family connection. "We're trying to find the cave where Big Bill Rockefeller hid horses. We've also heard that a family near here wrote a book about their conflict with him." Paul was determined. I hid in the background, embarrassed.

"Oh yes," the man said, with an amused expression. "The Rose-cranses. They live just up the road on the left. I'm sure they have a copy of the book. Everyone knows the story around here. Word has it he and his neighbors feuded for years." This man said it with a smile, as if he enjoyed informing us of a local secret. Much relieved, I thanked him and we drove up the road to the designated house.

Paul parked the car under the shade of a sweeping elm and walked up to the front door with Danny and knocked. I was too shy to leave the car. I am nervous about meeting strangers anyway, and I worried how we would be received. The elderly couple opened their door. "Come in," said the woman of the house. Emboldened, I left the car and joined Paul and Danny. This time I talked. "Hello and thank you." I shook her hand. "We heard you are related to the man who was a neighbor of Big Bill Rockefeller's. I'm related to him and I'd like to learn how he wronged you and the others in this community. I wonder if you might have a copy of the book we have been told about." I held my breath.

"Yup," said the wife indifferently. "We've got the book right here. You're welcome to read it, but you can't take it with you." She led us in as if she'd been expecting us, reached for the book from a dusty shelf, and handed it to me. "It's the family copy."

Paul, Danny, and I sat together on the screened-in porch. I could not possibly take in all the details while sitting in the house of my great-great-grandfather's rival, but I scribbled the title and author as well as the publishing house in my notebook and thumbed through the pages. The book referred to Big Bill under the pseudonym Rockwell, but there were actual photographs of him. I recognized them from some I'd seen in our family archives. Danny and Paul looked over my shoulder. After a half hour we thanked them profusely and told them we hoped my family would give them no more trouble. They smiled and told us where to find the cave in which Big Bill had hidden horses.

Some stories die hard. The darker the horse, the longer they last.

37

IN THE NEST OF MY HEART

~

When my mother was dying after surgery, my five siblings and I went to the hospital together to see her. Spring came early to New York City that year. It was a tepid day in March, as we stood in the front circle outside. The sun looked pale. I was grateful for the daffodils and buds on the trees. I hoped the returning life was a sign that she would wake from her coma.

At age eighty, my mother had entered the hospital for routine elective surgery. We expected her home in a few days. Tragedy followed. During the surgery, she suffered an arrhythmia on the operating table and went into cardiac arrest. Her surgeons decided to implant a pacemaker. The process caused a leak in her heart and she subsequently had a stroke. The doctor informed my family that my mother's kidneys had given out. Her body was losing fluids, and without life support she would not live long.

The night before we visited, we sat in a circle in my father's living room discussing the best options for her final hours. This was the hardest decision we had ever made. I was grateful for the work my siblings and I had done on our relationships with one another. It made it easier to discuss options without getting as much emotional baggage in the way. We finally decided to direct the doctors not to attempt revival.

At the hospital entrance we discussed how best to visit: how many at a time, who should go first. Before long I found myself at the doorway of the critical-care room. I was first in line.

I entered the room with trepidation. Her eyes, which had always been so quick to light up, were frozen to the left. I had never seen her so still. Stillness was not in my mother's character. She was a fiercely independent, active woman. Even if she were to recover, I suspected she would not be happy living with an artificial device in her body. My last conversation with her by phone had confirmed this. "Oh, Mum," I had moaned. "You must feel so out of control." She answered, "Yes. But the nurses are here, darling. I must go. I love you."

Now, bending close, I wondered if her frozen gaze was seeing her whole life before her. I stroked her forehead, my fingers running repeatedly through her tightly curled hair just like she had done to me as a child while lulling me to sleep.

"I promise we will take good care of Dad." I sensed this was what she needed to hear. I had always said what I thought she needed to hear. Sometimes that had not been easy for her or good for me. Today, I hoped what I reported would lend comfort.

Years before, she confided to me that if she predeceased my father, his loneliness would need to be filled by lots of company, if not another partner. What she had not shared was how important it was to her to feel her family's love. Part of her did not feel she deserved it. My role had been to help her believe she did.

With the end in sight, I continued stroking her forehead and bent close to her face. "Mum, we all love you and we're surrounding you with our love." A strange thing happened. Despite her lack of fluids, I noticed a lone tear seep out of her left eye and trail down her cheek.

Who says the ears can't hear when in a coma? I watched the last tear roll down her face for what seemed like an eternity. It looked like a tiny, transparent egg, such as I had once emerged from. I believe her last tear was brimming with love and gratitude. I kissed her good-bye.

In retrospect, my family realized that my mother had a prescient sense about her death. She had tied up many loose ends in the weeks before going to the hospital; last words of wisdom and wishes to employees; pleasant visits with all her children and many of her ten grandchildren. We later learned from the nurse who wheeled her into the operating room that she told her, as she was going into cardiac arrest, "I've lived eighty wonderful years." These were her final words, spoken with the courage of a soldier. My mother was a fighter. She had always wanted to live on her own terms or not at all. I knew she would not accept a pacemaker. Life drained out of her soon after her last tear.

Two weeks after she died, I dreamed I found a broken robin's egg on the path to the door of my house. It had been crushed by someone's foot. I looked further and found a nest of robins' eggs on the ground nearby. They were still whole, covered loosely by earth. I was excited that there were robins about to hatch right in front of my door.

I sensed this dream was somehow connected to the loss of my mother and the beginning of a new chapter of life for me. I opened a book, *An Illustrated Encyclopaedia of Traditional Symbols*, by J. C. Cooper, and found the page on birds. To my amazement I read, "Birds symbolize transcendence, soul and spirit, including spirits of the air, of the dead and of the ascent to heaven." In the footnotes I found, "Birds represent the ability to communicate with the Creator or enter into a higher state of consciousness."

I interpreted the crushed egg in my dream as the body my mother left behind and the unhatched birds as my mother's transcendent spirit. In the months that followed, I lived out the dream of birds hatching.

I "received" numerous letters from my mother as I wrote in my journal over the next year. Questions were answered through words that did not feel like my own. They spilled onto the pages faster than I had time to think. I felt her speak to me from a place of unconditional love. The letters helped me to heal my sorrow. Though I could no longer bring her body back to life, I discovered over time that the most important thing was living in the nest of my own heart.

My mother holding me,
February 1952.

38.

PUTTING THE HEART
INTO PRACTICE

～

P aul and I worked hard to teach our sons how to speak from the
heart. We reinforced social and emotional skills as a regular part
of their upbringing, but when they went off to college we had to let go.
My favorite example of how our efforts paid off occurred during Danny's sophomore year at Princeton. He joined a group of classmates for
spring break in Chicago to learn about community organizing and social
change. They were meeting with several local leaders about youth and
violence, and I thought it might be useful for them to learn about
CASEL and its roll in teaching life skills in the classroom that could ultimately prevent more violence on the streets. I introduced Danny to
Roger Weissberg, the president and chief executive officer of the Collaborative for Academic, Social and Emotional Learning.

Danny was not always amenable to doing "heart talks," as we referred
to them when he and Adam were growing up. On more than one occasion, I had to drag him back into the room to complete the resolution of

a conflict with his brother. Sometimes I wondered if the effort was worth it. His letter to Roger after their visit was vindication for my many hours of hard work and occasional doubt. I include Danny's letter with his permission, and the permission of his friend Melekot Abate.

April 6, 2009

Dear Roger,

I'm writing to thank you for so generously taking the time to meet with me and the rest of the group from Princeton's Breakout trip to Chicago, and to pass on a story I think you'd like to hear. Our discussion of social and emotional learning and the work that CASEL does was a highlight for our whole group, adding a very different dimension to our discussions of gun crime and community organizing, and particularly to the conflicts that inevitably arise in that process. For me personally, it was a wonderful window into a part of my mother's life that I've glimpsed from time to time, but which I'd never seen the totality of before. So thank you for both of those gifts.

And now for the story.

On our first night in Chicago we went to an Ethiopian restaurant, and while eating our injera and doro wat, we ended up discussing the fact that my friend Melekot (who is from Ethiopia) expects, on the basis of his culture's expectations of him, to earn more money than his future wife when he marries. The Ethiopian waitresses agreed—but this view was completely at odds with the view of gender equality held by a number of the girls on the trip. Although the discussion became somewhat heated, it ended with mutual respect and we moved on to our busy schedule—until the evening after our visit with you.

SEL had sounded like an interesting concept to our group at CASEL's headquarters, but it took on a new meaning when we arrived back at the University of Chicago Church, where we were camped out on the floor. As we all sat around after dinner—some writing reflections on the day, others drinking hot chocolate, and most of us talking—the conversation returned to the issue of gender roles in relationships. I looked up from my journal as the tension in the room began to rise. Melekot and several of the girls got more and more heated in their discussion of whether or not the idea of a wife necessarily earning less than her husband was sexist or not. Melekot argued that regardless of Western interpretations, it was a fundamental expectation of his culture that a man have the ability to support his wife and family as a primary breadwinner, even though he expects his wife to work full-time as well. The girls insisted that regardless of Ethiopian traditions it was a fundamentally sexist idea.

In the course of five minutes, three or more people were suddenly talking over each other and disagreeing on different levels; the argument had become two parallel tracks of accusations of sexism or, actually, perceptions thereof; and hurt feelings were growing all around, particularly between Melekot and his friend, Jillie.

Our little room, which was ironically right next to the sanctuary of the church, seemed on the verge of exploding. I stepped in to suggest that we apply some of the principles of SEL that we'd learned in the morning. There was a chorus of laughs. I persisted and eventually led Melekot and Jillie through a "heart talk."

When the laughter quelled I laid the ground rules. Speak from "I" statements, and answer the three central questions: what you didn't like, how it made you feel, and what you would have preferred.

As soon as we started the tension rapidly cooled. Bit by bit the misunderstandings and non-equivalent arguments were clarified. After about forty minutes the hurt feelings were assuaged and Melekot and Jillie ended up hugging warmly. A few minutes later I passed Jillie sitting on the stairs talking to her boyfriend. I couldn't help overhearing her say, "We just did the most amazing thing, and I don't even know how it worked . . ."

I was amazed to see this simple technique, which I used to despise, be so incredibly effective. The practical demonstration of the power of SEL was a wonderful experience, not only for me, but for our whole group. It got us all thinking—if only there could be SEL education in every public school in Chicago, what would it do to gun crime? Perhaps what we need to pass in the Illinois legislature is not a gun control law, but a mandatory primary school SEL education law. . . .

In any case, Roger, thank you so much for meeting with us and for all the great work you are doing.

> With appreciation from all of us,
> Danny Growald

The power of any learning is in finding its context. Danny called Paul and me right after the incident to thank us for training him, even against his will. Since then, SEL has become mandatory in Illinois public education.

ᔥ

When my elder son, Adam, played a home movie recently, the whole family was in for a surprise. Adam was twenty-five, old enough to have left home, return of his own volition, and know that whatever problems he suffered as a child are similarly difficult or worse in the homes of his friends. He was ready to look back. He popped in a DVD, taken when he was almost five, and pressed PLAY. What happened over the next hour still has me thinking.

I was in the room next door putting away recycled Christmas ribbon when I heard familiar voices. They were not the deep tones that now resonated throughout our house but the familiar high-pitched ones of long ago. At that time, parenting seemed like an eternity. But it had turned out to be much shorter.

I hurried into the room and called to Paul and Danny to join us. We sat down with Adam, mesmerized by the sight of a family Thanksgiving with Paul's relatives and friends in our former San Francisco house.

Eighteen people were squeezed around the center island of our kitchen listening to Adam recount the experience of helping slaughter our forty-pound turkey, Buster. He had been reduced to a large roasted bird with brown-glazed skin, ready to carve.

I heard myself from behind the video camera asking Adam to describe how Buster came to be here in San Francisco. I blushed, remembering uncomfortably how I paraded Adam in front of my family and friends, proud of his charisma and knowledge. It attracted attention like I had wished for myself as a child. Adam was dressed in his favorite blue-and-red-plaid shirt, blue jeans, and a top hat, like the master of ceremonies at a circus. His round cheeks were slightly flushed and his nose and eyes twitched nervously as he talked. He was under pressure to perform. I heard myself interrupt him to give Danny, then almost four, the spotlight.

I saw now what I was blind to then. I had asked my older child to perform and then encouraged the younger one to upstage him, as if Danny were me getting to take the stage from my domineering older siblings. I cringed. The video kept playing.

"I just want to point out," I heard myself tell everyone, "that *Danny* made all the place cards on the table." The emphasis on *Danny* made me cringe. In the film, he was darting about, clearly uncomfortable with the attention as he found a place out of view, under the table. I must have protected him like the fierce lioness I had wished for myself. As a young parent I had pressed REPLAY in an effort to finally have it my way.

To my relief, Adam stood up for himself. "I made the drawings on the walls as you enter the dining room," he announced. "And I made some of the decorations, too." Adam's nose and eyes continued to twitch as he piped in a high, commanding voice.

A dual feeling flooded me: I was proud of Adam's courage, but I felt suddenly guilty to realize that he was having to compete for attention not with his own younger brother, but with the undefended little girl in me.

When it was over, I looked around the room, reading everyone's faces. The expressions varied, but I could see that the DVD had plugged all of us into a direct line back to old emotion.

I asked our sons what it was like looking back. The selflessness of their responses surprised and touched me. Danny said, "I feel guilty about getting more attention than Adam, and seeing Mummy come to my rescue, even when I didn't need it."

Adam chimed in, turning to Danny. "You deserved attention, too, though, Danny, and I feel guilty about the way I kept trying to take it back from you. I'm sorry, bro."

Paul and I listened. We both took our sons' feelings seriously, but I saw, with some envy, how Paul did not dwell on the parts of his fathering that were not perfect. He was delighted simply to be reminded of that time in our lives. Fathering came as naturally to him as breathing. A look of nostalgia softened his face. I wiped my eyes.

"Danny, you're right," I said. "You were more than capable of sticking up for yourself. I think I was giving you the kind of protection and praise I wished I'd gotten from *my* parents—but that was my situation, not yours. And Adam, it wasn't fair to you, either. I can see now that I was living out a part of my own childhood in each of you. I'm sorry."

I felt the whole room sigh. I never feel I have done well enough as a mother, but something in that collective exhale, protected by the cocoon of our red-walled library, helped me to release a piece of my own self-doubt.

39.

TEARING DOWN THE FENCE

My sister Neva sets clear boundaries. I used to think she was shutting me out, but I have come to understand that she has good reasons for boundaries. When we were growing up, my family had very little privacy, both in the outer world and in our home. Our name voiced aloud in public turned all eyes on us. At home, without knocking my parents walked into our rooms in the morning to wake us up, bathroom doors were left ajar, and I felt guilty if I closed my door.

I remember spying Neva through a crack in the door to her room in New York City. She often sat in her reading chair in the corner. Books were her escape. She and I, like most of us, brought into adulthood whatever we suffered from as children. I became an easy target for her anger.

We are neighbors in the summer. My parents gave each of us a house in Maine. I got our cozy guest cottage and Neva was given the family house on a steep bank overlooking mine. Her terrace is screened from our parking area by a row of cedars, but I can hear her talking there from my bedroom, which is on the side next to her house.

For many years, my family was accustomed to walking back and forth across the two properties to reach the ocean or the swim and tennis club. There were no boundaries.

Our driveway ends at a curve in the main road and is very dangerous. When Adam and Danny started tennis lessons at the club, they cut across Neva's lawn. I noticed her becoming cool toward me. One day I received a phone call.

"Eileen. I have to tell you that I'm really very unhappy about having your family walk across my lawn."

I couldn't believe my ears. Her voice sounded shockingly like Mum's. What could have happened? I thought she loved children. She went on: "Bruce and I like to sit on our terrace in the middle of the day and we would rather not have your family running back and forth in front of us. And when we're not there, we are working on the third floor and we can hear you."

I felt like saying, *Excuse me for living.* Neva's words brought me back to the "you're not wanted" message that we both had received from our mother. I hated to admit my fear that Mum felt that way about me, too.

Neva was born eleven months after Abby, and my mother named her for her mother, Neva McGrath. Dad was away in the war. Mum called her mother to say she had just given birth to another girl and had named the baby after her. Mum probably thought she would be pleased to have a namesake. Her mother hung up the phone.

Neva's story is legendary in our family. I might have been more sensitive to her if I had acknowledged my own rejection. I thought I had escaped by striking a deal with Mum to care for her if she cared for me. Apparently not. Each daughter was rejected in a different way: Neva and me for being the most openly vulnerable of the four girls; Peggy for being my father's favorite; Abby, because she fought back.

Each day, during our vacations in Maine, after our sons went to the club, I ran out my back door to the stable, where I kept my horses. My path crossed Neva's back lawn for approximately fifteen feet. One day, as I was heading to the stable, I saw her weeding among the rocks I used to play on as a kid. She looked up, and I could tell by her scowl that I was in for more bad news. I tried to defray it by currying favor.

"Hi, Neva, I hope you don't mind my crossing your back lawn. We have stayed off the front one since you asked." I'm sure there was an edge to my voice. She responded in kind.

"Actually, I've been thinking about how you cross my back lawn every day, and it really is disturbing to me when I'm in my study. As you know, Bruce and I work there almost all day, every day. I would appreciate it if you would make your own path through the woods."

Good fences make good neighbors . . . Robert Frost might have understood her words better than I did. I was hurt to the quick.

A few months later, Neva surprised me by inviting me to see her therapist with her and agreed to visit mine in Burlington. I learned that she needs to have boundaries in order to feel safe. She learned that I need connection to feel comfortable accepting boundaries. We have opposite ways of engaging. I explained that her request for boundaries made me feel she didn't want me as a sister.

"Oh! That's not true at all," she exclaimed. "My greatest worry has been that you would move. Did you know I funded the extra parking lot, up the hill, out of fear that all the cars near your house would drive you away?"

Why hadn't she said this in the first place?

"I really like having you next door," she continued, "and I've been hurt that you can't seem to make time to see me."

I was consumed with trying to give my sons the kind of mothering I didn't get, and in concentrating on them, I had created my own boundaries.

Paul and I honored her request to build our own path from the back of our house to the stable. Our timing coincided nicely with the expansion of our house and a redesign of our garden. I borrowed ideas from the garden that my grandmother, Abby Aldrich Rockefeller, had built on the hill above us. I felt like I was bringing my grandmother down the hill and down to size. I would give anything to have known her. The renovations took almost five years.

Neva was remarkably tolerant of the construction. She is an expert gardener and oversees plantings in the family garden up the hill. I knew she was curious to see the end result.

My landscape architect, Dennis Bracale, received a Watson Fellowship to study East Asian and English design and did his thesis on the Abby Aldrich Rockefeller Garden. He poured his heart and soul into my gardens, finding just the right boulders to surround the manmade waterfall and place behind the seated Buddha on the winding path to the stable. The result was more beautiful than I ever dreamed.

Word got out and I was asked to include my garden on the local garden club's annual tour. I worried about Neva's need for privacy. Paul and I felt we shouldn't have guests use the stable path because it passes too close to her office. They would have to walk through Neva's pastures across the road and enter from our driveway. I had gained respect for Neva's needs, but I was still afraid to ask her permission.

I invited her to take a walk together. She arrived at my house and blurted out, "I tore down the fence."

"What do you mean?" I asked, trying not to look too shocked. We had put a deer fence between her house and mine. She rested her large, floppy hat on the table and looked quite pleased with herself.

"Yup! I had to break the post because someone had made it so fast there was no easy opening. Next year, we must tell them to put a latch on that fence."

I put my hand up to my mouth to hide my astonishment and said, "Good idea."

She suggested we drive her car to the nearest beach and take a different path from our usual one. I liked the idea of walking new territory together.

As she paused at the end of her driveway to look for cars, we faced the horse pastures across the street. I decided to ask my question and get it over with.

"Neva, I've been asked to put my garden on the tour next summer. I was wondering if it would be okay with you if they parked up the hill and came through your pastures."

I braced myself for reproach.

"I've been expecting this, and I already have it all planned out. I think they should just walk down through my garden."

"But Neva . . . there may be as many as two thousand people!" I protested, hardly believing my ears. "I thought of having them come the back way past the stable, but the noise would have carried to your office."

"That's very sensitive of you," she said, "but I really think this is the way to do it. And as to the number of people, I'll just hide for the day. They should see your garden."

~

There is nothing like a play to bring a group together. As children in the 1950s, my two brothers, three sisters, and I would dive into the dress-up drawer at the end of the hall and pull out hand-me-downs from my parents. In the overstuffed chest we found many pairs of real silk stockings from my grandmother, wide-toed low- and high-heeled shoes, fitted dresses with low waistlines, and hats with lace drooping over the front. From my grandfather, we had trousers, shirts, ties, and handkerchiefs. My mother periodically tossed in a few of her own discarded hats and gloves along with my father's old shoes and worn dress shirts. She never bought costumes for us until I was eight, when she finally relented and gave me my first cowboy chaps, vest, holster, and gun. Costumes gave me a sense of security against my older siblings. At ten, I became the proud owner of my only store-bought, FAO Schwarz Halloween costume. It was the outfit of a queen, complete with gold crown, purple cape, and white elbow-length gloves. In wearing it I could exercise another kind of power that was sorely lacking inside my own skin.

Rainy days were good for trying on different personas. My brothers and sisters and I experimented with costumes. Richard stuffed his oversize pants to become a pregnant lady. (He grew up to be a family physician and specialized in obstetrics.) I stuffed pillows above my belt, and perhaps that saved me later from desiring breast implants. I am still trying to balance the cowboy with the queen.

Our obliging and weary parents and nannies would sit through endless minutes of random stories and tenuous plots as we danced on and off "stage" in oversize shoes, and stuffed shirts and pants, with perpetual grins on our faces. As time went by, we turned our attention to other things and ceased our dress-ups. It wasn't until decades later, after the eventual loss of our mother, that we came together again to play.

It was Neva, in fact, who brought playtime back to all of us, though her impetus for doing so was deeper and more thoughtful than casual entertainment. For my fiftieth birthday, she suggested we all spend a winter weekend together in Vermont. I didn't know it at the time, but Neva's gesture was more than a birthday gift: she recognized, as did my other siblings, that I didn't feel part of the group and that if they didn't do something soon to reinforce the bonds among all of us, I might become more distant as the years went on and each of us became preoccupied with our own families and lives. We had such a wonderful time that it has now become a tradition to spend an overnight or two when each one of us reaches a turn-of-a-decade birthday. Given our numbers, and a ten-year age span, this happens with some regularity. The person being celebrated chooses what he or she wants to do for the occasion. These reunions have gradually lengthened from a dinner to an overnight to a full weekend. We have had a wide range of celebrations, from lobster bakes to cross-country skiing and canoeing adventures to a day or more of foraging for wild food followed by cooking a meal of our harvest.

Neva's sixtieth birthday celebration remains a favorite memory. She chose to have each of us play a part in the musical *Oklahoma!* Since saying no to the birthday person is a little like saying no to the president, we accepted our assigned parts and resigned ourselves to practicing a CD of the songs before the performance. Thankfully, Neva planned a seriously abridged version. And fortunately for the very small but captive audience, we can all carry a tune.

I was thrilled to be given the part of Laurie, even though it meant I had to sing "People Will Say We're in Love" with my brother David. He was my hero growing up, but turning an adoring eye toward him as he threw his arm around me in mock romance was a first.

There was one small hitch to my siblings' performance. Aside from the few minutes or hours we had each given to learning our lines, we had exactly three hours to rehearse. We established from the start that we would not memorize our lines. This gave some relief to our high-achieving family. Nevertheless, we wanted to give a better performance now than we had done as children for our eighty-nine-year-old father and a few other family members and friends who had agreed to be the audience. The rehearsal began and we left most of our old expectations behind.

Neva had found an accompanist and attempted to orchestrate us. Without the piano, the audience would have found it painful to hear us. This was a little like directing bees in a hive. Abby protested being given a male part, Richard and Peggy quibbled over who should stand where on the stairs, David balked at singing a solo, and I asked for more lines.

Despite our disagreements, when the time for the play arrived we were as excited as when we were children pulling clothes out of the dress-up drawer. Our costumes were minimal: hats and aprons for the ladies, bandanas for the men. My father was given the seat of honor. We cautioned him not to expect too much and he reassured us he was just happy to be included.

Neva's birthday celebration, in addition to years of individual therapy and working together, gave all of us a second chance to move beyond whatever we suffered from as children. My father laughed at our antics and lyrics and wiped a few tears from his face. Somewhere in the distance, I could hear my mother joining him. Harmony among one's children is every parent's dream.

40

CLEANING HOUSE

~

My sister Abby started having nightmares a month before our family came to celebrate her sixtieth birthday. She had invited my father and my siblings and me to her farm in New Hampshire for the weekend. Dad would only join us for Friday night, but Abby feared her farmhouse was too messy for him and he would disapprove. When she told me on the phone that she had not been sleeping well because of her worry, I saw for the first time how vulnerable she was. I decided to see what I could do to help.

As a teenager, Abby had been a powerful influence in our family. She convinced Neva, Peggy, and Richard to join her in ganging up against our mother. Mum couldn't bear to have me fall sway as well, and for the next ten years she kept us apart. We went away to different schools and came home on separate vacations. We were strangers. I believed we had nothing in common, until she called about her birthday. I felt a kinship for the first time and hatched a plan.

I called my brother Richard and asked to charter his six-seat plane to fly my housekeeper and helpers to New Hampshire for the day. Flying would ensure we had enough time to get her house ready for the weekend. He readily agreed.

We were graced with a sunny day, in the low sixties. Fall colors were at their peak as we flew over the Green and White Mountains. Abby met us at the airport in bare feet, as usual. Her white hair hung wild about her shoulders. It blended with her beekeeper's suit, worn for gardening and tending her horses, chickens, pigs, and sheep.

Abby proudly showed us around her vegetable garden. We admired the overflowing rows of cabbages and fences of tomatoes. "Look at the size of these Brandywines," she said with obvious pride. She twisted off one of the biggest, reddest tomatoes I'd ever seen and handed it to me. "You should grow these, Eileen. They're hardy." *Hardy* is a sister to *resilient*. I was enjoying our tour. She plucked a melon from its vine and held it up for each of us to smell its fresh skin, sweet as a newborn's bottom. "Isn't that just the best smell?" She loved sweets when they came from the earth. I began to see a new side of Abby. Maybe we weren't so different after all.

Chickens pecked around our feet, looking for fallen seeds and fruit, and horses whinnied from the hill as she led us to her house. "Now you have to be prepared. It really is quite a mess. I just can't believe you all came to help." Abby showed us the rooms.

My housekeeping crew went at the bathrooms and first and second floors. I took the third-floor dormitory surrounded by shelves filled with children's books and mouse droppings. "Listen, Eileen," she began. Listen is often her first word of a sentence. "This is really very nice of you. I hope we can have all six of us sleep up here." Her footsteps were already lighter as she went back downstairs. Many of the books had been part of my own childhood and I enjoyed getting to know Abby by those she had saved. The Uncle Wiggly series were all in a row beside Uncle Remus, Thornton Burgess's Old Mother West Wind series, and horse books like *Black Beauty* and *Misty of Chincoteague*. I removed each one and dusted it, along with my memories.

Wasps had nested in the skylight. I opened the window gingerly and flicked a cloth at them. They, too, were messy housekeepers and it took soap and water to clean the sill. Finally, I vacuumed the room and made each bed. When I was all done, I chose books that matched each of my siblings' tastes, as best as I knew how, and put one beside each bed as a kind of place card.

Abby made a huge pot of stew from her garden to feed us lunch. The flavor was rich with gratitude. I had never heard her say thank you so much. Her expression was genuine, as was my desire to ease her anxiety. We finished by four in the afternoon and flew home, tired but happy.

Our housecleaning had the desired effect. Abby's nightmares ceased and she began to look forward to her birthday weekend. When the family arrived, she proudly showed us through each room, telling everyone how I had brought a cleaning crew. "It made all the difference. Look how clean it is." Dad showered her with complements. "Why Abs . . . it all looks so beautiful." I had never seen her so happy.

The next night, after Dad had left, the six of us went up to the third floor. We joked about how this was like a nursery room for the six of us. My siblings loved finding books by their bedsides. Abby grabbed the Uncle Remus book I had chosen for her and flopped down on the king-size bed in the middle of the room. I lay next to her, and the others listened from other beds as she read aloud the story of Br'er Rabbit. We were transported to childhood, only this time I had the place of honor next to Abby. She squeezed my hand and continued.

Abby thanked me many times after that weekend. She called often in the weeks following, and I could still hear the joy in her voice. Something had shifted. We had never known affection for each other, but one night at the end of the call she surprised me.

"I love you, Eileen."

"I love you, too, Abby," I responded. We had never said these words to each other before. I had found my missing sister.

41.

PASSING THE TORCH

❧

Chinese Export, Imari, or Chamberlain Worcester? Since I was eight, and old enough to sit at the grown-up table, my father has taught me about fine china. He has a lifetime collection with a knowledge and appreciation to go with it. Tonight, we are having dinner together, just the two of us. He is sitting at the head of the table. I am at his right, the place of honor. A white linen cloth with no wrinkles adorns a table set for four, just for balance. The unoccupied place settings across from each of us remind me of how good it feels to leave spaces in life. He often has company at dinner, so I love the empty seats as much as the bowls we are examining.

A flower arrangement decorates the center of the table—peonies and narcissus—and to either side are matching pieces of the china service in the shape of square dishes. They hold my dad's famous white after-dinner mints, "a digestif," he used to say, from a little store in New Jersey. Growing up, they were the only candy we ever saw in the house.

Four silver candlesticks are placed in pairs between the flowers and the candy dishes. Their flames shed soft light on the table. Dad and I turn over the dinner plate in front of us. I share his delight in design and color. He comments: "I like this Chamberlain Worcester. Your mother and I bought it in London shortly after we were married." Dad knows where he bought everything. The butler pours our soup.

After we are both served, we spoon the soup from the surface, just like Dad taught me when I was a child. "It's cooler there," he used to say. In between swallows he tells me how this set is very similar to one that used to belong to his mother. A nostalgic look sweeps across his face and I can feel his love of her still. The appreciation of beauty is a way of connecting to her as well as to the artisans who made the bowls.

We examine the warm orange band around the rim and the gold inlay on the hand-painted flowers. I imagine unknown artists—a short woman with delicate hands, a tall man with a steady gaze, and a child bringing water for more "slip." I can almost see them. I cup my hands around the bowl as if clasping their hands in mine, and the warmth of homemade sorrel soup seeps into my fingers and out to my father.

The sharing of beauty and soup connects us. We spoon it into our mouths, tasting the sweet-and-sour flavor as its warmth spreads through us. Dad reminisces about the time he and my mother bought this set together as newlyweds. "We enjoyed this service together for fifty-five years," he reflects, with a wistful smile. It has been twelve years since Mum died and his eyes look down as if trying to bring her back.

The soup has awakened memories in my dad. As I swallow, it dawns on me that my stomach is home to my third chakra. Dad would not be familiar with this Sanskrit word for an anatomical center of energy. I wonder whether I should share with him how the third chakra is the source of emotion and personal power. Could he see the bridge among soup, emotion, and power? I see meaning in coincidence. He sees memories. I want to tell him that the stomach is the chakra for social and material concerns. It is the place where we deal with feelings of self-acceptance and acceptance from others. Even at his ripe age of ninety-three, with a lifetime of success and acclaim, he, too, is susceptible to these feelings. We are both made human out of the same clay, just molded differently. I decide I don't need to tell him. A little soup drips from my spoon onto the tablecloth as we continue draining our bowls together. Somehow it doesn't matter.

In my family our own bowls are usually overflowing: too much to do and too little time in which to do it. Raised as we all were with the conviction that those who are in a position to make a difference have an obligation to do all they can, we are still learning to leave our bowls a little empty, like the extra places around the table, with room for rest and for the unexpected. I am no exception.

My dad and I finish our bowls of soup. He wipes a small dribble from his mouth with a white linen napkin and takes a final look at the bowl before it is cleared. I am glad we've had this time together. It's been a full meal in the first course.

It has not always been so easy. We are both the youngest of six and have sometimes run up against each other. But the old patterns of service, large enough to hold us both, bring out the best in us.

We talk about the book he is writing and how the photographs, which span his life, are helping to remind him about what is most important. He says, as he has many times in recent years, that of all the things he has done, he is most proud of his six children.

I steal an after-dinner mint to help me digest his words. Fueled with new confidence, it is a small rebellion, as he used to disapprove of his children taking things out of order. But he no longer seems to mind or has given up trying to change us. There is comfortableness between us.

The butler removes the bowls and places our plates for the next course. We look up and our eyes meet for an instant. The plates and flowers against the white tablecloth and the matching peppermint candy bowls are in that moment forgotten. Dad's pupils, reflecting the light of the candles, are like little bowls: dark in the center, light brown and blue toward the rim. One eye spills a little fluid over the lid, just like a drop of soup—small excess from the full bowl of life. And for a moment we are connected to what really matters.

〜

My extended family is rather like a giant bowl. My great-grandfather, as one of the early industrial entrepreneurs, shaped and molded our expanding circles into workaholics and public servants.

When I was in my twenties, I thought the whole world rested on my shoulders. As a young idealist wrestling with my conscience over my privileges of birthright and good fortune in life, I felt a moral obligation to make a difference. I believed that the only way to justify my opportunities was to work harder and do more than I felt like doing. Work was not the problem. It was the feeling that I had to do it all by myself. I didn't know my limits and I knew even less about how to work with others. As I got to know younger members of the next generation, I felt relief in learning I was not alone. My niece Rebecca, almost thirty years my junior, became one of my guides.

The year was 2000. We were gathered at our family estate in June for our annual multigenerational family weekend. The purpose of these

weekends is to maintain family unity, discuss business and personal issues, and share our common values. Spouses are included, as are children age eighteen and over. Younger children have babysitters and
spend the day by the outdoor pool of the Playhouse, which my grandfather, John D. Rockefeller Jr., built in 1927 as a place for our family
to congregate.

Grandfather planned the estate with an eye to the expansive views
across the Hudson River and the sheer cliffs of the Palisades beyond.
What I love best about the property are the many specimen trees.
Huge weeping beeches drape their leafy branches to the ground like
eighteenth-century hoopskirts. A grand old sycamore stands at the entrance to the circle drive, arms outstretched as if greeting every visitor.
The history behind these trees is broader than their girth. To me, they
symbolize my grandfather's love of nature and his vision for the future.
He personally decided which trees to plant.

Grandfather lived a life of unrelenting duty and accomplishment. I
believe he saw trees as a symbol of roots, and he built the Playhouse for
subsequent generations to find comfort in one another's company. He
gave us his "responsibility gene," but our weekends together remind me
that relaxation and recreation are as important as duty and service.

Grandfather provided a comprehensive blueprint for recreation. The
Playhouse includes a reversible nine-hole golf course, indoor and outdoor tennis courts and swimming pools, a squash court, two automated
bowling alleys, a gym (which throughout my childhood had a huge
trampoline with climbing ropes to jump onto and swing high above the
floor), a card room, a kitchen, and, best of all, an ice cream soda fountain
by the outdoor pool.

The tall, framed front doors open to a wide set of stairs bisected by an iron handrail. Two portraits are immediately evident, like pages from a family album. On the left is one of my great-grandmother, Laura Spelman Rockefeller, and at the top of the stairs is a companion portrait of my great-grandfather.

A wide hallway leads to a card room and bowling alley at one end and a kitchen and small dining room at the other. Circular stairways on either end of the hallway lead to the second floor. Upstairs is a billiards room with a vaulted ceiling and views out to the golf course. The narrow hall leading to it has odd-shaped closets tucked into corners along its length. As a child these provided the perfect setting for such games as Murder in the Dark and Beckon, Beckon, a protracted variation of hide-and-seek.

Midway between the two ends of the second floor is a balcony overlooking a spacious, wood-paneled living room with portraits of my grandparents and my father and his four brothers and one sister. The presence of family is everywhere. As a child I spent many hours imagining conversations with them as I spied on grown-up family members below.

An oversize Romanesque horse sculpture stands on the carved stone fireplace mantel at one end of the Victorian living room. It reminds me of my grandfather's conviction that we humans are not more powerful than nature. The ceiling has two oval plaster wreaths resembling embroidery. They are carved with the initials of each of my grandparents, Abby Aldrich Rockefeller and John D. Rockefeller Jr., and their six children. The outer one has the initials of my grandparents plus Abby, John, Nelson, and Winthrop. The inner wreath is inscribed with the initials of my uncle Laurance and my father, David. Laurance and David were the fourth and sixth children. The choice of their initials was seemingly random. Yet mysteriously, the owners of the initials on the outside circle were the first to die. I still get goose bumps when I look at the ceiling.

The room is lined with comfortable couches and chairs arranged for conversation and serves as a meeting place for the fourth generation, called the Cousins.

As one of the youngest of the Cousins' generation, I joined the discussions, in 1970, at the age of eighteen. My first meeting was memorable. Twenty-one cousins, who had navigated the turbulent 1960s together, were having lively discussions ranging from the morality of the Vietnam War to the imperfections of parents to contemplating streaking a dinner party at Kykuit, the family mansion up the hill. They were still rebellious and their bond from years of shared experience made it hard for me to feel I belonged. I didn't know how to insert myself in a way that felt appropriate or welcome, but by the time I was twenty-five they recognized me as a leader and elected me chair of my generation. I appreciated the honor but it was a lonely role.

My extended family has now grown to over 200, and 120 members are active participants. Separate generational meetings start the day, followed by the plenary Family Forum.

To me, the most interesting part of the day is the afternoon, when we separate into small groups to discuss designated topics or to join an intergenerational dialogue. Over the years, the dialogue has become an effective vehicle for feeling connected to my cousins. Strict rules of conduct govern what quickly becomes a very intimate and confidential personal sharing. It was at one of these dialogues that I first took notice of my niece Rebecca. It is with her permission that I tell the following story.

Sixteen of us sat in a circle to discuss our chosen topic for the day:

the New Millennium. Many of my generation were worried about the plight of our planet. Global warming and environmental decline were accepted as fact in our family long before it became an international debate. Yet despite widespread efforts by many around the world, things were getting worse. My family has been involved philanthropically in environmental protection—from preservation of wilderness, farmland, and islands to species extinction and biological diversity—but climate change trumps them all.

My cousin Laura designed the intergenerational dialogue in 1992. She explained the rules: There is a rotating timer. The person before the one speaking holds the watch. Each person is given two minutes without interruption to share his or her feelings. Confidentiality is required and no judgments, advice, or interruptions are allowed. I listened to the cousins from my generation share their anxiety and concern about the future. An impending sense of gloom filled the room.

Then it was Rebecca's turn. As a twenty-year-old and a member of the fifth generation, her mouth formed into a wide smile of optimism. She spoke about her hope for the world and how she was going to change it. Her blue eyes sparkled as she shared the perspective she had gained during her semester in Belize, studying the attitudes of local people toward a newly created national park. She was going to make the world a better place.

"You guys don't have to do it all yourselves," she exclaimed. "There are others of us wanting to make a difference and I'm going to do my part to change the world. I am hopeful because I have seen change and I know it can happen again."

Tears brimmed in my eyes as her can-do attitude conjured up memories of my own idealism at her age. I realized in listening to her that I had let my early visions and stories gather dust. Layers of work and worry over the years and distractions from parenting had dulled my optimism.

The room felt brighter and more open as her enthusiasm sent smiles around the circle. For the first time in my life I realized that family leadership was transitioning to a new generation and I was no longer the youngest. My place in the family was shifting as others climbed up through the ranks to assume new roles. It was sobering to come into middle age and have to give up my place in the family. In six years both my sons would be gone from home and I would be looking for a new identity. I felt insecure, yet I was relieved in knowing that the burden of leadership was not on my shoulders alone.

My generation had grown up hearing the mutual back patting of our prominent uncles at the Christmas family luncheon. Sunday lunch in December became an annual history lesson of the family's good works, as well as a reinforcement of values set mostly by men at a time when women's liberation was on the rise. Their toasts acknowledging one another for public recognition felt lopsided. Our uncles celebrated notable appointments and public service works, such as my uncle Nelson and uncle Win being reelected as governors of New York and Arkansas, respectively; my uncle John starting the Population Council; my uncle Laurance saving land in the Virgin Islands; or my father, David, founding the Trilateral Commission. They also commended my cousin Jay when he became a U.S. senator from West Virginia. They neglected to talk about less publicized deeds, including the good work of their only sister, Abby, oldest of their generation, who created public gardens throughout New York City. My generation was working to make a difference, too, but we had chosen a more private path. Our efforts were often overshadowed by the uncles.

As a teenager, I listened to these family toasts with mixed emotions. On the one hand I was proud of my uncles' accomplishments and concern for improving the common good, a value passed down from our grandfather and great-grandfather, but I also felt daunted as I approached young adulthood. The value of serving society is so strongly held that it's impossible to feel you are doing enough. Our patriarch and his son had set the bar impossibly high. They invested a lot of hard work and money curing infectious diseases, improving medical education, building universities, restoring national monuments around the world, and creating national parks and museums in North America.

Not everyone can say her grandfather was an early financial supporter of biomedicine, fostered the emerging field of public health, or restored Versailles. The implication around the table of our collective family was that *big* was the only visible *good*. This fit with the rise of capitalism, but it diminished the achievements of my generation. We could not compete with our fathers or uncles or grandparents. We chose quieter paths, went incognito, and found as much value in helping a few people as in helping a nation.

My father's generation acknowledged public duty over private acts of philanthropy. We cousins and I wanted our efforts to be recognized by our elders, but the challenges facing us included diminished funds and greater numbers of people and problems in the world. This required new strategies and imagination. We became doctors, psychotherapists, teachers, and social workers, and we worked with others to create and lead organizations for service and social change.

In 1985 my brother David and our cousin Laura Chasin invented a ritual called "Passages," to acknowledge every member of the family who wishes to be presented to the family. Each year, people whose birthdays have reached milestones are contacted to ask if they would like to be part of the family ceremony. If they say yes, they invite a family member to stand with them and describe their interests and accomplishments.

The ceremony takes place under the great sycamore tree on the family estate. A different leader is chosen each year as an announcer to provide a brief introduction and conclusion to the ceremony. White fold-up chairs are placed in a circle on the lawn, and roses stand in a bucket, ready to be handed out after each person is presented. A family member takes pictures. Each presenter is given two minutes.

The Passages ritual is a time to acknowledge personal qualities, like being a loving person who cares about her friends and family, founding an organization to foster mutual understanding, being someone who makes others laugh, or co-authoring an initiative to build a more peaceful and sustainable world. Little-known facts are revealed, like having read one hundred books in the past year or having developed a passion for elephants.

This is a far cry from becoming governor again, but it seeks to place a different kind of value on us as individuals, celebrating our passions and our cores, as well as our accomplishments.

At the end of the ceremony, we stand in a circle to hear the names of all new family members born during the year. We also honor the memory of anyone who has died in the past year, inviting the bereaved to stand in the center of our circle as we join hands and sing "Amazing Grace." In this way we remember the whole and each family member or spouse remains forever in our circle.

42.

PLANTING SEEDS

❧

First let me mention again, in my own defence, that I have a mild form of dyslexia. It's an annoying aspect of my inheritance. My *b*'s sometimes turn upside down into *p*'s, and vice versa. What happened in the garden was not so surprising; what happens while gardening often holds surprises and lessons for me.

It was close to dusk when I finally had a moment to plant the fava beans in our kitchen garden in Vermont. Our gardener, Aubrey Choquette, had thoughtfully sprouted the seeds several days before and laid them in between layers of wet newspaper in a tray. Each one had a little arm extending from its flat, kidney-shaped body. Some of the arms stretched up and others curved at the elbow, but all were pointing at something.

The earth at my feet had a straight furrow in it, carefully scooped along the front of a birch frame, which would serve as a support for the beans to climb on. I bent down and divided the tray in half so Paul could plant his on the other side of the grape arbor. Then I began to place them in the furrow.

I have always been too impatient to bother soaking seeds, so I had not taken the time to contemplate whether the little stems that grow out from them are in fact arms or legs, shoots or roots. I arbitrarily decided that they must be arms reaching for the sky and planted them with the pointy parts facing upward. I did this very carefully, making sure that each one had a good chance of bursting through the soil after I had covered and tamped it down.

Something deep inside was nagging me. My sense of direction has often been 180 degrees off, so I decided to ask Aubrey, who knows everything about growing plants.

"Aubrey, do those little shoots point upward or down? I mean, are they sprouts or roots?"

Aubrey was too polite to tell me I had made a mistake. "It doesn't really matter. They will find their way down."

I considered this.

"You mean they really are roots? Oh, but of course. Things can't grow until they have their roots in the ground."

He assured me that even though I had planted them upside down, they would find a way to put their roots down before sending shoots upward.

"Is this the way with all plants?" I asked, trying to cover my ignorance—with the possible exception of dyslexic plants.

"Well, as far as I know . . ." and his voice trailed off, so as not to dent my ego.

I laughed, seeing a side of myself clearly. Of course I would think the roots were arms reaching up. My life force wants to stretch skyward and jump for joy, but without grounding it has no balance.

I marvel at the potential for everything to grow, even when planted upside down. A seed doesn't need to know it is a fava bean. It just does a quiet somersault and keeps growing.

⟶

I have always loved digging potatoes. They hide earth's little treasures below long hills of soil, there for the finding. Big ones, little gnarly ones, round and oblong ones, you never know what will be unearthed as your fingers burrow into the dark below each plant. They remind me that mystery is just a few inches below the surface.

The fall that our sons drove off to Princeton University together, I felt a pit in my stomach. The unknown of what lay ahead needed some careful cultivation. I looked at Paul with tears in my eyes. Our partnership in parenting as we knew it was over. It would never be the same again. Paul held me, letting my tears drench the handkerchief he had pulled from his pocket.

When I dried my eyes I felt a need to do something together. "Let's go dig potatoes," I entreated. I could tell from the tight muscles around his mouth that he needed distraction and grounding just as much as I did. The air was dry under the strong rays of summer's final warmth. We put on sunblock, picked up several white plastic buckets and a potato fork from the workshop, and plodded to the production garden.

Paul pressed his foot on top of the fork and carefully pushed it into the soil along the potato hill to loosen the potatoes from their hiding places. I pulled the dried plant, revealing some of its earthy, brown children clinging to their umbilical cords. I placed them in a pile on top of the earth to dry. We moved to the next plant in the row.

It was surprisingly hot work. Paul soon had smudgy streaks down the sides of his face from where he had wiped away the sweat. I knew I must look the same. In a burst of elation at the freedom of being alone together, I stripped off my shirt and pants and sat in my undergarments between the potato rows. Paul did the same and we laughed away the tears.

Twenty years of parenting is a lifetime. No amount of potatoes could replace the warm and growing bodies of our sons, but it was a good start. I grew new appreciation for the term *grounded*.

The next few weeks were purposely full. We were grateful for staff meetings, meals with friends, movie dates, and dinners together. But something was tugging at me from inside.

One night as Paul and I were driving home together from our office, I said to him, "I think we need a new partnership. With the boys gone, we could too easily fall into our own work and drift apart."

"We will never drift apart," he comforted, always the optimist and perhaps more confident in general. I wasn't yet convinced. Marriage is like clay. You have to keep it moist and knead it or it will crack and lose its malleability. I had been sculpting an idea.

"Would you be willing to partner with me on my philanthropy?"

I had felt alone in this work for years, dutifully following my family's example of doing good in the world through giving money. I had discovered it is a lot easier to spend money than to give it wisely. Paul and I discussed our philanthropy and he supported my desire to start organizations in mind/body health and social and emotional learning. He offered good ideas but was respectful of my inheritance. I had needed time to grow my desire to share.

Trust cannot be bought or bargained for. It has its own timing, which evolves like the relationship that nurtures it. Our first ten years had been a testing ground, which almost culminated in separation. After we pulled through, I shared my income with Paul equally. The last outpost was philanthropy. We were in our twenty-sixth year of marriage. I sensed a second harvest in our partnership.

"I think we could do a lot together." He was alive with ideas. I was surprised to feel how my body suddenly relaxed. Burdens carried over time can feel as natural as a backpack up a steep trail. Only after we lift them off do we know the lightness of being. I felt like dancing.

Two weeks later, Paul came home and told me about a young woman he had been introduced to who had just moved back from San Francisco to her native state of Vermont. "She helps not-for-profits apply business practices and principles to social issues and has an international perspective from living and working in Europe and Latin America. I think we should meet her."

"Why?" I asked naively, forgetting for the moment that I had started the conversation.

"I think she might be helpful to our philanthropy."

"But we are already working with Rockefeller Philanthropy Advisors," I said tartly. My roots are loyal and I was not willing to jump ship, especially as I had been the founding board chair of our family's philanthropic advisory vehicle. However, they were in New York and I was living in Vermont. It might be nice to have someone nearby. We scheduled an appointment.

Joanna Messing arrived at our house exactly on time. She was wearing a petite print dress. I was drawn to her lively dark eyes and black corkscrew hair. She smiled warmly as she shook our hands. The three of us sat down to get to know one another.

At the end of two hours, we asked her for a consulting proposal. I immediately wrote Rockefeller Philanthropy Advisors, told them how things were evolving, and asked them for a proposal to work on crafting a philanthropic plan. I told them I hoped they would emphasize strategic thinking in their proposal. My loyal side wanted them to win the contract.

It was not to be. The winning line in Joanna's proposal was her mention of "your accountabilities." In thirty-four years of doing philanthropy and working with various wise and passionate family advisers, no one ever talked to me about my own accountability. I could feel the page opening to a new chapter in philanthropy.

The next six months were spent with the three of us scribbling on large newsprint. We brainstormed all the ways we hoped to make a difference in the world. Paul and I share a love for long-range visions. The only constraint to our enthusiasm was the size of our budget and a belief that part of it should go toward community grants. I was enjoying the partnership. It was so much more fun than all the years I had spent making decisions on my own. We decided to create a family foundation in hopes that our sons would add their own ideas to ours.

We spent hours at the beginning clarifying our values. Then we made lists of our interests: social and emotional learning in schools, parenting education, the creation of a compassionate culture for nurses, the preservation of traditional cultures and community, the promotion of local agriculture, pollinator protection, and the stemming of climate change.

The last subject stopped us in our tracks. It underscored on a macro level everything else we had listed. If the climate keeps changing, our natural and human systems will fall into chaos. The parenting classes I wanted to start in high schools and at birthing seminars and Paul's desire to protect pollinators would have to find another way of coming into being. We decided to limit our giving to climate work in this country and see how successful we could be.

In the course of our discussions I began to appreciate how differently the three of us thought. Paul was by far the most long-range thinker. I contributed intuition and sensibilities where personalities and relationship building were concerned. Joanna did a good job of keeping us in a relatively straight line of thought, teaching us the differences among vision, strategy, and tactics. We all agreed on measurable results, but she knew how to implement the metrics in grant-making and seeking.

It was an exciting day when we finally agreed on our shared vision of philanthropy: to stem global climate change by cutting carbon emissions in half by 2030. We took the advice of Dr. James E. Hansen, director of the NASA Goddard Institute for Space Studies at Columbia University in the Department of Earth and Environmental Sciences: "... the only hope for keeping a planet that resembles ... the past 10,000 years is to halt any new CO_2 emissions from coal and to phase out existing coal emissions promptly."

Our strategy was to stop the construction of nearly two hundred proposed coal-fired power plants in the United States from being built and to show the financiers of coal that it is no longer a good investment. Our tactic was to support the major not-for-profits on the ground and fund financial analysis of coal, from mining through combustion. Within four years we had helped to stop 160 of those 200 plants.

The Growald Family Fund involves both our sons. We call upon them for strategic and aesthetic advice. Paul and I allocate funds annually to both Adam and Danny to give to causes of their own. They talk to us and to Joanna about how best to leverage their interests. Like the potatoes Paul and I unearthed, Adam's and Danny's ideas will stir the earth of our collective interests and bring new ideas to the surface.

43.

OUT OF THE CANYON

～

> Strong convictions are the secret of surviving de-
> privation; your spirit can be full even when your
> stomach is empty.
>
> —*Nelson Mandela*

We are just going to hike until lunch." My sister Peggy's alto voice was certain and persuasive, as usual. "I've been to the oasis before and it's a really beautiful place. The staff from the lodge is going to bring our picnic there so all we have to carry is our water and a few snacks."

The year was 2008. We were camped by the Fish River, below the edge of what's called the Grand Canyon of Namibia. Peggy and a few other investors had recently acquired a large tract of land where they were building an eco-lodge. They had found multiple petroglyphs near the oasis and she wanted us to see them. My brother Richard and his new wife, Nancy, Peggy, Paul, and I had hiked to the bottom of the canyon the day before, over many loose rocks, with Peggy's ranch manager, Ian. Our tents had been set up ahead of time, next to the river, and we had enjoyed a relaxing evening around the campfire.

Today we were on a tight schedule for a very exciting reason. Today we would soon meet Nelson Mandela. Peggy had known him for several years, through her work with the antiapartheid movement. She arranged for us to fly in a charter plane from the top of the canyon to Johannesburg to have dinner with him. Nancy, Richard, Paul, and I had been looking forward to this for months. Afterward we would go on safari to Botswana with my dad; I hadn't been to Botswana since my first job out of college.

I was looking forward to again seeing the Savuti wilderness where I had camped for three weeks in 1974, but I was even more excited at the prospect of meeting the great leader of South Africa. I was counting the hours.

"Are you sure we will be able to find our way to the oasis in time for lunch?" I asked cautiously, remembering other adventures with her that had required twice the length of time and resulted in more danger than anticipated.

"I wouldn't be suggesting it unless I was," she answered testily. Persistence had been her ally in getting her way. It had also helped her found a not-for-profit organization, Synergos, in 1986, to bridge grassroots, political, and business leaders from around the world. Her mission was clear: to forge new ways to overcome poverty. All I wanted was a sure way to reach the oasis.

Peggy does everything on a large scale. From the time I was a teenager, I watched our dad take her under his wing. It seemed he wanted her to carry out his work in the world. She's well suited to the task. I admire the way she navigates foreign countries, people, and ideas, but I haven't always trusted her when it comes to safety. As a child she rode the fastest horses available and encouraged me to voluntarily fall off our donkey so I could learn to relax when the real fall happened. I never did quite understand her logic. Now we were with her in one of the driest and most remote places I had ever seen. I did not know then that hiking in the Fish River Canyon is recommended only for the brave and hardy who have passed a medical examination.

I looked up from where we were standing to the canyon rim, near where I imagined the oasis sat, a fifteen-hundred-foot vertical cliff of sandstone and shale. I did not relish the idea of climbing up there or possibly falling. Peggy explained, "We'll be hiking along the river until we reach the canyon that leads to the oasis. I'm sure there's an easy way in." Her eyes were on fire with excitement. The truck, which had come down to our campsite to collect our tents, food, and other gear, left in a trail of dust up the rough dirt road.

I packed my small first-aid kit in my backpack, along with a few extra clothes, just in case it didn't turn out the way she imagined. I had been on "short hikes" with her in the past that ended up being over twenty miles. We six picked up our daypacks and water bottles and started off along the river.

The sun warmed quickly, from forty degrees at dawn to over ninety degrees. Richard and I decided to take a swim. We found a flat rock, stripped down, and went in. Richard did not look carefully before diving and cut his elbow almost to the bone. My first-aid kit was already coming in handy. I placed one of the butterfly Band-Aids tightly across the cut and we continued.

A tawny eagle circled above us. I wondered whether this was an auspicious sign, but I kept my thoughts to myself and walked close to Paul. Better not to be an alarmist.

We passed the base of the first and second canyon. Peggy and Ian discussed whether the third was it. "I'm sure it's not," said Peggy. Ian admitted he had never been to the oasis before. *Why hadn't he told her earlier, and why hadn't she asked?* Peggy confessed, "Well, I've only hiked down from the oasis to the river, not up. I thought you knew the way." Had I known this before we left, I would definitely have said no. But we were committed now and the next canyon was just around the bend. Paul and I talked in low voices about when we should turn back. We decided to defer to my doctor brother.

Five canyons and five hours later, Richard and Nancy, who had stayed quite a distance in the rear, caught up to us. Richard took a stand.

"Peg, this is not working for Nancy or me. It is now almost two o'clock and even if the next canyon is the right one, it will be a difficult hike up, and we have probably missed our chance to meet Nelson Mandela. We're almost out of water. We are playing with death. I can't speak for the rest of you, but we are not going any farther."

I was deeply relieved. Somehow, I had worried I would not be listened to if I spoke first, but now that Richard had voiced his concern, Paul and I echoed him. He was the doctor, after all. He was still taking Gleevec, the medicine for his chronic myelogenous leukemia (CML), from which he was now considered almost symptom-free, but the medicine made him prone to severe cramps.

After a weak protest from Peggy, she agreed to return with us to our campsite and wait until we were found. Ian ran ahead to see if he could intersect the truck, whose trail of dust we had seen speeding along the rough road on the canyon wall above us. By now they were searching for us.

Our water was almost gone. Richard volunteered to be the first to drink from the river and let us have the rest of his water, as he would need antibiotics anyway for the cut in his elbow. We decided to walk straight back, crossing the river where it bowed, to get to the campsite earlier. As it was, we were not sure if we would make it by nightfall.

A small plane circled in the distance. We were sure this was the charter we were supposed to be on and that it must be looking for us. We shouted and waved our arms, but after several passes it disappeared. My heart sank. We were hungry, thirsty, and worried. Dusk was descending fast.

The final ford across the river was deeper than the others. We realized it was imperative to keep our clothes dry to stay warm. I had only met Nancy a few times before, but without hesitation we undressed from the waist down at the near side of the river. Holding our clothes and boots above our heads in one hand, we grasped each other's hands for balance as we crossed. I looked over at her and said, with a twinkle in my eye, "Nancy, welcome to the family."

We laughed until our sides hurt. It was a good relief from the tension. My humor masked how bad I felt for her and how scared I was for all of us. Peggy's love of adventure had turned our innocent outing into a life-threatening situation. The worst thing, beyond our physical danger, was that we were going to miss meeting Nelson Mandela.

It was dark when we reached our original campsite. We had been hiking for almost ten hours and had eaten only a few raisins, two power bars between the six of us, and a few tiny apples. Our water was almost out. Richard shared his water bottle around so he could fill it from the river. At that moment his leg went into spasm. His body was severely lacking in electrolytes anyway from the Gleevec, and the lack of food and water exacerbated the cramp in his leg and a swiftly oncoming headache. We were now entering a stage of crisis.

I had one packet of Emergen-C in my first-aid kit. I tore it open, poured it into his canteen, and gave him two Aleves from my bottle of pills. Luckily, it worked. We made our way down over rocks to our former campsite.

The temperature dropped like a stone to forty degrees. We huddled together in our shorts and light hiking shirts to warm ourselves. I fumbled around in my backpack and found an extra long-sleeved shirt and hat for myself and a spare hat, shirt, and socks that I passed around to the others.

Paul stirred the fire to see if there were leftover embers from our campsite that morning. Luckily there were. He and my brother collected enough wood to last for the night and revived the fire. We had nothing to do but lie down in the sand and wait for our rescue.

There was no moon, nor was there any habitation or electricity for fifty or more miles in any direction. The stars were as bright as I imagined them to be at the time of cavemen. We were surviving much like prehistoric humanoids depicted in the petroglyphs, cold, hungry, and empty of anything but each other's company. The fire was a godsend. It warmed our heads as we lay near it. Laughter covered the undercurrent of worry and fear. Here we were in one of the most remote places on earth, huddled together in survival mode, all on Nancy's first family trip. Peggy was clearly relieved that we weren't expressing our anger at her. We were furious and disappointed, but this was not the time to verbalize our feelings.

I wondered aloud, "Where is Ian? Has he run into a leopard? Has he found the truck?" There was nothing to do but wait and stare at the magnificent stars. I thought about the tawny eagle and realized it probably had been a sign. Next time I would stand up to my sister.

An hour or so later we heard footsteps. Peggy jumped up and yelled. It was Ian. He had not found help, but he was back safely. He pulled a space blanket out of his daypack. It was just big enough to share with Peggy. They lay on the other side of the fire while the other four of us spooned each other for warmth. Any time one of us needed to turn over, the rest of us rolled with them like hot dogs on a grill. This produced loud giggles from Nancy and me, but we seemed to be the only ones who didn't sleep. Despite our being in the middle between Richard and Paul, we were too cold to doze and had to get up every hour to warm ourselves by the fire.

The good thing about having no food or shelter is that, if you survive to the morning, all you have to do is get up and start moving. That is what we did. As we had not been rescued, we all filled our water bottles from the river and started walking up the road that the Land Cruiser would come down, knowing we would intersect it at some point. The plane that was supposed to pick us up yesterday would soon be looking for us again.

Richard kept saying, "I just wish we had a mirror." The words had played in my head since yesterday. *We must have something*, I thought to myself. I had already looked in my first-aid kit for a mirror. I had also checked everyone's clothes for something shiny. No luck again. Ian walked in front of me with his backpack on.

We heard the plane in the distance, along the river, starting its search. Peggy and Nancy tore off their white shirts and waved them together in the air. The plane circled twice but didn't see us. We were beginning to despair. I kept thinking we *have* to have something that will work as a mirror. My eyes fell on the netted side pocket of Ian's backpack, and suddenly it clicked

"Ian's got the space blanket!" I shouted. "That's our mirror."

Ian dropped his pack like a hot potato. I pulled the space blanket out and Peggy and Nancy spread it with Paul and me. A three-by-five-foot shiny reflection gleamed at the plane on its third (and probably last) time around. This time it dipped its wings and headed straight back to the airstrip. Nancy and I burst into tears. The others hooted with glee.

I was wiping tears from my eyes when I heard Peggy and Richard say, "Eileen, you are our hero." They would tell the story many times to the rest of my family. I felt seen. And I'm glad we all lived to tell the tale.

❧

Two months later, Paul and I returned to South Africa to take our sons on safari. It was our last window of opportunity before they both got too involved in their work to travel. They had never been to Africa, and we wanted to introduce them to one of the great leaders of the world. Peggy made up for our mishaps in Namibia and kindly arranged for the four of us to have a private meeting with Nelson Mandela.

You know you are in the presence of a strong man when he sits with his back to the door. Nelson Mandela was seated in a wing chair facing away from us when we were ushered into his office in Johannesburg. We took turns shaking his hand and he invited us to sit down around him.

Peggy had told us to call him Madiba, a respectful greeting referring to the name of his clan and its nineteenth-century Thembu chief.

After we were seated, his assistant, Vimla Naidoo, asked if we would like something to eat or drink. A table at the side of the room had a spread of soft drinks, cookies, and sandwiches. We were too excited to eat but, to be polite, we all asked for water.

Madiba jested. "I will have Cuban rum, Vimla." To which Vimla responded, "Sorry, Tata, but we are all out." The tone of her voice told me she had heard this joke before. Right away I felt at ease.

I began the conversation by thanking him for seeing us and reminded him that my sister Peggy had arranged this meeting. He had just turned ninety. I did not expect him to remember how my family of four came to be with him now, but the mention of Peggy brought a smile to his remarkably wrinkle-free face.

"I am very fond of your sister and of your father," he said. "How is your father?" I told him he was very well. My dad is three years older than Nelson Mandela, but he considers Mandela one of his heroes. I told him this.

"Yaas. Yaas," he said thoughtfully, nodding his head in the affirmative. His voice was soft but gravelly. "And he is one of mine."

We had come prepared with questions. I went first. "Madiba, what is one thing you have learned in your life that you would like to share with our sons?"

He thought a minute. "It is never only one person who makes change and it is important to remember that. It is always a collective effort with one person being put at the head of the pack. One person is necessarily more visible but there are many others who are of equal importance and influence to the cause."

I knew he was thinking of his role in South Africa. I thought back to my days with the CASEL leadership team. He was right. Many people gave him all the credit for ending apartheid. But he knew differently. This was not false modesty. He really meant what he said. Then he moved on to his other favorite subject, education.

"With education no one will starve." He looked deeply at both Adam and Danny, as if taking them in for the first time.

I thought of one of the quotes I had underlined in his autobiography, *Long Walk to Freedom*, which I was holding for him to inscribe before we left.

Children wander about the streets of the townships because they have no schools to go to, or no money to enable them to go to school, or no parents at home to see that they go to school, because both parents (if there be two) have to work to keep the family alive. This leads to a breakdown in moral standards, to an alarming rise in illegitimacy and to growing violence which erupts, not only politically, but everywhere.

He could have been talking about our country. I felt sad to realize that the situation is very much the same in the United States today.

Madiba turned to Danny and continued. "When I was a child I was a good stick fighter. It was the tradition of my Khosa tribe to stick fight. The left hand was used for defense and the right for attack. I have scars." He pulled up his loose sleeve to show him. "I am proud of these scars because they remind me of my roots. But I think that stick fighting should be eliminated because it is violent."

Danny challenged Nelson Mandela as only a twenty-year-old can do. "But if stick fighting is an intrinsic part of your clan's culture, wouldn't its elimination be erasing part of your cultural heritage?"

Madiba's eyes twinkled. He liked the challenge of youth. "Yaas. Yaas. That is gooood for you to think about these things. I would eliminate stick fighting but I would keep the dances. I like my traditional dances. I always join in when I go back home. I would like for my people and other cultures to keep such traditions."

There was a pause. I thought of my favorite quote from his book:

No one is born hating another because of the colour of his skin, or his background, or his religion. People must learn to hate, and if they can learn to hate, they can be taught to love, for love comes more naturally to the human heart than its opposite.

I felt a lump in my throat. How could this man, who had suffered so many indignities, still call for the human heart to open to love? It is one thing to write about it. It is quite another to live from a place of love, even in the face of bigotry and hate.

It was Paul's turn to ask him a question. "What advice would you give our sons?"

Mandela summed it up in one word. "Travel." He turned and looked at Adam, perhaps seeing something beneath his skin. "Have you ever been to Georgia, Russia?" Adam blushed and said, "No? But we housed an international student from Georgia a few years ago." Madiba continued, "Yaas. Yaas. There are some interesting things going on over there. It is important to travel. It gives you perspective."

Madiba had already opened our eyes. He was right about traveling. I was glad Paul and I had made the effort to bring our boys to South Africa, for it is easy to remain isolated in the United States. We have to see other cultures with our own eyes to gain perspective. I had told the boys before we met Madiba that in 1985, the year Adam was born, talks for reconciliation against apartheid were beginning. In 1988, when Danny was born, the US Congress passed its sanctions bill and other countries began to impose sanctions against South African apartheid. In 1990, the year their paternal grandmother died, Madiba became president of the African National Congress. At the time, this made little impression. They would look differently now at these events in history.

I remembered back to how shaken my parents were after first visiting South Africa together in 1960. I was eight years old and they were gone for six weeks. Every day I followed their itinerary on a map with a red pencil. My mother hated being gone so long and she came home distraught over seeing horrific conditions of racism and brutality toward black South Africans. It changed how she viewed black people and she despaired that there would be a bloodbath before things got better. In 1994, two years before she died, she got to see Nelson Mandela become president of South Africa. It was a great day in our house and a huge step forward in the world. Her stories influenced my sister Peggy's decision to devote her life to eradicating racism and poverty.

Our meeting with Mandela had originally been scheduled to last for fifteen minutes. It was now approaching an hour. Vimla gave me the nod and I asked Madiba if he would be willing to inscribe my copy of his book. Vimla wrote down the correct spelling of my name and Madiba inscribed it with the following words: TO EILEEN. BEST WISHES. MANDELA. He had already given my family and me the best wish we could have imagined.

Vimla took a photograph with my camera, which I now have framed in my office. The four of us are standing around him as he remains seated in his wing chair. Paul, Adam, and Danny are on either side of him. I am leaning over, holding his hand. He is looking directly at me and we are laughing. Despite all the troubles in the world, we are connected for a moment by something resembling love.

Growald family with Nelson Mandela, 2008

44.

COURAGE

～

My brothers and sisters and I were seated around a fireplace at the Mount Washington Hotel. The mountain's snow-patched face filled the frame of a window in our suite. We had gathered here on this early spring afternoon to celebrate my sixtieth birthday. I had been anticipating this occasion for five months. I wanted to tell all of them together about a pivotal conversation I had had with Richard, which I felt would lead to expressing something important about my relationship with each of them. I had worked hard to get to this point. I wanted to stand before them and take responsibility for my past actions. It was a rite of passage.

A chill ran up my spine as I looked at Richard and David on either side of the fireplace. Neva was sitting on a chair to David's left, and Abby and Peggy were on either side of me on the couch. My hands felt hot and my throat tightened. I forced myself to take a breath and begin.

"As you all know, I had a powerful conversation with Richard in

October. I have been waiting these past five months to share it (with Richard's permission) in front of all of you."

I swallowed dry air, paused, and began again.

"In the past I would have told you one by one, but this feels too big, and I wanted to be sure I had anchored the change in myself before revealing the details."

My siblings sat very still. They had been waiting for me to grow beyond my righteous victim. I was terrified.

"The conversation with Richard was the hardest I've ever had. I wanted to run out of the room and forget the whole thing, but we had agreed to try to work through a lifelong pattern of hurting each other.

"Last summer I barged into Richard's home on our family island just before he was about to start a new kind of guided meditation. I interrupted his preparation time, spewed negative energy, and criticized him thoughtlessly for things he had done. I left without realizing how upset he was.

"When we met in October, Richard was able to express his anger to me, but the heat had gone from his words. He asked me gently if he could tell me how my behavior hurt him. I hesitated, gathered my courage, and said yes.

"He told me that I had criticized the friend he'd had lunch with that day. Then I had called him a messy blueberry picker and launched into a review of our recent cruise together. He'd been furious.

"I felt humiliated. I pushed back tears and pondered my response. It would have been more familiar to explode in self-defense, but surprisingly, the image of my book saved me. I remembered back to last spring, when I received my first rejection letter from a potential literary agent. I called my editor and talked it through. I was teetering between despair and determination, but my desire to publish gave me courage, and

I chose determination. If I could take the higher road then, I could do it now."

I felt my sister Abby's hand reach out for mine and saw tears glistening in her eyes. I looked across to Richard. His warm smile came straight from his heart, as if to say, *I'm with you.* I gathered my courage and continued.

"I looked Richard in the eye and said, 'I see what you are saying, and I'm sorry I have hurt you. All my life I have only seen the ways in which you and others have hurt *me*. I didn't consider how my own angry barbs might have affected others, and I'm sorry I've been insensitive. This was not easy to hear but I appreciate your honesty. I won't be perfect going forward, but I will do my best to be direct in expressing my feelings.' "

I stopped to wipe my eyes, and Peggy put her hand on my knee. I felt taller. My siblings remained uncharacteristically silent, giving me all the time I needed. I could feel their hearts softening and I took a deeper breath before concluding.

"Now, I want to tell each of you something I love about you." I looked to Richard first.

"Richard, I love your patience and kindness. I appreciate how you asked if I was ready to listen before you told me how I'd hurt you. Do you know I still have the *American Heritage Dictionary* you gave me for Christmas when I was about fifteen years old? I've kept it on my desk wherever I was, ever since, even while writing my book on the computer. You have encouraged my intellect and my honesty. Thank you for being my teacher."

Richard put his palms together and gave me the Buddhist bow of peace, *Namaste*. His graying hair had receded from his forehead and his freckled face looked more open.

David was leaning forward in his chair. Thick glasses and a beard hid most of his face, but his kind blue eyes shone through.

"David, you have always been my protector and friend, as I have been your adoring little sister. A few years ago, you asked me to drop the 'little' and simply become your sister. I have done that, and I love you for your steadfast encouragement, loyalty, and love.

"You gave me my first eye shadow—a little plastic case with two shades of blue and a white. I still have it! And do you remember that you gave me my first leather miniskirt when I was sixteen? Our parents would never have given me something so sexy, but you saw it was time. Thank you."

David blew me a kiss and said, "I am glad to have you as my sister, and no longer my little sister."

Neva was next. She sat with one leg draped over the other. Her china white skin suited her air of reserve and she looked at me with diffident sweetness.

"Neva, I have told you this before, but I love your goodness. In my forties I came to see that underneath your prickles and need for boundaries you have a very sweet heart. Without your insisting on clear property lines, I would never have built such a beautiful garden and path behind my house in Maine."

"I knew you would!" she exclaimed, with the joy of a young woman who's just been given a huge bouquet of flowers.

I turned to Abby. She was barefoot in spite of the season and she pushed a haphazard bobby pin into her long, white hair with a hand calloused from years of gardening.

"Abby, I didn't get to know you until you turned sixty, but I am so glad to know you now. I love and appreciate your deep empathy and passion. Your playfulness is delightful. Remember the time you were the cello and I was the harp?"

Abby's laughter poured out of her like chamber music. She turned to the others, saying, "You should have seen us. We reversed roles and I actually played Eileen, like she was a cello, and she plucked me like I was a harp! We danced with each other. It was great fun."

Peggy was last. She has been my most constant companion of the group, and the one with whom I've had the most complicated relationship. My occasional feelings of "less than" were not present as I spoke.

"Peggy, I appreciate how well you listen, and I love how you care so deeply about our whole family. Thank you for having the stamina and passion to do your international work in helping people out of poverty, and for being willing to be out there with your heart as well as your head. I will always remember our dance of two vines intertwined, yet free of one another."

Peggy leaned into my shoulder and put her arms around me. A huge sigh released from my depths. The hardest part was over. I looked at the smiling faces around me. If I could have ascribed a color to the room just then, it would be yellow, for innocent love.

A few days after my birthday weekend, during an early morning meditation in my hot tub, I had some revelations about my bond with Mum and how it had impacted my sibling relationships. I wrote all five of them an e-mail, which they've given me permission to print:

Dear Richard, David, Neva, Abby, and Peggy,

Notice the unusual order of your names! It feels good to mix them up, like changing a pattern. I am still imagining you just as you sat in the Mount Washington Hotel. Relating my conversation with Richard and telling you how much I love each of you brought me to the other side of a fairy tale. I want to share my revelations.

I was sitting in the hot tub yesterday when I experienced bad heartburn. I had had it several times in the night and suspected it was related to fear. Instead of drinking Diet Coke, which I often do to get rid of the pain, I laid my head back and let my feelings surface. When tears came, I understood what was beneath my burning heart.

By the age of three I had assumed the role of caregiver to Mum. I wanted to be friends with all of you (or even one of you), but you were a lot older and not interested. I don't blame you now. There was such a sense of scarcity in our family, and given your bonds with each other, I was left with Mum. Our relationship was born of my desperation for survival and belonging. I made an unspoken contract with her.

I subordinated myself to Mum, agreed to take care of her and love her above all others. In order to secure her love I felt I must reject those of you who were openly rebelling against her. In return for my loyalty, I thought she would love and protect me.

I lived up to my part of the bargain but no matter how hard I tried to please her, or take her side, she did not live up to her part of the bargain. She told me I was too dependent on her and sent me off to boarding school.

I know now that she had too much on her plate to love anyone unconditionally, including herself. I felt let down again and again but I didn't dare show her the full extent of my hurt or rage for fear I would lose her altogether. I didn't realize I already had.

I believed that Mum loved me best, and depended upon me for support more than anyone else; that she treated me as special. This magical thinking served me for many years, but it also kept me enslaved. This was my fairy tale. In admitting it to myself, my heartburn disappeared.

Another interesting by-product of moving beyond the fairy tale is that for the first time, I feel free to love each of you. I'll take you in any order, any time! I no longer have to keep my allegiance to Mum.

It has been as hard for me to trust and accept your love of me, as it was to love each of you without fear. I don't have fear now. I've put some of the photos of Mum away, along with the fairy tale. I'm really, really, really glad that you are all still here, and still willing to take a chance on your youngest sister, who has now become your peer.

I'm sorry about the barbs I've shot at you throughout my life when I was angry or hurt. They were a substitute for the real feelings which none of us were allowed to express. I hope you understand that the barbs kept my fairy tale alive until I was ready to let it go.

I'm free to choose now, and it feels good to be falling in love with each of you.

Eileen

45.

ONE LAST LOOK

❧

My father's ears were tuned for frogs as we left the restaurant. It was a hot summer evening and we had just finished dinner at the Blue Hill at Stone Barns Restaurant in Pocantico Hills, New York. When I was a child, its stone and brick buildings housed my grandfather's milk cows. I still remember the sweet smells of clover and milk on their bovine breath as their sandpaper tongues licked my face. The field just north of the barns was once grazed by cows. In the spring their milk tasted of onion grass. Now it is lined with vegetables like a Tuscany landscape. Chickens and sheep occupy other fields. Meat and vegetables are brought with reverence to the restaurant kitchen where every morsel is given special attention in both preparation and presentation. A single baked onion is served on a plate. After cooking slowly for twenty-four hours, even this humble vegetable is given center stage. Humble turns out to be the theme of the evening.

After many tastes of food bursting with flavor and freshness, my dad and I walk into the night to his car. Our stomachs are happily sated but not too full. Sounds fill the night air in much the same way. My father is listening.

"Are those frogs I hear?" he asks, hopefully. At ninety-five his ears are less certain of sounds than in his youth, but his curiosity is as sharp as ever.

"I think it's just crickets and katydids," I say as I listen for the deep *wallop* of bullfrogs or the persistently high-pitched *chereep, chereep* of green frogs. We are both disappointed. But my dad does not give up.

"Let's go to the back porch when we get home and see if we hear them," he says. For years frogs sought mates in a tiny pond at the base of the hill behind our house. Their songs of seduction filled our dreams at night. We cling to our hopes as we arrive home and find our way in the dark, past the familiar layout of cushioned furniture framed by colonial columns. The porch faces west over an expansive lawn dipping down the hill where memories of childhood sledding come to rest at the foot of a three-hundred-year-old white oak. Beyond it are fields filled with cattle, walking trails, and finally the Hudson River. The Palisades rise from the other side of the river to receive the setting sun in its transition from day to night.

Dad rests his cane against the sofa and eases himself down. I sit next to him. We listen. Crickets and katydids are audible to the right and straight ahead. We turn our heads to the left, expecting more variety down the hill at the frog pond. But we cannot turn up the volume or variety of sounds.

"I used to hear so many frogs," Dad laments. "About ten years ago we dredged the pond. They said it had to be done for some reason. After that the peepers never came back. I wish I knew what happened to them." Grim reality sinks like a stone to the floor of our stomachs.

For a man who spent his career with the Chase Manhattan Bank, bringing home more heads of state than I can remember, this is a humble moment. Not a single peeper is heard. Their absence focuses his attention on the little things that share the right to live. If dredging can eradicate whole species from a pond, how much more destruction will it take before they are gone everywhere? I wonder if my grandchildren will ever know the frogs that my dad longs to hear again. Listening is the first step to preserving the world for the next generation.

If my dad listens to the world beyond himself, my uncle Laurance felt guided internally, through Spirit. Their initials, carved into the inner ring of the Playhouse's ceiling, have come to represent for me the yin and yang of their generation.

In 2001, three years before he died, Uncle Laurance made a decision that initially sent seismic tremors through our extended family. I did not make peace with it until Paul and I visited the property in October 2011.

Some places hook your heart and never let go. For me, the JY Ranch in Moose, Wyoming, is one of them. I owe everything to my Grandfather Rockefeller, who first visited the Tetons in 1927. He was so moved by the inspiring views of jagged peaks and sagebrush valleys that when he saw the beginnings of sprawl in the Snake River valley, he vowed to protect the area and quietly bought thirty-five thousand acres. By 1950, he had contributed thirty-two thousand acres to the United States government for the Grand Teton National Park. He kept the remaining land, including a dude ranch called the JY, and made it into a family retreat.

From the 1930s until 2003, six generations of his family unpacked their bags in the rustic log cabins and relaxed before the same views, one and a half miles across Phelps Lake to the craggy mountains rising

beyond. We came as Grandfather's guests until 1960, when he passed
the ownership of the JY on to his third son, Laurance. Uncle Laurance
continued the generous tradition of inviting family to stay at his ranch,
free of charge. My family and I visited many times over the years, finding balance between service and solitude, city and wilderness, opulence
and simplicity. We drank in the dry, pine-scented air, the fields painted
red and yellow with wildflowers, and the smell of pinesap oozing from
the logs in our cabins.

The JY Ranch was a place where all six branches descending from
our grandfather ran wild. We canoed across the lake at night, jumped off
a thirty-foot-tall boulder into the glacial water by day, stalked elk and
moose, rode bareback, and played capture the flag on horseback. We
helped wrangle the horses before sunrise, caught trout in the lake and ate
them for breakfast, and hiked for miles among alpine wildflowers and
leftover winter snow. My parents' idea of the perfect vacation was to ex-
haust ourselves physically and find rejuvenation in natural beauty.

Red Mathews was the manager of the ranch for many years, through
the fourth generation of family guests. He stirred up the dust with
laughter and practical jokes, a healthy relief from my adult family members' sense of duty and service. Red was the only person who could swear
in front of my grandfather and get away with it. He had red hair and an
irresistible laugh. He inspired us to short sheet beds, put elk turds in the
olive bowls, and dare to ride faster and hike farther than we ever
dreamed.

Romances flourished at the JY and braided together different
strands of family. My mother's parents honeymooned there when it was
still a dude ranch before Grandfather bought it. My uncle Laurance
and aunt Mary honeymooned there, and my mother became legendary for shooting a bear while on her matrimonial pack trip with my

father and Red. The first time I took Paul there, he proposed to me. We continued visiting the JY with our sons, Paul's and my parents and friends, my brothers and sisters, and their children.

At night we occasionally shined a flashlight on a curious bear just outside our cabin. One time, I visited with Paul during the rutting season for elk. We listened to their high-pitched bugling from opposite hillsides across the lake.

There were quiet moments, too. We sat on the porch of the main lodge, reading a book or watching fish rise in the lake before dinner. I liked to read my cousins' and their children's entries in the guest books, recounting the horses they rode, the number of moose they counted at the salt lick by the cabin across the bridge, or the miles they had covered, hiking and riding among the Grand Tetons. The JY Ranch was the only place that was home to every member of my Rockefeller family.

Everything changed in February 2001. Uncle Laurance made a decision to give the ranch and its surrounding acreage to the Grand Teton National Park. He didn't tell his plan to anyone in the family until he completed the deal. I believe he felt a spiritual calling to give it back to the public. He also wanted to avoid conflict. His wife, Mary, had predeceased him, and I suspect he felt he must make this decision on his own.

He sent a letter to his children and the rest of the family telling them that they could no longer come to the JY, as he would be dismantling all the buildings and restoring the ranch to nature for the public to enjoy.

The family was stunned. How could he do this to us? We had never meant to take his generosity for granted, but the ranch had come to feel like a permanent fixture. Had we not shown him how deeply grateful we were? Of course, he had the right to do with his land as he wished, but why hadn't he prepared us? His children and many of my other cousins, and my brothers and sisters were dismayed. Uncle Laurance became the target for the anger he had so wanted to avoid. E-mails and phone calls shot back and forth among his children and their cousins. Several of his children confronted him in person. My cousin Ann Roberts, Uncle Nelson's eldest daughter, wrote him a letter that finally opened his heart. With her permission I include it here:

> So dear Uncle Laurance, I am standing here in my grief and sorrow, feeling how deeply this family is rooted in the JY, how much love and memory is there, how sacred that place is to us, how torn open your children must be—and surely there is more meaning, memory, and feeling there for you than any of us can know . . . and I am asking how I can be with you to find . . . a way . . . forward . . . that honors all that you believe in as a conservationist and all you have so eloquently spoken to regarding family values, traditions, the meaning of sacred place, and the importance of the family harmony we have strived for, for so long. There is, I deeply believe, a way for this to happen that honors all that is good—it is never too late for that.

I will never know just how Uncle Laurance felt in receiving this letter, but after much deliberation he consented to giving the entire family three more years in which to say good-bye. The family breathed a collective sigh of relief.

By early fall of 2003, the last guests had packed their bags and the buildings started coming down. My cousin Larry, Uncle Laurance's only son, found several family members who shared his desire to keep the buildings. They bought some land in the valley and had all the cabins reinstalled with the same furniture, paintings, books, Navajo baskets, and rugs put back in exactly the same places.

My uncle died the following summer, on July 11, 2004. His job was complete.

I did not visit the ranch again until Paul and I went to the Environmental Grantmakers Association retreat at the Jackson Lake Lodge in October 2011. We asked Larry if we could spend one night at his ranch before the meetings started. I was ambivalent about the visit. I wanted to see the familiar cabins, but I was nervous about going back to Phelps Lake, the site where they had stood for over seventy years on family land.

We arrived at Larry's ranch late at night. The sky was brilliant, and coyotes yipped and howled in the distance. We were shown to the main lodge, where we had stayed many times. Everything looked the same. I had a flash of delusion. Perhaps this was all just a dream. I would wake up the next morning and hear the splash of a moose stomping along the edge of the lake.

We woke at dawn to the sound of horses whinnying outside our window. There was no Tetons, no moose, no lake, just horses grazing in a vast, windblown field. This was the morning for our pilgrimage back to Phelps Lake.

We drove to the beautiful visitor center of the Laurance S. Rockefeller Preserve, within the Grand Teton National Park. It was located at the start of the trail leading to the site of our family's former ranch.

Paul and I walked in silence. The dirt roads, which I remembered driving on to get to the ranch, were no longer in evidence. Trees had been planted and gravel removed. The cold morning air chilled my fingers and I felt a ponderous weight in my heart. It beat loudly with the ascent to over six thousand feet.

I wanted to dream the past, to see the ranch house by the corral and cross the stream over a brown, wooden bridge to find a moose and calf at the salt lick. I was sure we would pass the boathouse, or at least see a canoe tied up along the dock, and then we would be there. The recreation hall (or "rec hall," as we all had called it) would be first to greet us. I couldn't wait to see the bronze sculpture again, called *Appeal to the Great Spirit*, by Cyrus Dallin, of an American Indian bareback on a horse—his arms outstretched, with chest lifted to the sky—in surrender pose. I was not quite ready to surrender my dream.

I could almost smell lunch being made in the dining room, just past all the cabins. I listened for the triangle bell. It would still be there, hanging from an iron arm on the landing outside the dining-room doors. I was sure it would, because the air smelled the same as always, of trout, pine sap, and a hint of sage.

Somewhere along the trail, I became disoriented.

We arrived at the lake. The people we passed en route had gone the other way and we were blessedly alone.

I recognized the two rocks a few hundred yards out, used as perches for ducks, and the boulder we had jumped from was still visible, far along the right edge of the lake. I looked down at the water, still and clear as a looking glass. It reflected the mountains I've known all my life.

Paul reached for my hand and wove his fingers through mine. My sense of geography was somewhere between knowing and missing. Paul pointed to Static Peak, the mountain ridge where we became engaged thirty-one years ago. Nothing in the view had changed. Everything in the human landscape, where the buildings once stood, was changed forever.

Paul and I turned to walk along the path that used to pass between the cabins, and my eye lit on something shiny embedded in a tree ten feet from the water. I moved closer and saw it was a hook. Its companion was lodged in a tree five feet away, like old friends that once held each end of a hammock. Something of our human past had remained, after all. The trees refused to give them up.

We walked to where the main lodge should have been, where the bedroom we had slept in the night before was no longer. We stood on the site of the wooden terrace and hugged. I was too numb to cry. I walked a few feet to the tree we had posed under many times as a couple and a family. It was slightly thicker but still there. Paul and I said a prayer of gratitude for the tree, the lake, the mountains, and our memories. We sat on different rocks to meditate and acclimate ourselves to this new chapter of the former JY Ranch. Not a soul was heard. I appealed to the Great Spirit to accept this change. My heart opened and I felt a presence of Grandfather and Uncle Laurance.

Uncle Laurance seemed suspended between spirit and shadow. He had chosen his spiritual vision over family and tried to avoid their reaction. Grandfather's hand was on his shoulder, half comforting, half sharing the dilemma.

I reflected on the one time Uncle Laurance and I had dinner together, how his blue eyes looked up from his slightly lowered head. I asked him whether he ever felt shy.

"*Well*. You are very *perceptive*." I can still hear his voice. I told him I was shy, too. In fact, sometimes I felt so shy I couldn't even look at my own eyes in the mirror. We laughed like schoolchildren caught in the act, and the bond between us deepened.

The air was as still as my body. I felt a clearing inside, like the water in front of me. My sorrow over Uncle Laurance's decision was starting to fade. Perhaps he, too, had appealed to the Great Spirit. I believe that together with Grandfather, Uncle Laurance realized that this land we all have loved and held so dear for three quarters of a century was not really ours to hold.

Beauty cannot be contained because it is the twin of spirit. We can no more own beauty than we can own a star. We look and we feel inspired, moved, overjoyed, or grateful, but it doesn't come with us when we die. I believe Uncle Laurance saw this in the magnitude of the gifts he had been given by his grandfather and father, which each of us in my family have received in one form or another.

I looked up from under the family tree where each of us had stood, wanting our picture taken with the glory and the beauty beyond us. We can own a photograph, or the land that forms its backdrop, but ultimately beauty owns us. It *is* us, in all our shapes and colors, in our various moods, in every season of our lives. We *are* beauty, and each of us belongs.

Acknowledgments

❦

The working title of my memoir was *Family Matters: Stories to Invite You Home*. I considered this title out of a longing for connection with my family of origin. I thank my late mother, Peggy, and my father, David, who I grow closer to with every year, for giving me this one, amazing life. Six years of intensive inner exploration while writing my life story forged deeper bonds with my family and enabled me to finish my book; but not without help from many. First and foremost I want to thank my siblings—David, Abby, Neva, Peggy, and Richard—for supporting my growth, being willing to grow yourselves, and for sharing yourselves candidly. Special thanks to you, Neva, for giving me the first glimmer of belonging, when you brought the six of us together for my fiftieth birthday. Thank you, David, for always being there for me, and thank you, Abby, for teaching me that it's never too late to grow close. Thank you, Peggy, for encouraging all of us to do the work, and for loving me even when I was annoying. And Richard, thank you for being my wise teacher. It feels good to be at home with all of you.

I used to think I had to do everything by myself. I would never have started writing this book had I known how many people would be required to bring it to completion. First I needed a coach, then an editor, then readers, advisers, friends, and family. The list kept growing until I surrendered to the adage "It takes a village to raise a child." I am grateful to Karen Thorkilsen for helping me get started, and for teaching me it's okay for a writer to have a messy desk. (Creativity is a messy business!) Thank you, Lynne Blackman, for making sense of my mess. Your countless hours as my longest-standing editor (with Vernon as your backup) were invaluable. I appreciate your teaching me everything from structuring stories to digging deep, and even showing me where to put the commas, those little pauses that we all need. Thank you for friendship and occasional mothering, like I wished I'd had. Thank you, AB, for introducing me to Lynne, and for helping me find the connections I longed for as I discovered my core. Thank you, Jim Levine, of Levine Greenberg Agency, for your vision, tenacity, and quiet confidence, seeing the possibilities in my book when many others had turned it down. Your idea for the title helped make it universal. Thank you for finding David Rosenthal at Blue Rider Press, who gave me Sarah Hochman, my alchemist of an editor. Sarah, you helped me dredge order from chaos, and your belief in me as a weaver of words as well as people and yarns brought me farther than I ever dreamed. I also owe a debt of gratitude to Michele Hiltzig of the Rockefeller Archives, for finding priceless images on a dime, and to Patrick Groenewoud, who organized my father's photographs so well he could find what I needed. Special thanks to Nikki Fitzcharles and Tausha Sylver, for their invaluable support in completing myriad details.

Throughout my six years of writing I depended on the ears of numerous friends who listened to me read my stories. To all who were at Paul's and my thirtieth wedding anniversary, know that I appreciate each one of you. And special thanks to my sister-in-law Sue Cohn Rockefeller, who found multiple audiences for me and was unwavering in her support. Additionally, I extend deepest gratitude to my dear friend, Rachel Naomi Remen, M.D., for sharing her wisdom and support and giving me the first quote to promote my book; and to Holly Duane, my fellow adventurer and closest companion since first grade, for being there with a warm shawl or a giant handkerchief throughout; and to my dear friend and neighbor Ginny Rowland, who helped support me in many ways, including the cover photo shoot taken with sensitivity and skill by another cherished friend and photographer, Bob Eddy. They all joined my focus group, along with Diane and Sol Pelavin (who gave me my first written feedback) and my cousins, Cindy Franklin, Mary Louise Pierson, and Mary Morgan (who shared a room with me for a week at the Vermont Studio Center while writing her own memoir), Rebecca Reynolds and Henry Weil, Chez Winter, Kate Gridley and John Barstow (who gave early advice regarding publishers), and Kathy Wonson Eddy, whose help was equal to her husband Bob's in bringing me blessings of love and support. I am also grateful to the Blue Mountain Center, for letting me write for a week in my old room when it belonged to my late friend, Harold Hochschild. I also want to thank my late mentor, Norman Cousins, who first believed in my ability as a writer, and the late educator and role model, Walter Clark, who gave me hope.

Finally, I come to my nuclear family. Adam and Danny, without you I would not have written some of my favorite stories. You have enriched my life beyond measure. Thank you from the bottom of my heart for being teachers of honesty and accountability. And Paul, your belief in me and your encouragement every inch of the way has kept me going, even when I wanted to give up. I owe most of what I know about love, marriage, and partnership to you. Thank you for enthusiastically sharing my passion for nature, the pursuit of emotional intelligence and personal growth, for leading family dinners together when the boys were growing up, and for bringing sacred ritual into our family. These seeds, more than anything else we've done as parents, have helped transmit our values. May the love we have together, and as a family, bear fruit beyond our site.